IMAGES
of America

AROUND NAPPANEE

HOMETOWNS OF THE HERITAGE TRAIL

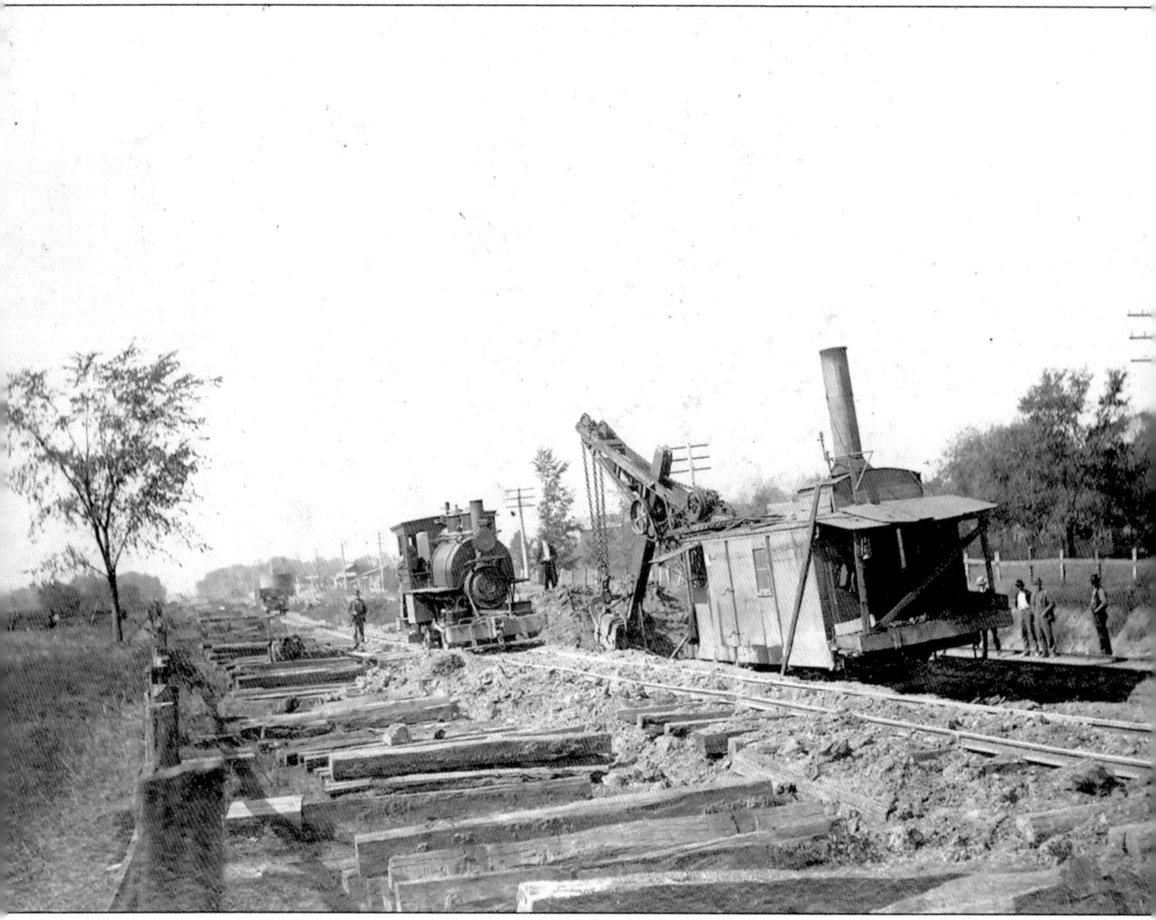

One wonders if these gentlemen could have possibly known the impact of their contributions as they became part of this 1874 endeavor. That spring and summer, these tracks were being laid to form a railway of the Baltimore and Ohio train system, which would connect Sandusky to the east and Chicago to the west. Upon completion of this project, an event of magnificent historical significance occurred—the evolution of a town called Nappanee. These diligent workers were not only creating the foundation for a new railroad, but the foundation for a new city as well. (Photo courtesy of Nappanee Public Library.)

IMAGES
of America

AROUND NAPPANEE
HOMETOWNS OF THE HERITAGE TRAIL

Amy (Lant) Wenger

ARCADIA
PUBLISHING

Copyright © 2003 by Amy (Lant) Wenger
ISBN 978-0-7385-3154-0

Published by Arcadia Publishing
Charleston, South Carolina

Printed in the United States of America

Library of Congress Catalog Card Number: 2003107007

For all general information contact Arcadia Publishing at:
Telephone 843-853-2070
Fax 843-853-0044
E-Mail sales@arcadiapublishing.com
For customer service and orders:
Toll-Free 1-888-313-2665

Visit us on the Internet at www.arcadiapublishing.com

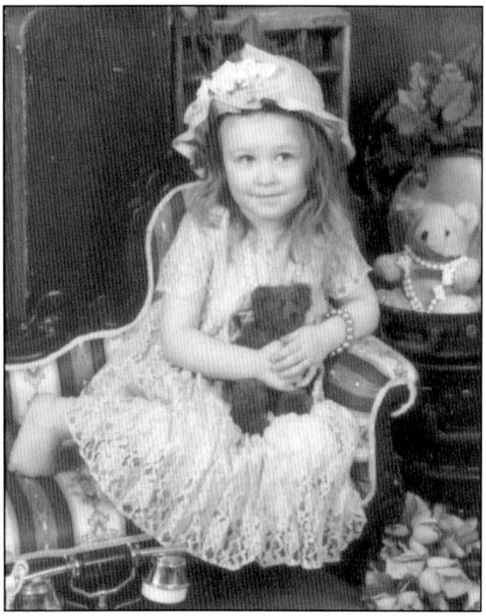

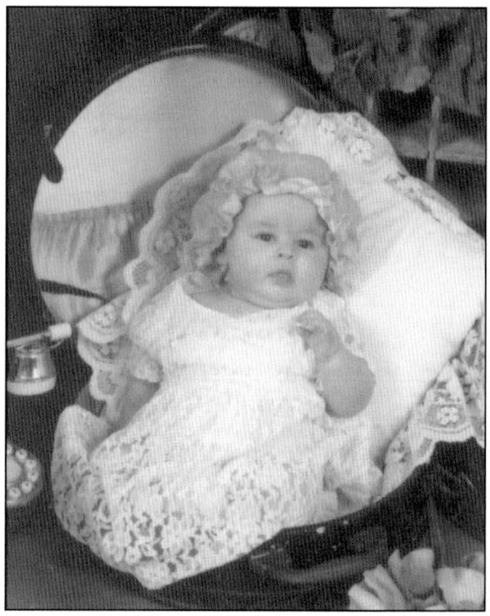

For my beloved husband, Larry Wenger Jr., my friend and soulmate.
For our precious daughters, Hannah Gabrielle and Rebekah Grace,
the darlings of my heart.
For my parents, Robert and Karen Lant, and my sister, Sarah Gilmer.
Your years of love, guidance, and faith inspire me always and will forever.
And I give praise to our Lord, for bestowing upon me a glorious family, a blessed life,
and a spirit resplendent in joy.

CONTENTS

ACKNOWLEDGMENTS

Mr. Larry Andrews, Executive Director,
Nappanee Community and Economic Development
Ms. Linda Yoder, Ms. Peg Dudzinski, the Nappanee Public Library,
and the Evelyn Lehman Culp Heritage Center
The Nappanee Historic Preservation Commission
Mr. and Mrs. Bruce Hunsberger and the Victorian Guest House
Mrs. Linda Hartman and the Wakarusa Public Library
Mr. and Mrs. Jay Klein, the Wakarusa Historical Society,
and the Wakarusa Historical Museums
Ms. Diana Zornow and the Elkhart County Historical Museum
Mr. and Mrs. William Johnson
Mrs. Betty Hochstetler
Mr. and Mrs. Kenneth Wenger
Mr. and Mrs. Merrill Yoder
Mr. and Mrs. Melvin Crilow
Mr. and Mrs. Dean Henry
Mr. and Mrs. Robert Culp
Mr. and Mrs. Howard Hochstetler
Mr. and Mrs. Robert Shigley
Mr. Bruce Rogers
Mr. Raymond Dausman
Mr. Robert Lant
Mr. Steve Ervin

May God bless all of you for your contributions—
I could not be more appreciative or more thankful.

FOREWORD

What distinguishes one community from another? Author Amy Wenger reveals the history of Southwest Elkhart County and details the important foundation upon which the vibrant community of today is built.

Today, Southwestern Elkhart County can boast of being home to one of the top ten small towns in America, a first class educational system, over 60 churches, a skilled workforce, and some of the richest agricultural land in America. To a great extent, today's fortune is a result of the area's rich Anabaptist history.

Being a descendant of Daniel Banter, an Anabaptist and founder of Union Township, Elkhart County, I am aware of our community's strong religious heritage. The Anabaptist heritage is made up of the Amish, Mennonite, German Baptist, Brethren, Old Order Mennonite, and Dunkards. The Anabaptist culture is defined by hardworking, honest, trustworthy, deliberate-thinking, community-spirited people whose daily lives exemplify their strong sense of moral and ethical values. Migrating from Germany and finally settling in Northern Indiana in search of religious freedom, the early pioneers of our community held religious and family values very high. Throughout this book you will see how those traits are still the foundation of our community's moral and ethical value today. The late George Apley once said, "It is worthwhile for anyone to have behind them a few generations of honest, hard-working ancestry."

As reported in the 1876 *Wakarusa Sun*, "We are impressed that Nappanee is blessed with citizens that do not spend their time talking about things, but go right to work and everything undertaken has been a success." We are where we are today because of who we were yesterday.

Larry Andrews
Executive Director
Nappanee Community and Economic Development

Introduction

There is something quite exquisite about the humble beauty and the modest, unfettered ways of life that dwell across rural Elkhart County. It is truly an ambience, a modicum of blissful charm that often eludes definition with merely a few succinct words. For those who live or have once lived there, there is a genuine and unwavering sense of loyalty and pride, to be able to say, "That's my hometown." And for others who have been so fortunate as to happen upon the area, they often come away enchanted, captivated by the notion that these small towns are able to embrace a reverence to their heritage, appreciate the blessings of the present, and find hope and wonderment for the future.

Within the pages of this book, *Around Nappanee: Hometowns of the Heritage Trail*, readers will be introduced to the seven communities of Nappanee, Wakarusa, New Paris, Jimtown, Locke, Southwest, and Foraker. Through the cultivation of carefully researched information, plus a photographic tapestry of vintage images, these pages capture but a glimpse into the window of rural Elkhart County and the lives of its people.

One reason tourists feel so drawn to this area is to have the opportunity to observe the lifestyles and mannerisms of the Amish. Elkhart County, combined with the adjacent LaGrange County, is one of the most visible populaces in the nation for Amish residents, along with settlements from Lancaster County, Pennsylvania, and Holmes County, Ohio. The city of Nappanee, which boasts a population of nearly 6,800, can attribute well over a third of that number to the Amish who live in and around the community.

Visitors often come with questions regarding the Amish beliefs, and there are various attractions in and around Elkhart County that serve to answer those questions in ways that are of the utmost respect and honor to the peacefully pious Amish society. One such destination is Amish Acres, which strives to offer its guests a culturally and visually stunning experience amidst an 80-acre setting that is one of the most historically integral sites in the state. On this land, which is located just west of Nappanee, lived several generations of the county's first Amish families. The ancestry began with Christian Stahly, who arrived in America from his native Germany in 1835 and settled on the future farmstead in 1842.

After being owned by several generations of family members, Stahly's property was sold at a public auction in 1968. A group of local businessmen, comprised of LaVern Pletcher, Richard Pletcher, Gordon McCormick, Freeman Borkholder, and Ivo "Pete" Heckaman, banded together to purchase the farm and its outbuildings. In 1970, Amish Acres, Inc. officially premiered, with several other additions and renovations added to the complex over the years. The original main house, which was built by Noah Nissley in 1893, still stands and is the centerpiece of

Amish Acres. Elaborate tours are conducted at the graciously restored Stahly-Nissley-Kuhns farm, which is now listed on the National Register of Historic Places.

The Nappanee community also provides a pleasant atmosphere for shopping and sightseeing which blends the best of timeless traditions with modern conveniences. Borkholder Dutch Village, which is west of Nappanee and one mile north of U.S. 6, has over 450 craft and antique vendors in a remarkable atmosphere which has an airy, outdoorsy feel, but is in fact enclosed—and air conditioned! Right next door lies Mary's Pastries, where homemade breads, pies, cakes, and other tantalizing delicacies make for a sumptuous sampler of Amish and Mennonite recipes. Nappanee's downtown corridor, and at several points eastward, is lined with dozens of antique shops and dining establishments. It is easy to see why, in 1997, *Time Magazine* selected Nappanee as one of its "Top Ten Small Towns."

The town of Wakarusa, with just under 1,700 residents, boasts its fair share of noteworthy sights as well. The Wakarusa Historical Society, with a membership that includes some of the community's most distinguished and respected citizens, sponsors a museum that is as much a source of intrigue as it is a mission to preserve local artifacts, photographs, and personal remembrances. There are a number of small buildings that line the Wabash Avenue facility, including the former depot, with an assortment of rail cars that nobly earned a final resting place in a fitting arena. In honor of the late Dean Garber, one of the society's most active members, there is "Dean's Shed," a marvelous collection of antique tools and other woodworking relics. The tiny cabin known as "Grandma's Haus" provides a look into life as it was when Wakarusa was first coming into fruition as a town, more than 150 years ago. A crowd favorite is the "Little Red Schoolhouse," which upon crossing the threshold into entry, transports patrons to an early 20th century classroom, complete with chalkboards, desks, books, and other school memorabilia.

Another spectacle not to be missed is the Bird's Eye View Museum, just south of the center of Wakarusa. DeVon Rose serves as owner, curator, and creator of the most astonishing miniature replica of the town *c.* the 1960s. It is fascinating in and of itself for the fact that he has perfectly recreated the town in diminutive scale, down to the very last detail. But even more awe-inspiring is the process by which he achieves the prolific diorama, by using ordinary mediums such as popsicle sticks, cardboard from cereal boxes, and bits of string.

For those who wish a respite from the occasional mania of city life, a passage through any of the other communities yields a number of hidden gems, like the Jimtown Historical Museum, a wealth of bed and breakfasts, homespun eateries, and other countryside amenities like roadside stands with freshly baked goods and luscious produce. It is an amble along some of the most tranquil and beautiful scenery in northern Indiana.

In conclusion, I must say that it was my heartfelt and sincere privilege to have had the opportunity to chronicle this journey through the annals of local history. This area holds a tremendous amount of nostalgia for me. My husband, Larry, and I met in Nappanee in 1992, and we still cherish the friendships that have been nurtured there over the years.

This compilation was also a genuine labor of love for me—in more ways than one. It took me almost a year to complete this book, in part due to the sheer volume of the region I was wanting to profile. But also, as the workings of the book evolved, I took a brief hiatus to celebrate the birth of our youngest daughter, Rebekah Grace, who arrived on November 30, 2002—fittingly, not long after Thanksgiving. Our eldest daughter, Hannah Gabrielle, was, and still is, delighted to be a big sister.

And now, without further delay, allow me to welcome you to this magnificent little corner of the world we know as southwest Elkhart County, Indiana.

One

NAPPANEE
Where Simple Pleasures Abound, The Heart's Treasures Are Found

The city of Nappanee presents quite a tranquil, idyllic panorama across the southwest corner of Elkhart County. It is a region which has become one of the most traversed destinations in the state, as visitors from around the globe come to tarry for a spell in a place where in some respects, there is a certain peace amidst the worries of the world, and the distinction between past and present seems as far away as the horizon. It is a place where kindness and pleasantries are still handily doled out with smiles and an amicable spirit.

Yet the area is also recognized for its schools, industry, recreation, and housing. All the while, Nappanee has succeeded in maintaining a definitive symmetry between bygone eras and the modern day world. But over 130 years ago, the land which would eventually become Nappanee was nothing more than a low marshy plain among patches of timber. It was a land with little prospect. A few families were scattered here and there, living in simple log cabins or small frame houses, but it didn't appear to be in the realm of possibility for a town to ever spring forth.

In the late 1860s, executives for the Baltimore, Pittsburgh, and Chicago Railroad, later the Baltimore and Ohio, saw otherwise. It had been a longtime desire of the company to establish a railway connecting Chicago to Sandusky, Ohio; to have the tracks run across the three states in a fairly uncomplicated, straight execution across the plains. When the preliminary route was mapped out, the proposed railroad fell in line just a couple of miles south of a small village called Locke.

During the course of the years 1872 through 1874, property owners along the proposed B & O railroad were approached to sell portions of their acreage so that the project could commence. Once the proper clearances had been secured, the tracks were laid out with a fair measure of speed. By the latter part of 1874, the railroad was nearing completion, and the neighboring town of Locke saw that it would be an advantage to offer some assistance to the effort, seeing as how it would greatly improve the scope of business to have access to the railroad. So a group of businessmen built Locke Station, which would serve as a depot and a passenger waiting area.

In November of 1874, John Culp Jr., Henry Stahly, and Daniel Metzler platted out a broad tract of land for the purposes of establishing a community. They, too, had the wherewithal to realize the opportunity at hand, and they chose to christen the new town Nappanee, a name also shared by a city in Canada, and derived from an Indian word meaning "flour." Just weeks later, on December 6, 1874, the new train schedule for Locke Station was in full operation. Locke Station, with Henry Eby serving as the first station agent, was Nappanee's first building.

In the months that followed, growth was so rapid and keenly palpable that progress was acknowledged on a fairly frequent basis. A written history of the county published in 1881 noted of Nappanee, "the place makes a very presentable appearance, far better than many of the older and larger towns of the county." Most of the folks who, only years earlier, had committed to Locke as their chosen site of home and business, were savvy enough to observe that their futures might fare far more successfully if they were to relocate to Nappanee. And a great majority of the merchants did just that, literally uprooting and moving entire buildings south and east to the new village.

Within a year of its founding, Nappanee was home to no fewer than seven sawmills and woodworking shops. A post office was instituted in due time, along with a drug store, a hotel, a dry goods and grocery store, a boot and shoe shop, and a blacksmith.

Other businesses rose up rapidly, but perhaps none is more characteristic of the community's heritage than the craft of kitchen cabinetry. Joseph Strohm's Planing Mill and Box Factory, one of the seven original mills, was later sold to Spencer and Eshenbaugh, which was subsequently purchased by Coppes Bros. and Zook. The latter was later joined by Mutschler Bros., but eventually the Coppes Bros. company and the Mutschler Bros. establishment parted ways. Each venture garnered a solid, reputable following and were very much an integral force in making products that were found in households all over the country. Coppes Bros. turned out the Coppes Napanee Kitchens and the Dutch Kitchenette, while Mutschler Bros. achieved fame with the Porce-Namel tables and Porti-Built custom kitchen. Antique collectors have traveled from great distances to come to Nappanee in search of these valued, timeless mementos of local history.

As the 1880s approached, it was evident that other services would need to be added or enhanced to supplement Nappanee's mushrooming population. For example, the first documented schoolhouse to serve the youngsters of southwest Elkhart County is said to have been located on the west side of North Main Street, in the area of where North Main Street Mennonite Church now stands. It was a simple, single-story frame building erected on a farm, and was in use between roughly 1858 and 1867. By the 1870s, students attended classes at a temporary school, on the second floor of a building on the northwest corner of Main and Market streets. One could speculate that the parents were not pleased with that arrangement, considering the questionable nature of the business occupying the lower level—the Porter Saloon.

Residents of Locke and Union townships gathered in 1878 to hear about a proposed four-room brick schoolhouse, and although the plan may have seemed quite logical at the time, many thought the money would be ill-spent, and that there would never be enough pupils to warrant so much room. But better judgement won out, and the building was completed in 1879, on the east side of Main Street, three blocks north of the center of town.

Those who worried that the schoolhouse would have empty seats faced an entirely different issue within just a few years—how to address overcrowding. The school campus was large enough to allow for two additional wooden frame buildings, each with a number of rooms. By the mid-1910s, there were so many first grade students that even the expanded school complex could not accommodate them all. Some of the children had to be shuttled to the basement of the Methodist Church for sessions

In 1916, ground was broken for a new high school, to be built on the same lot as the brick school facility. It was opened to the upper classmen in 1918. One of the frame buildings was later torn down; the other was moved to 601 North Main Street to be remodeled into a residence. So for approximately 20 more years, the old brick schoolhouse served the students in the lower and junior grades, while the new building was reserved for high school youth. By the mid-1930s, once again, the school-aged children outnumbered the available space. So an addition was created, an identical building to the high school facility and located directly to the south. It was unveiled in 1937 as the Central Grade Building.

Other changes came to pass to keep pace with the swelling student population. The 1879 brick schoolhouse was razed in May of 1937, and in 1947, Nappanee City Schools absorbed Scott Township and a portion of Jefferson Township. So the Community Park building was opened to students in grades one through six and called the Park School. While that school was in operation, a new South Side Elementary School debuted in 1954 on South Main Street.

Meanwhile, plans were being made for a new junior-senior high school to be known as the East Side School, sprawled along the intersection of Van Buren and Jackson streets. It was opened to students in January of 1958. Once those students had vacated the Central School location, the children of the Park School were sent back to Central School, which would from that point on be known as Central Elementary School. That building ceased to function as a school in 1992, but still has a vital role in the community.

Then, in 1962, Nappanee, Wakarusa, Union Township, and Harrison Township schools consolidated to become the Wa-Nee School Corporation, so the decision to have Nappanee be the host city for older students resulted in the development of NorthWood High School, which welcomed students in 1970 and was dedicated in 1972. Middle school students now attend the NorthWood Middle School in Wakarusa, while elementary school students, depending on where they live, are part of Wakarusa Elementary, Nappanee Elementary, or Woodview Elementary. The Nappanee Elementary School is the former East Side School, and until very recently, the NorthWood Middle School utilized the old Wakarusa High School facility. An entirely new building complex, the second incarnation of the NorthWood Middle School, was opened in 2003.

Nappanee, a city that never would have been if not for the destiny and dream of a railroad, has grown into something of a rural metropolis. It is a place where yesteryears are cherished, and tomorrow offers endless promise.

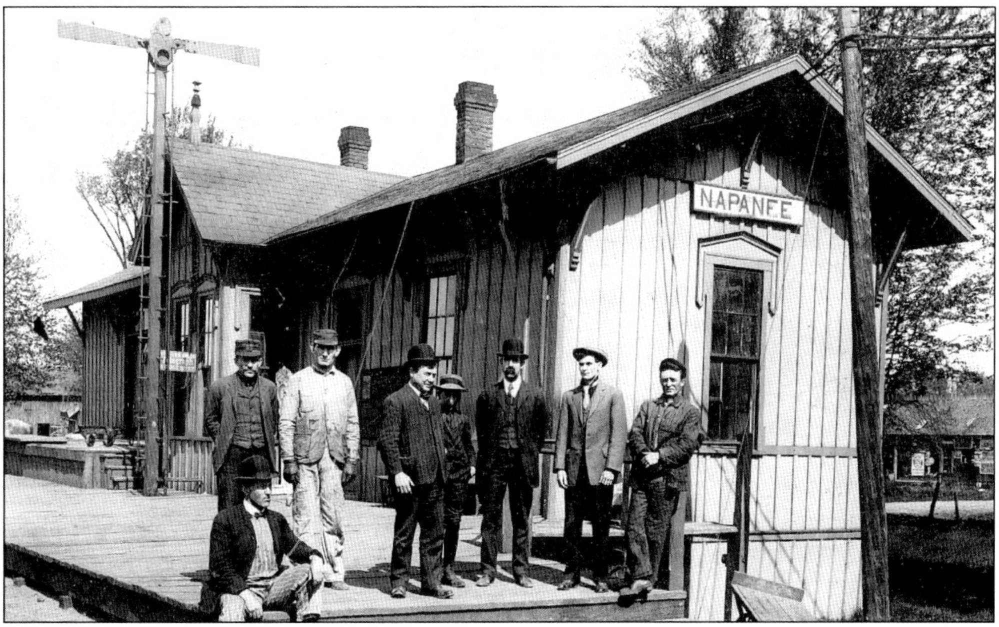

This is the original B & O railroad depot and passenger station, as it appeared c. 1900. The building was originally known as the Locke-Eby Passenger Station, christened as such owing to the town of Locke providing the means to have the depot erected. On the evening of December 6, 1874, freight and passenger service debuted along the new rail corridor, and the published train schedules of the weeks to come would feature "Locke Station," which was in essence the earliest days of "Nappanee." Shown in the photo are, standing from left to right, Oscar Walters, chief clerk; Charles Klotz; Charles Whiteman, B & O agent; messenger boy (partially hidden); Lemuel Sechrist; telegraph operator Sheller; Firm Troup, clerk; and an unidentified trainman. Another unknown trainman is seated at far left. With the creation of the new, and current, brick facility in 1911, this frame structure was relocated to the Tobias Kuhns farmstead southwest of Nappanee, where it enjoyed a renewed life as a storage unit. (Photo courtesy of Nappanee Public Library.)

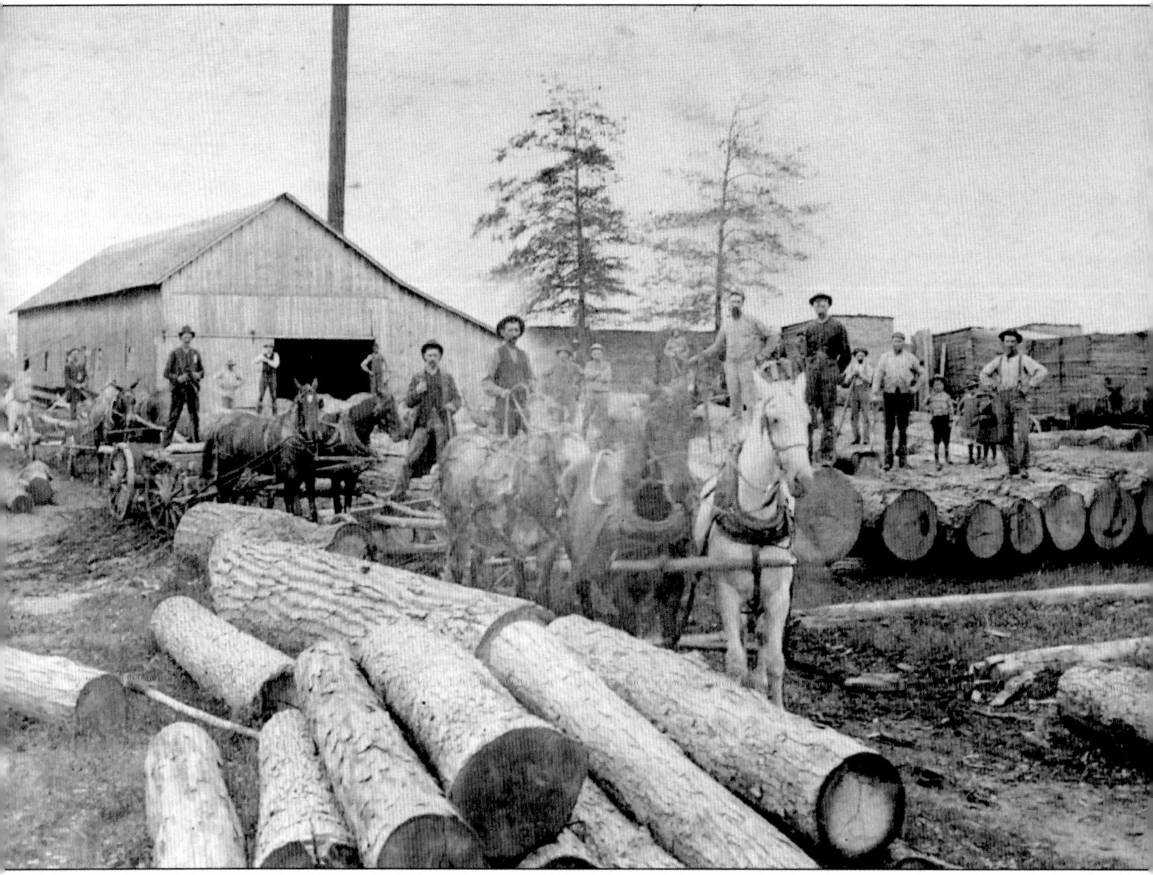

Without question, the image shown here illustrates the origins of one of the longest running and most successful business alliances in the history of Nappanee. What began at the Coppes Bros. Sawmill, seen here in 1876, evolved into a leading player in kitchen cabinetry. In the earliest days of the sawmill, it was actually owned by brothers John and Frank Coppes, along with J.C. Mellinger, and was called the Saw Mill of J.C. Mellinger and Co. In the years that followed, several changes of ownership transpired, but it wasn't long until the turn of the century ushered forth one of the most celebrated local inventions—the Napanee Dutch Kitchenet. A very popular amenity of the modern home in the early 1900s, this invention is often referred to as a "Hoosier cabinet." It offered such features as a sliding center section with a porcelain enamel work surface, mounted drawers and tambour doors allowing for all of the most basic kitchen items in one storage unit. The Napanee Dutch Kitchenet reached the zenith of its popularity in the 1920s when then-president Herbert Hoover authorized a study to analyze the excess momentum generated by homemakers in the kitchen. When the study revealed that "seventy-five percent of time and energy" could be saved by using the Napanee Dutch Kitchenet, boxcars brimming with the products were shipped to such large-scale department stores as Macy's and Gimbles. (Photo courtesy of Nappanee Public Library.)

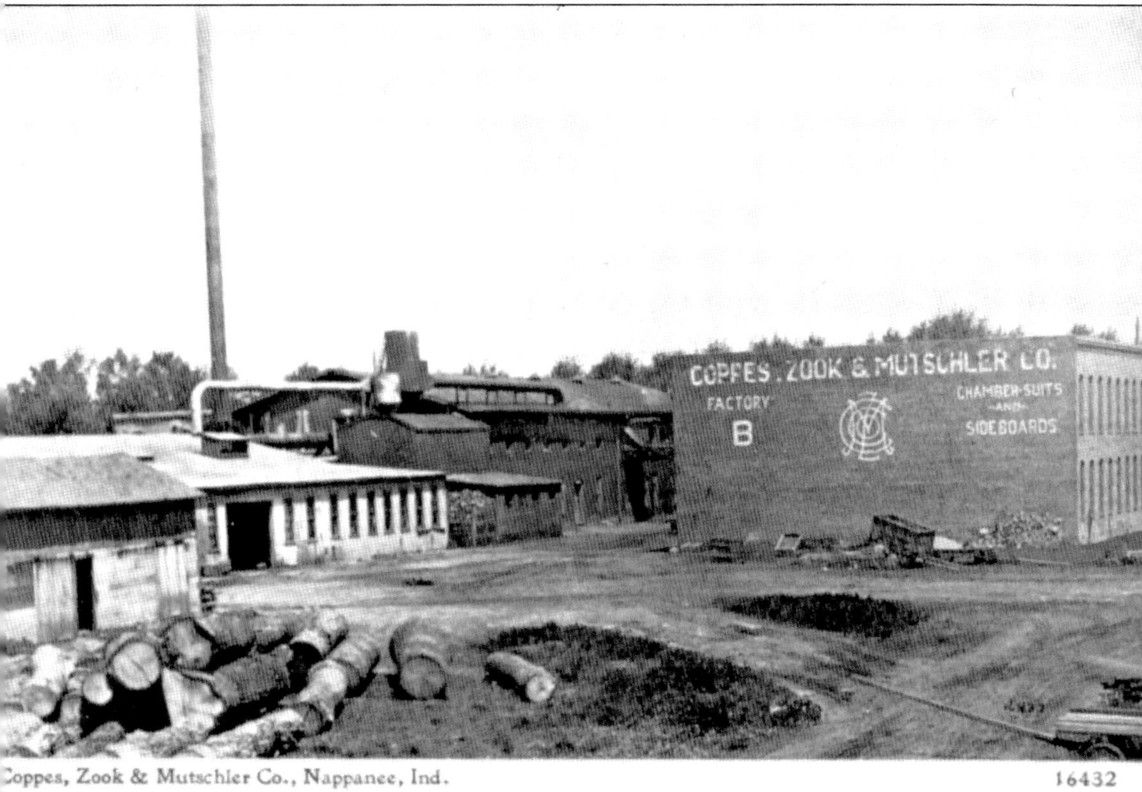

This represents another phase of the Coppes, Zook, and Mutschler entrepreneurship, as it sprawled along the East Market Street thoroughfare. This photo shows a broad view of the factory grounds, with "Factory B—Chamber suits and sideboards" visible in the background. There is even a company logo, incorporating the three initials, on the side of the building. (Photo courtesy of Mr. and Mrs. Dean Henry.)

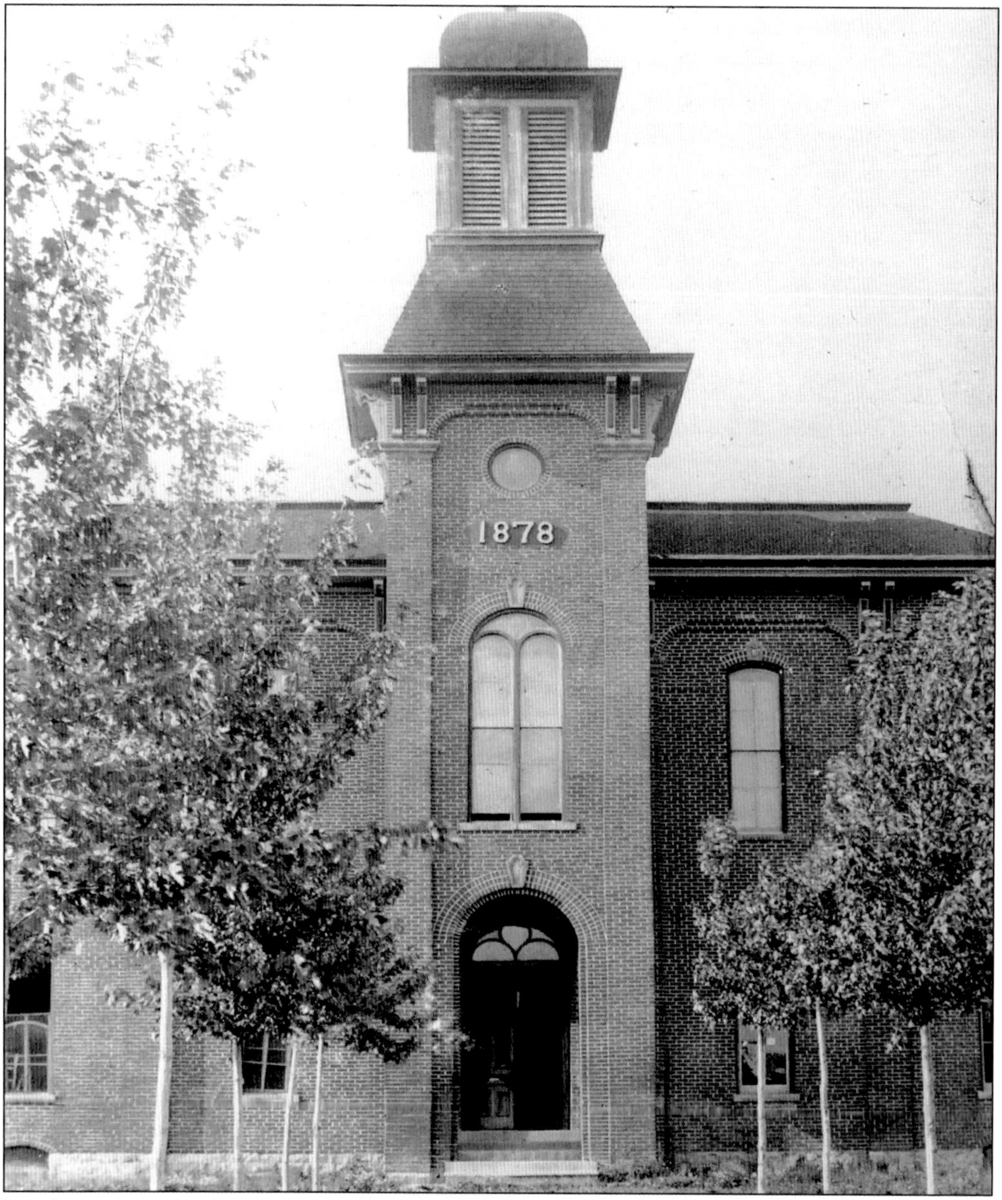

Just four years after becoming a city, Nappanee became the site for one of the most classically designed schools in the region with this, the first brick school building. When the proposal was first brought forth to the residents of Union and Locke townships, the idea to create the spacious, four-room schoolhouse was met with, to put it mildly, an unfavorable response. The belief was that there would be far too much space to accommodate what was perceived to be a meager lot of students. But the project forged onward, and by the spring of 1879, two of the four classrooms were completed. D.M. Best was the first principal, and Miss Florence Stauffer was the assistant. There were also two teachers at the graded school, where students convened for about seven months out of the year. By 1880, there were 160 pupils. Construction costs for the two-story facility were approximately $6,000. It was located three blocks north of the town square on the east side of North Main Street. The building was razed in 1937, coinciding with the arrival of the new Central School campus. (Photo courtesy of Nappanee Public Library.)

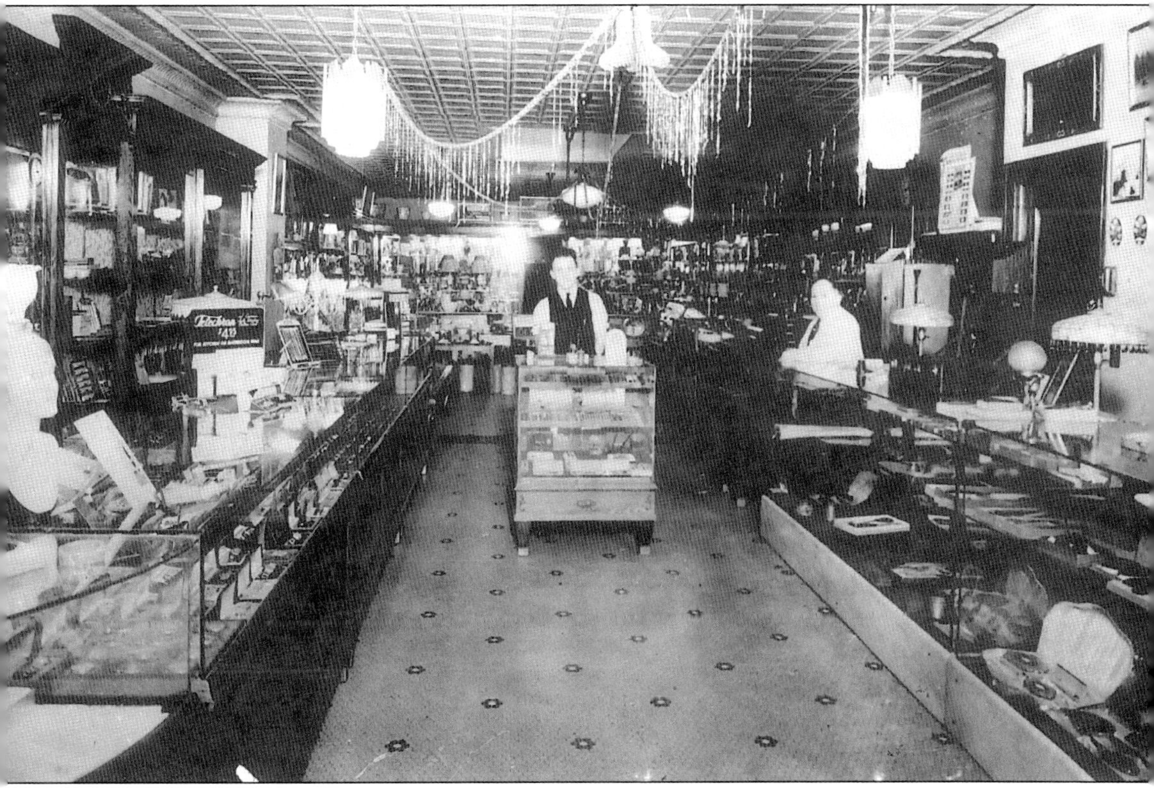

Reed and John Newcomer are shown here in what is now regarded as the oldest business in Nappanee—E. Newcomer & Son jewelry store. Located at 107 South Main Street, it has held sway as part of the retail landscape since its founding in 1880. The business was launched by Enos Newcomer, who was newly married at the time and looking to start a business venture. He purchased his beginning inventory from Peter C. Stahly and opened his doors to customers, only to lose nearly his entire stock to burglars a short time later. Undaunted, he reopened the facility, and as the business garnered respect, more generations of Newcomer men would take the helm in years to follow. Enos's son, John, became part of the business in 1902 and was made a full partner in 1905. Ownership later was taken by John Reed Newcomer, but his sudden passing left him with a short reign. Reed, as he was called, left behind his brother James to become his successor in 1953. James ran the business until 1978, followed by his wife, Margaret, who took ownership until 1980. The shop is presently under the management of Brad Newcomer, James and Margaret's son. (Photo courtesy of Nappanee Public Library.)

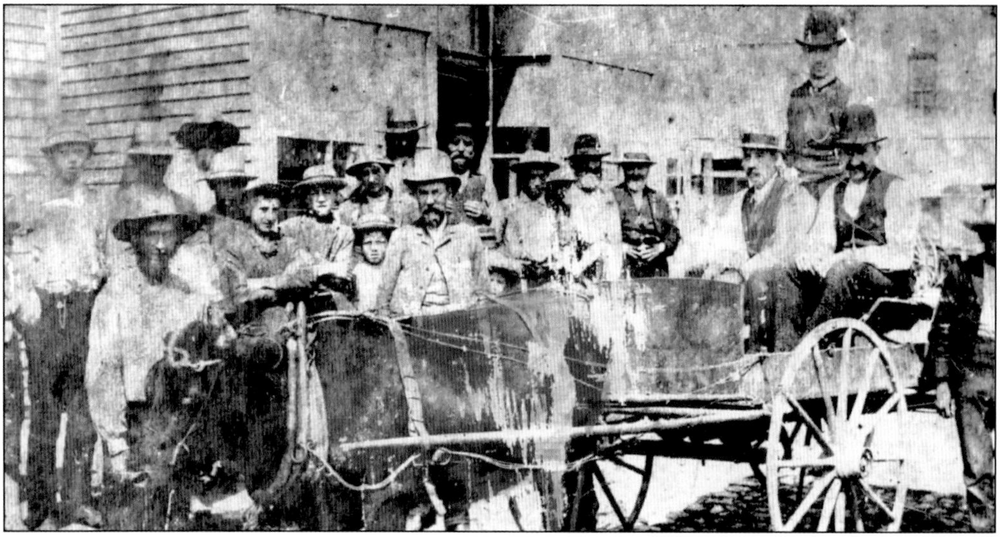

This vignette from 1883 depicts the David Binkley Drug Store, which was moved from Locke to Nappanee by John Peddycord, soon after Nappanee was platted and the B & O railroad laid in 1874. It stood on the southwest corner of the original plat, or what we now know today as the intersection of Main and Market streets. Mose Stahly is the owner of the ox and cart, and is standing at the head of the ox. Stahly was a building contractor and helped to create another Nappanee landmark, the Hartman store. Joseph Spicer, seated at right in the cart, was the superintendent of the Water Works, and John Metzler, at the left side of the cart, was one of Nappanee's original settlers. Standing in the cart is Chauncey Miller. Binkley himself is seen alongside the ox, with full beard and mustache. Behind Binkley, in the tall, light-banded hat, is John Hartman, and to his left, George Stuckman. (Photo courtesy of Nappanee Public Library.)

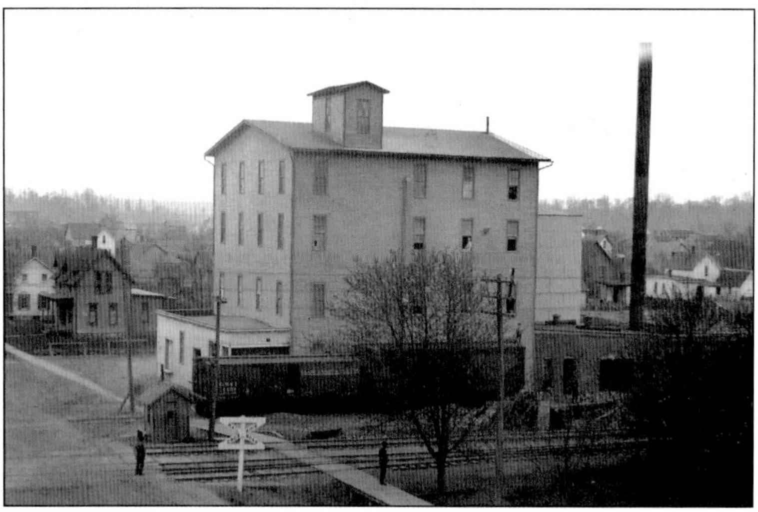

The Coppes Bros. and Zook flour mill, is seen here in about 1900. Initially known as the Nappanee Milling Co., Inc., the business began in 1886 under the ownership of the Coppes brothers Frank, John, and Sam. The name would quickly change to Coppes Bros., and when local attorney Daniel Zook entered into the partnership in 1890, the business became Coppes Bros. and Zook. This entrepreneurship encompassed not only milling flour, but a saw mill and a box factory as well. By 1902, Coppes Bros. and Zook purchased the Nappanee Furniture Company, and were joined by Albert and Charles Mutschler to form the Coppes, Zook, and Mutschler Co. While the other ancillaries of this business would move in different directions over the years, the flour mill was eventually sold to other ownership in 1920. (Photo courtesy of Nappanee Public Library.)

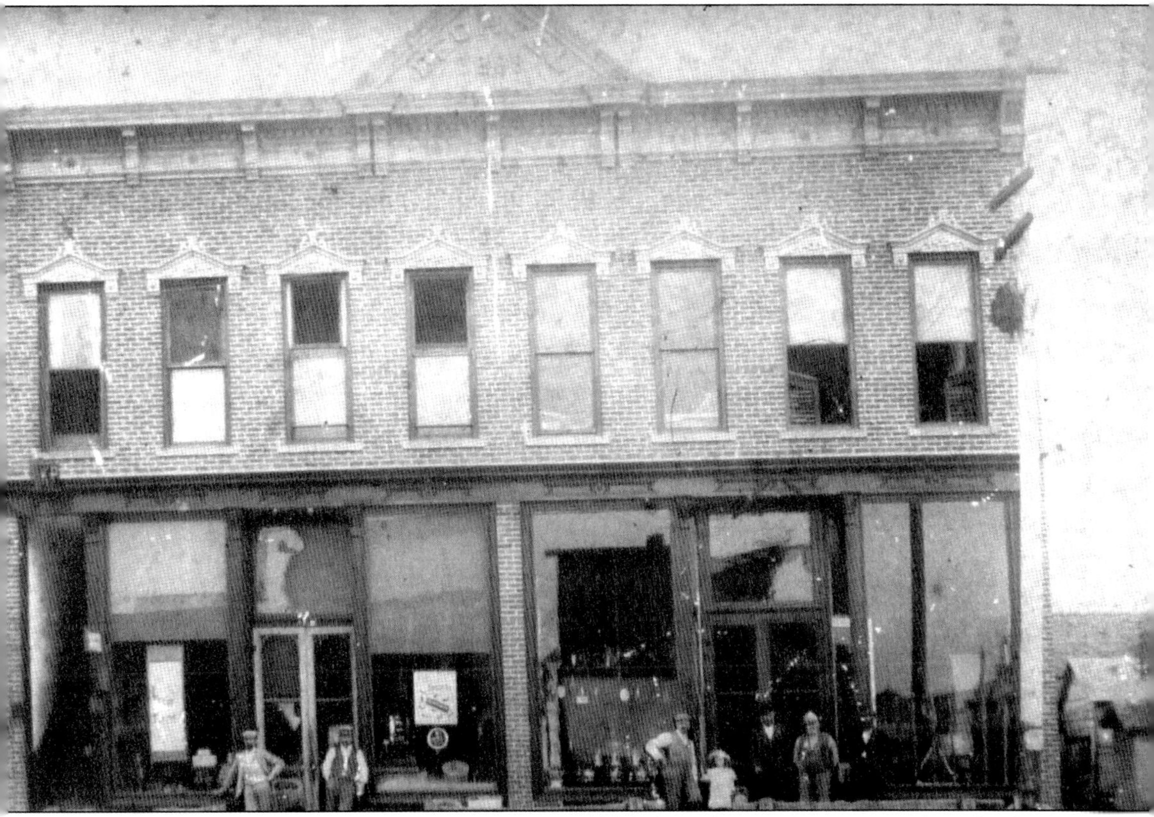

Construction of the Bechtel Building began in 1887, but the death of Samuel Bechtel in an excavation accident put the project on hiatus until 1888, when it was finally completed. Bechtel's widow was always an avid supporter of the project, even beyond the passing of her husband. She would eventually take up residence in the upstairs apartment, while the remaining space was used as a dry goods store, a barber, a tailor, and a Masonic Lodge. The structure was formed in the common commercial style of Italianate architecture, and once sported a triangular shaped pediment that read, "Bechtel, 1888." Located at 151 East Market Street, this building is now the home of Martin Hardware. With its three floors of merchandise and splendid customer service, the store is one of Nappanee's most unique retailers. (Photo courtesy of Mr. and Mrs. William Johnson.)

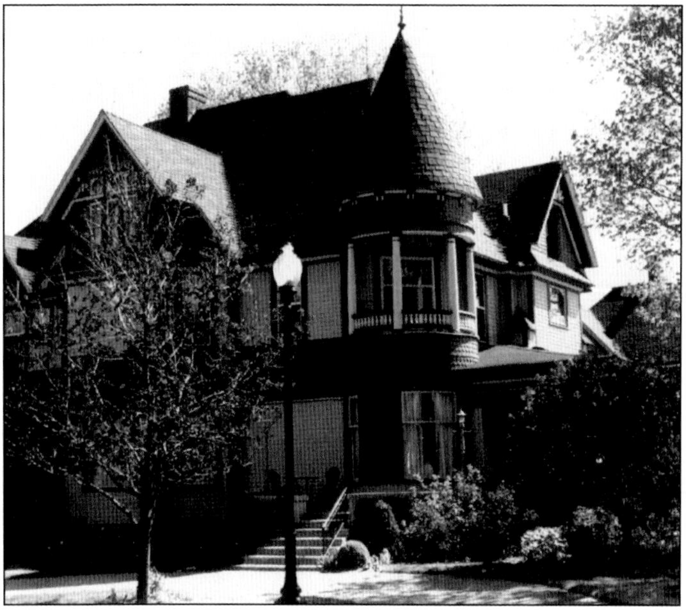

Easily recognized as one of Nappanee's crown jewels, this is the former home of business magnate Frank Coppes, located at 302 East Market Street. Built in 1887, this was considered at the time to be the most elegant, posh house in the community. Though the house did not originally feature indoor plumbing, a cleverly designed system was integrated to collect water and channel it into the home. A third floor wooden cistern would collect rain water, which was siphoned into the basement and then pumped up by hand through a network of pipes into the kitchen. Some of the garnered water supply was put to a more artful use, as was illustrated through the five fountains found in the second floor bedrooms. The house also featured a parlor, a library, a cupola room off the master bedroom, and an elevator used to haul wood from the basement. Four generations of the Coppes family called this home and today it serves as the Victorian Guest House Bed and Breakfast. The facility is run by the husband and wife team of Bruce and Vickie Hunsberger. (Photo courtesy of Mr. and Mrs. Bruce Hunsberger.)

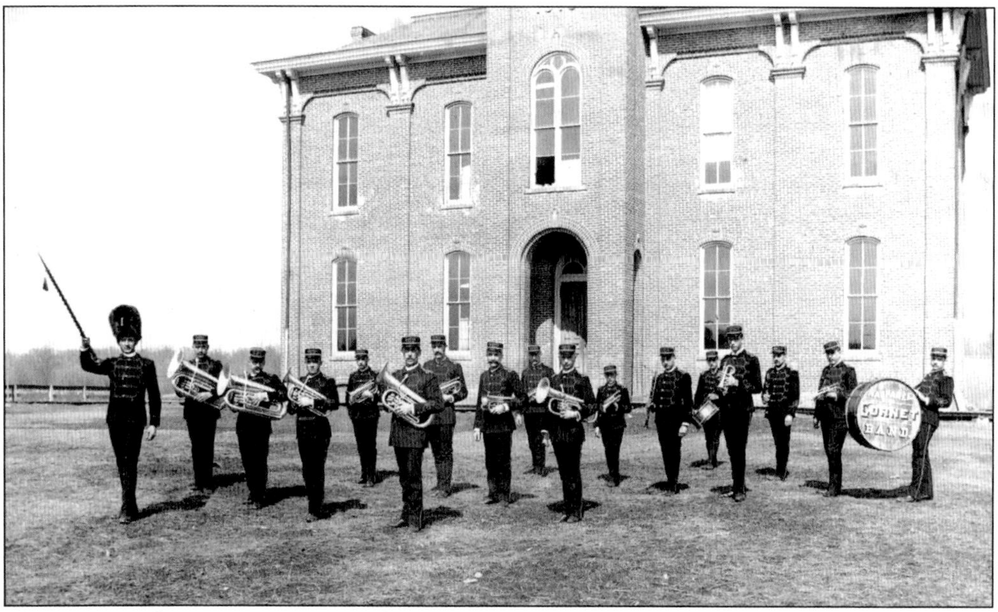

This troupe of musicians comprised the Nappanee Cornet Band, in a photo taken in 1888. The men are posing in front of Nappanee's first brick school building. (Photo courtesy of Nappanee Public Library.)

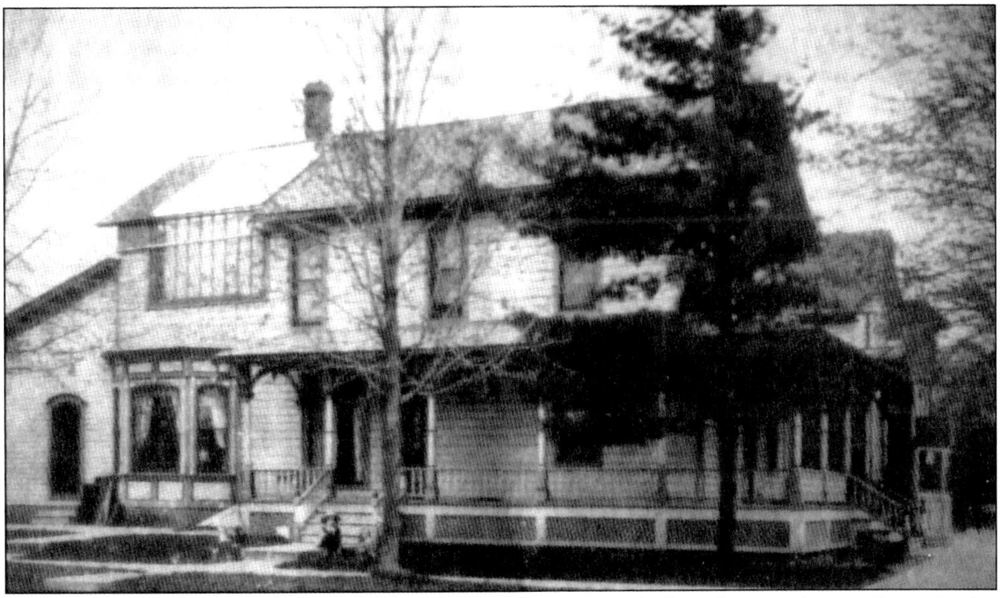

Taken in 1890, this photograph shows another of Nappanee's finer homes. It was formerly the business known as the Keller Photography Studio and Bicycle Shop, and eventually became the home of Dr. Cripe. It was later the town's first library, officially opened on February 5, 1921, on the same site as the current library facility at 157 North Main Street. The first librarian was Rachael Stier, and the materials on hand included 1206 books, 35 magazines, and 3 newspapers. When the present library facility was being constructed in 1936–37, this building was relocated to 352 West Walnut Street, where it still stands. (Photo courtesy of Mr. and Mrs. William Johnson.)

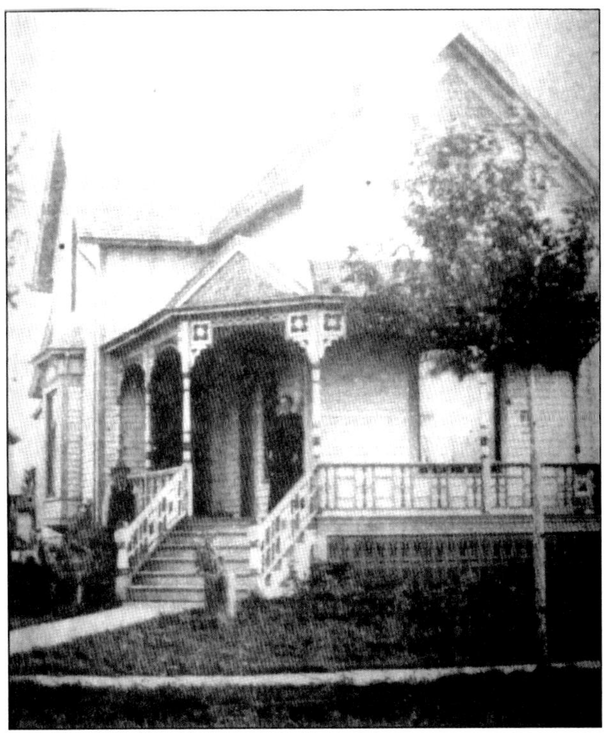

Known by local historians as the Tillman house, this residence is located at 358 East Walnut Street. It was built in 1890 for Guilford Leslie, courtesy of a land grant by then-president James T. Polk. The home was later sold to James Tillman in 1897. (Photo courtesy of Mr. and Mrs. William Johnson.)

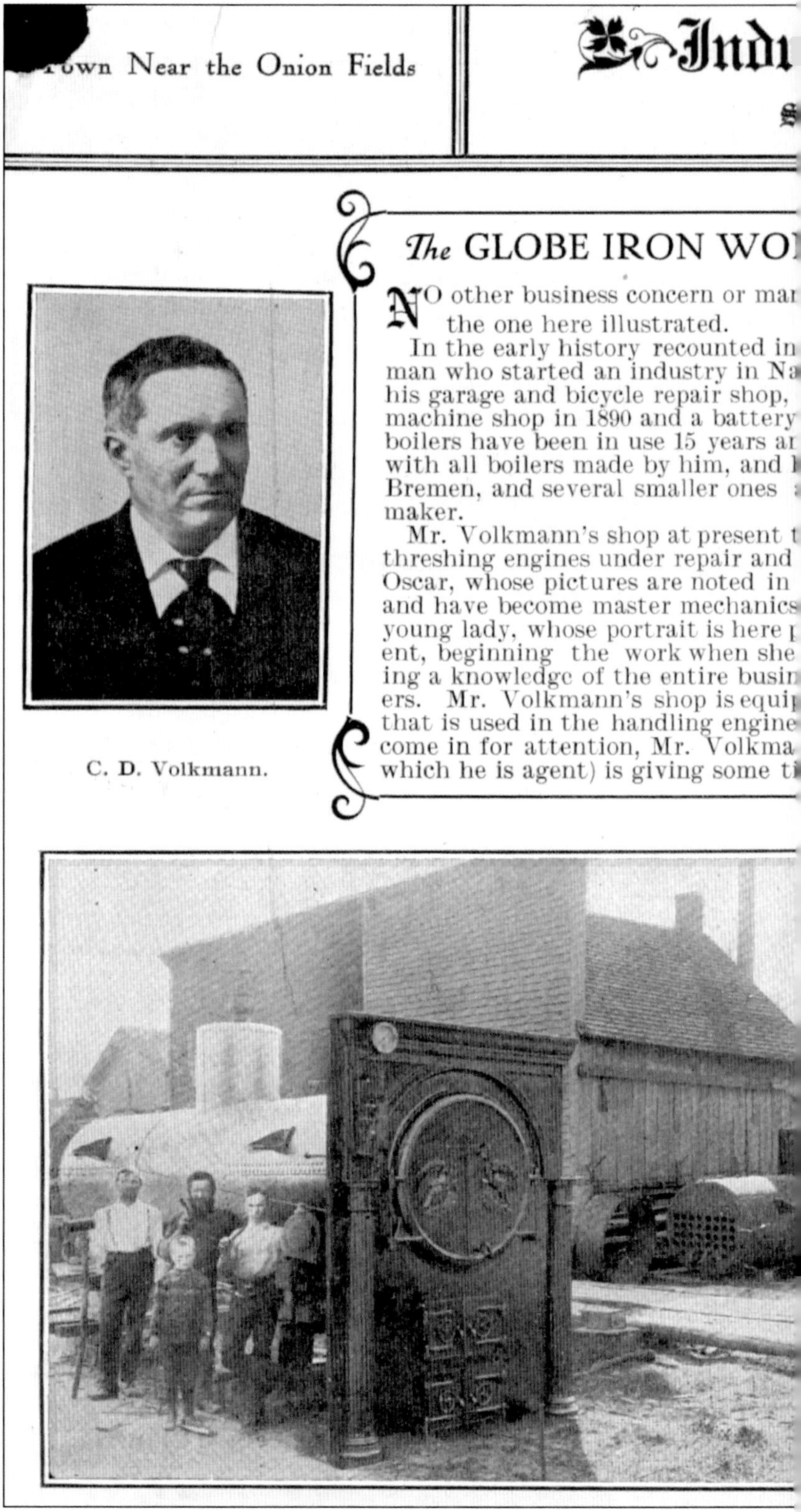

...own Near the Onion Fields

Indi...

The GLOBE IRON WO...

NO other business concern or ma...
the one here illustrated.
In the early history recounted in...
man who started an industry in Na...
his garage and bicycle repair shop,...
machine shop in 1890 and a battery...
boilers have been in use 15 years a...
with all boilers made by him, and ...
Bremen, and several smaller ones ...
maker.
Mr. Volkmann's shop at present ...
threshing engines under repair and...
Oscar, whose pictures are noted in...
and have become master mechanics...
young lady, whose portrait is here ...
ent, beginning the work when she...
ing a knowledge of the entire busi...
ers. Mr. Volkmann's shop is equi...
that is used in the handling engine...
come in for attention, Mr. Volkma...
which he is agent) is giving some t...

C. D. Volkmann.

A special advertising section of the local newspaper documents the beginnings of what was Nappanee's first industry, the Globe Iron Works. Charles D. Volkmann, "machinist and boilermaker," raised a machine shop and boiler factory at the southeast corner of Elm and Lincoln streets, and as the brief article details, went on to further notoriety as one of the city's first automobile owners and repairmen. (Photo courtesy of Nappanee Public Library.)

400 to 500 Bushels Per Acre

. D. VOLKMANN, Machinist *and* Boilermaker.

g establishment can show more marked progress than

azine, will be found that Mr. Volkmann was the first
It was a blacksmith shop on the lot where now stands
rated here. The one illustration shows the boiler and
just being completed for the furniture factory. These
ver had a hammer touch them. This is equally true
de a total of ten boilers for people of Nappanee, one in
places, all bearing testimony to his skill as a boiler-

ıstrated, the picture being taken when he had some 23
epairs at his machine shop. Both his sons, Charles and
llustration as mere boys, have grown to man's estate,
e parent's instructions. Miss Volkmann, an excellent
with that of her father, is book-keeper, and correspond-
school girl. In this she has become proficient, acquir-
en taking orders for repair work the same as her broth-
tools, lathes, planers, drills, etc., in short, everything
nd general work. Since the automobile business has
owned the first car in Nappanee (the Oldsmobile for
air work in this line.

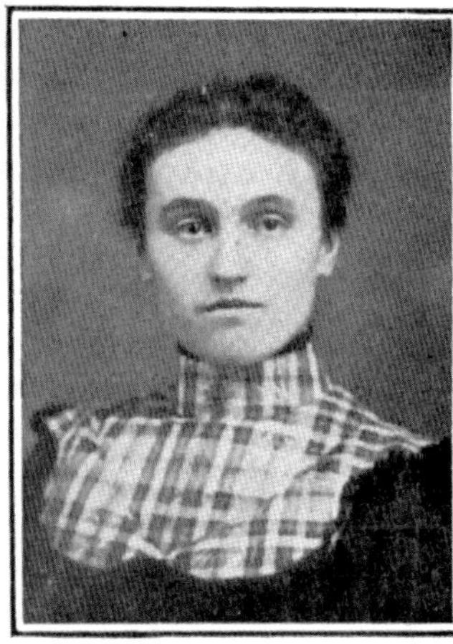

Miss Lucinda Volkmann.

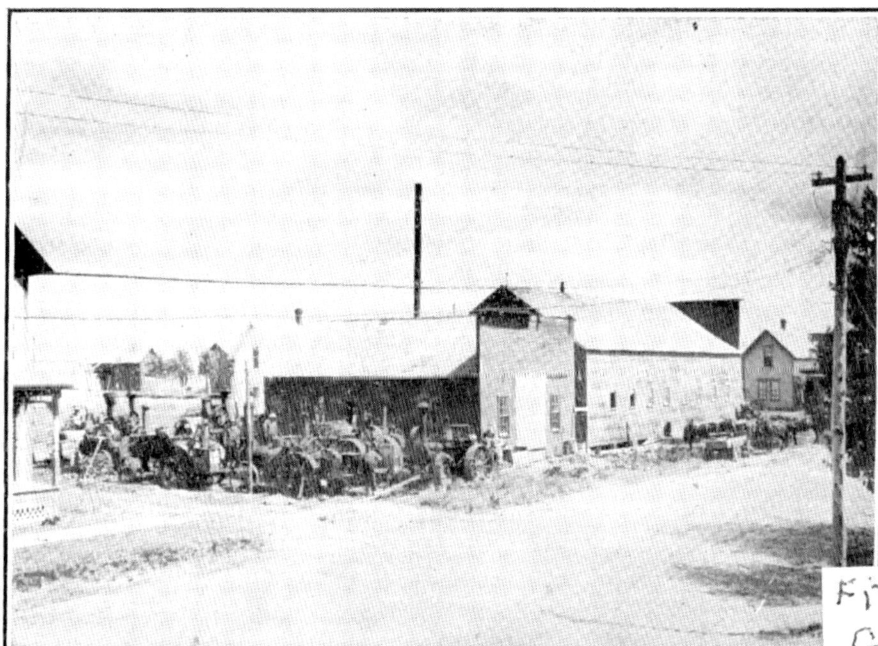

Firs
Gl

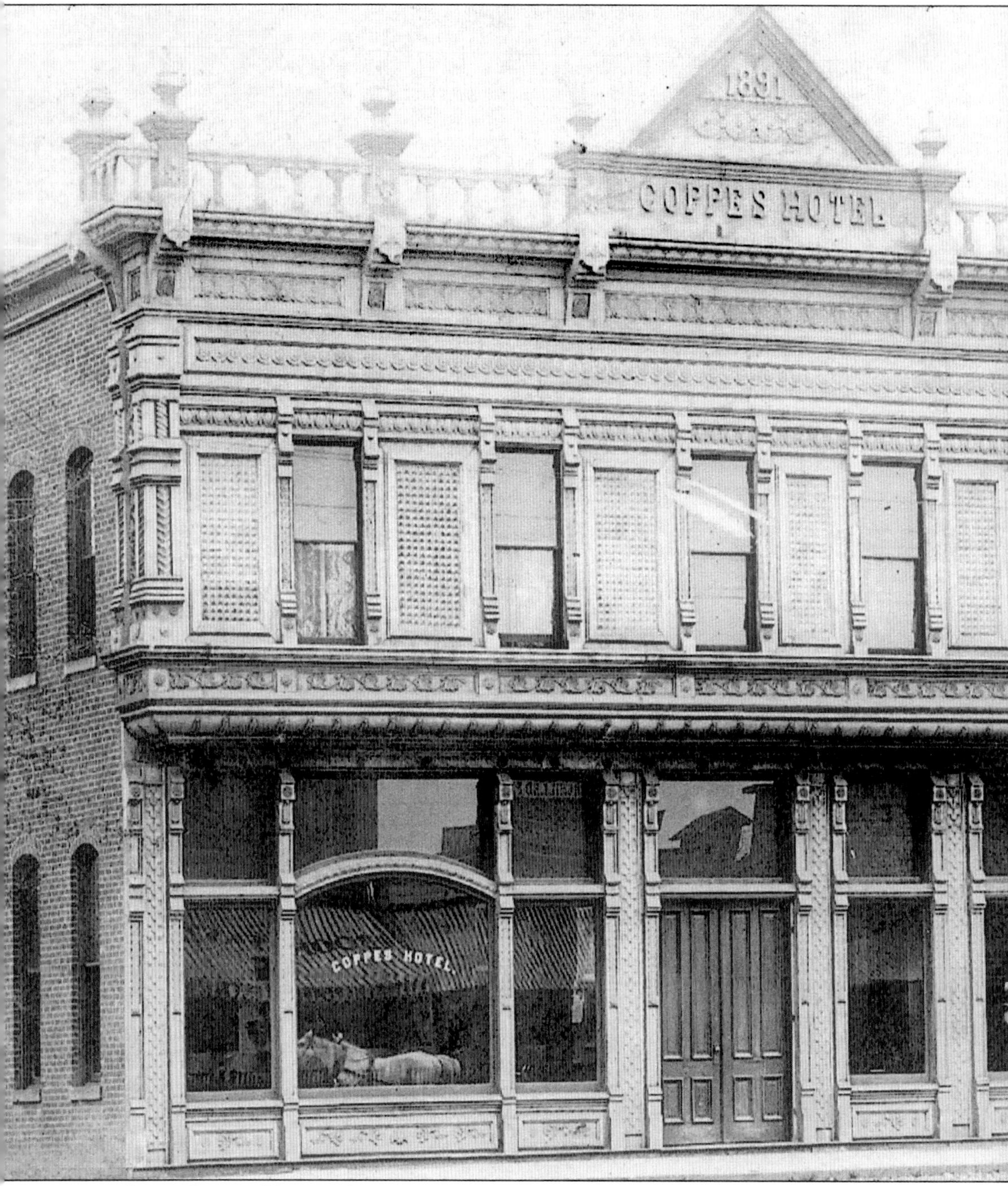

In the opulence of late 19th century America, the Coppes Hotel was looked upon as one of the finest establishments of its kind in the state. The illustrious landmark encompassed much of the south side of the 100 block of East Market Street. It was financed primarily by Samuel Coppes, at a cost of $17,000, and was completed in 1891. Initially, the first floor offered sleeping quarters and a spacious dining room well-suited for the company of local dignitaries. An evening of lodging at the Coppes Hotel could be had for two dollars. The second floor was reserved for use as Coppes Hall, an entertainment venue for a host of showcases, which lasted only until the

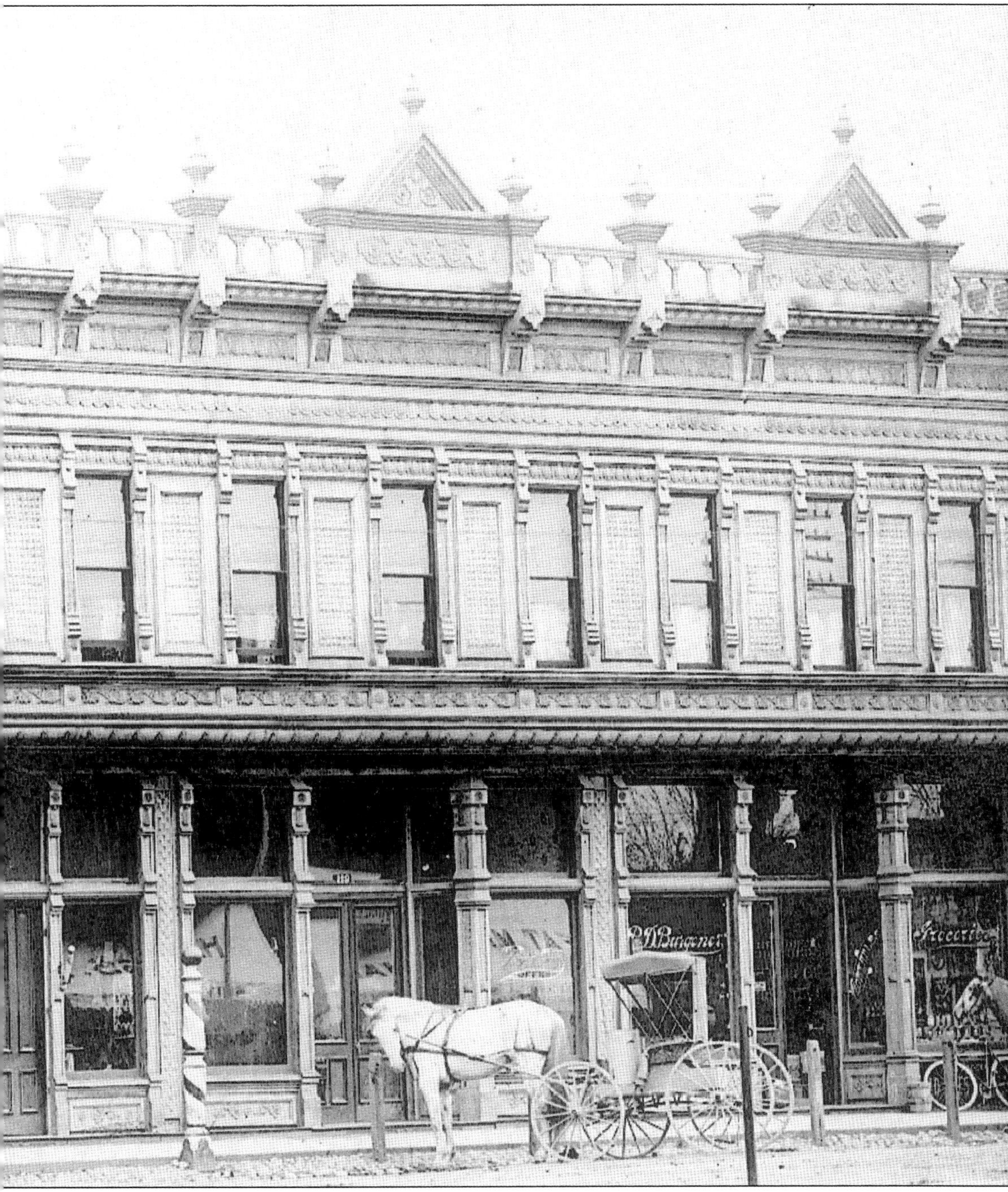

debut of the city's new Auditorium in 1899. After that time, the upper level was converted into seven additional guest rooms. J.Q. Hamilton and Ben Warren served as landlords for the Coppes Hotel prior to 1899, and were succeeded by L.B. Branham, who with his wife, Rilla, took over the management until well into the 1930s—a reign that ended with the death of Branham. The hotel was demolished in 1964. Today it is the site of KeyBank. (Photo courtesy of Nappanee Public Library.)

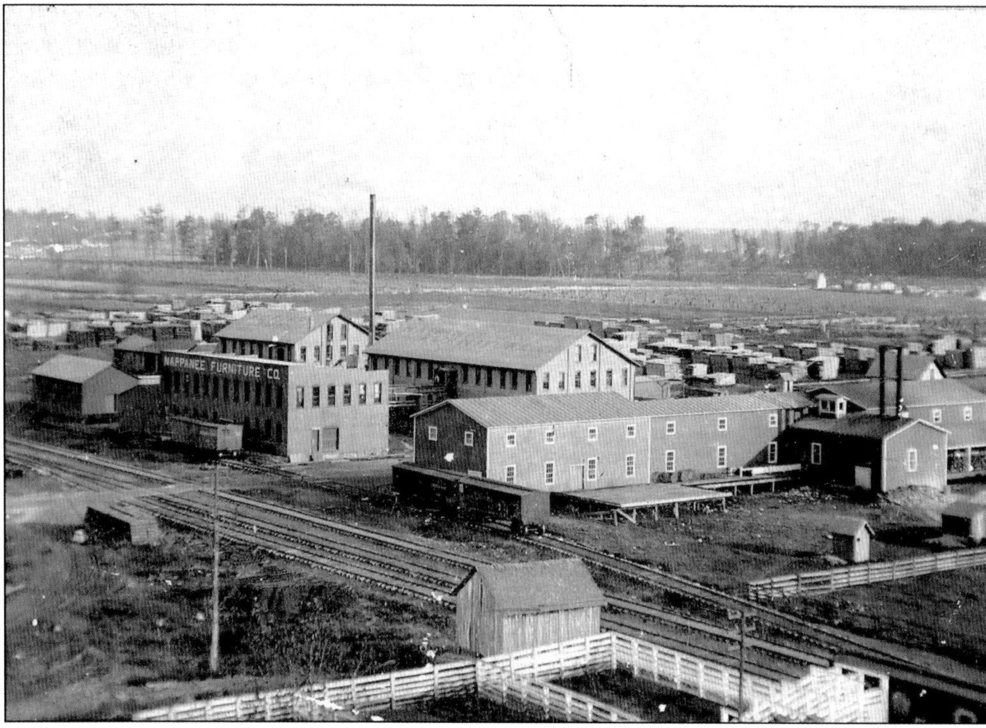

The Nappanee Furniture Company is seen here around 1895. The factory is on the east side of South Madison Street, and the canning facility is on the west. The stockyard is visible in the lower part of the photo. (Photo courtesy of Nappanee Public Library.)

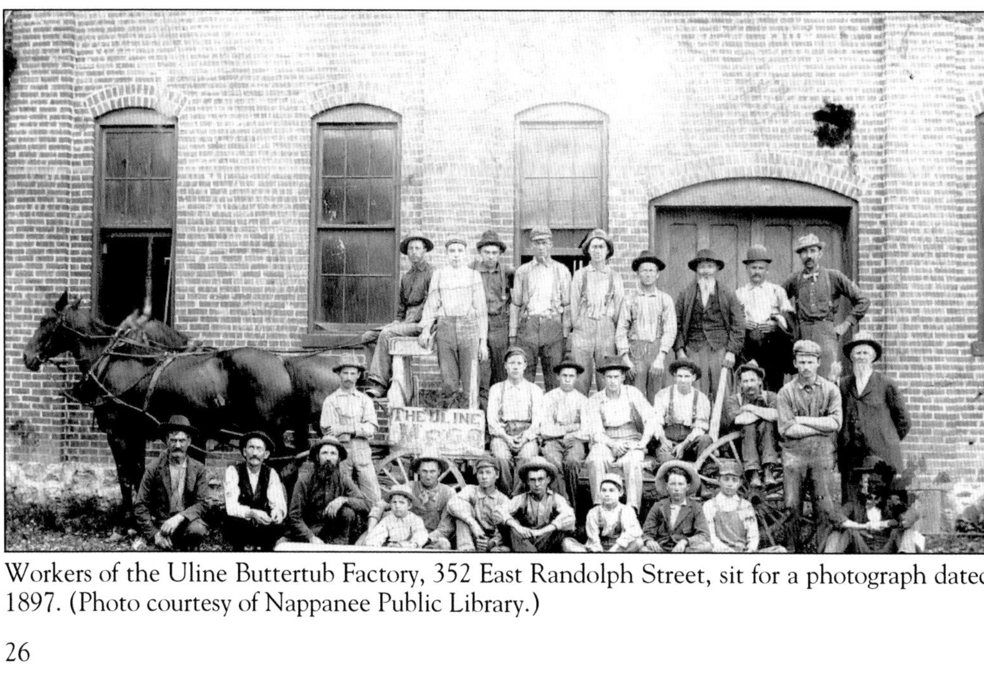

Workers of the Uline Buttertub Factory, 352 East Randolph Street, sit for a photograph dated 1897. (Photo courtesy of Nappanee Public Library.)

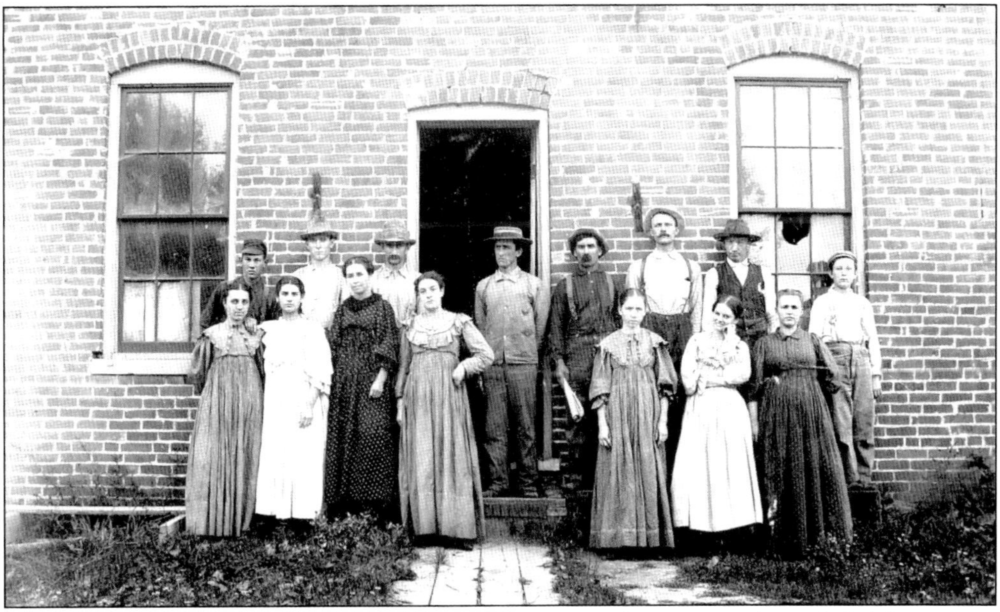

These are the employees of the Stauffer Box Factory as they appeared in 1897. The precise location of the factory is not known, but it was in close proximity to the Coppes Bros. & Zook facility. A July 14, 1897 *Nappanee News* article documents a fire at Stauffer Box Factory, where it is noted that "Lumber sheds and a driveway only separate the building from the brick factory of Coppes Bros. & Zook." The only person that is identified is the third woman in the front row—Mrs. Charles Tobias. (Photo courtesy of Nappanee Public Library.)

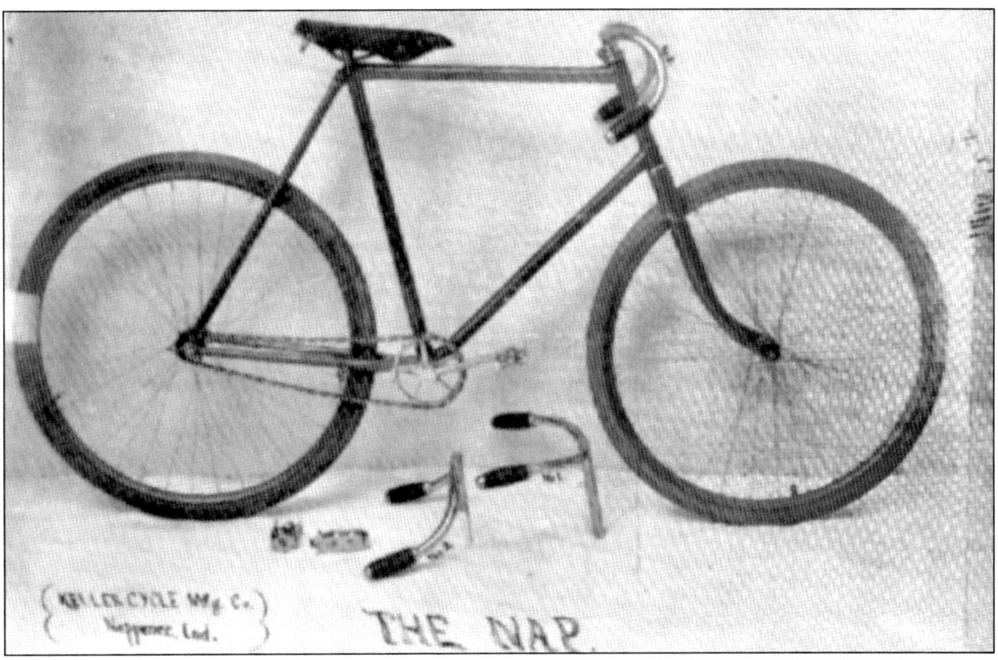

This intriguing piece of machinery was "The Nap" bicycle, which was produced by the Keller Manufacturing Company of Nappanee. This model was created in 1897. (Photo courtesy of Nappanee Public Library.)

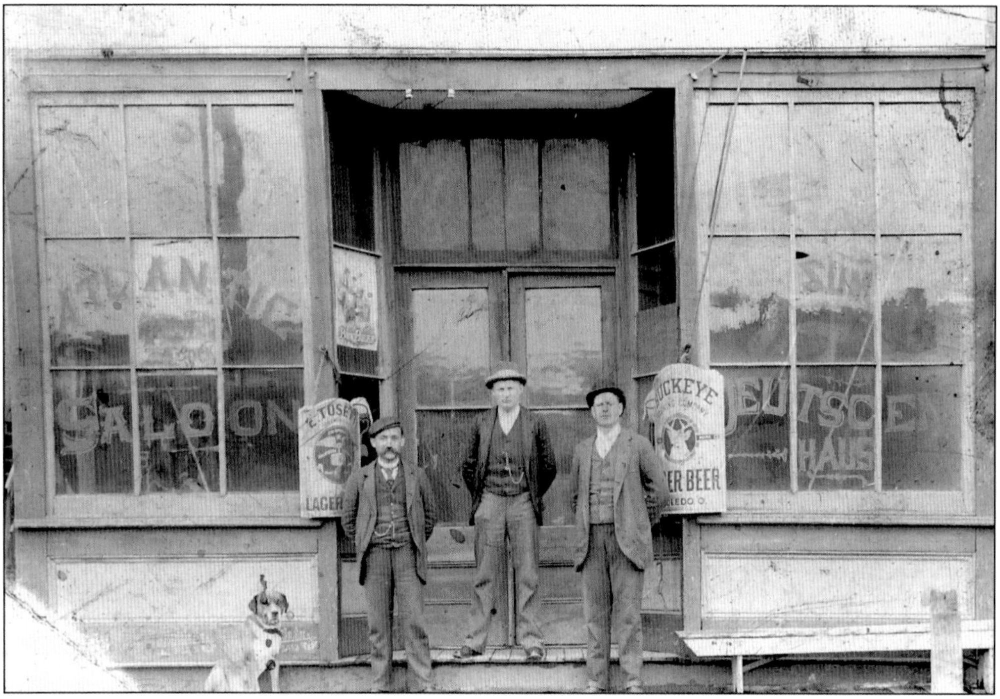

This 1897 photo shows Mahler's Saloon, owned by Charles Mahler. The business was located in the 100 block of West Market Street. (Photo courtesy of Nappanee Public Library.)

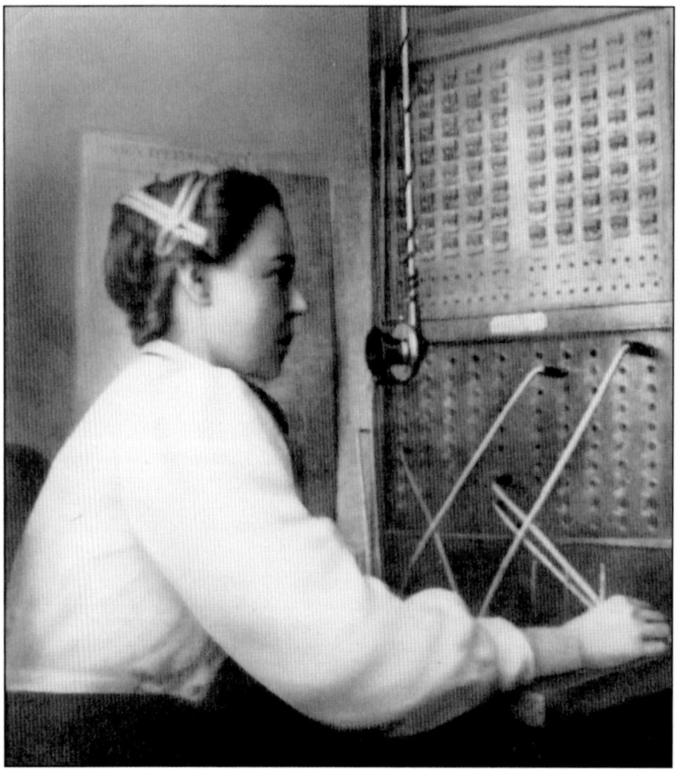

In 1898, Lydia Weber made local history by becoming Nappanee's first telephone and switchboard operator for the Nappanee Telephone Company. (Photo courtesy of Nappanee Public Library.)

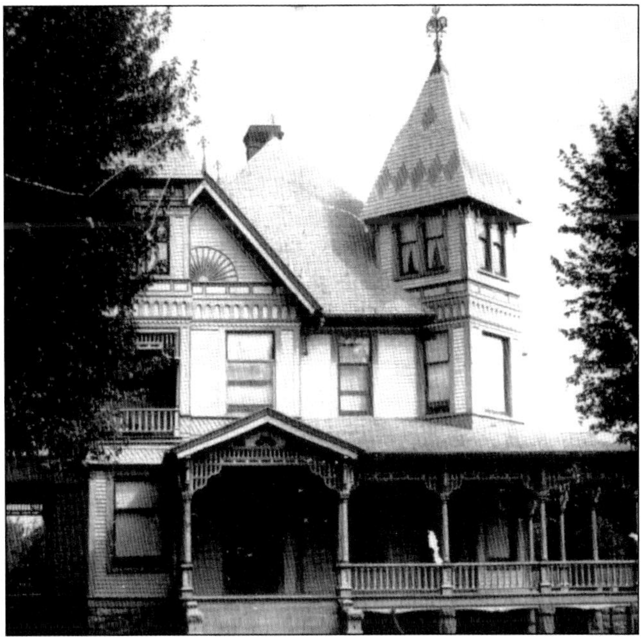

Another one of Nappanee's most legendary dwellings, this is the John Coppes house, built in 1898. This Queen Anne-styled structure was the home of John and Malinda Strohm Coppes, the first couple to be married in Nappanee. John Coppes was also one of a trio of brothers who achieved renown as part owner of the Coppes business empire. The original design of this house featured high-pitched roofs, a tower, and a port-cochere which was connected to the Daniel Zook residence just to the west. The interior of the house was something of a mirror image to brother Frank's home, which was located directly to the east, across the road. Other lavish features of this house included water fountains in each bedroom, art glass windows, and a hand-cranked elevator in the basement, which was used to haul wood. In 1950, the house was purchased and renovated for use as the Masonic Temple. It also serves as the Elder Haus, a facility that provides recreational opportunities for senior citizens. The house can be found at 258 East Market Street. (Photo courtesy of Nappanee Public Library.)

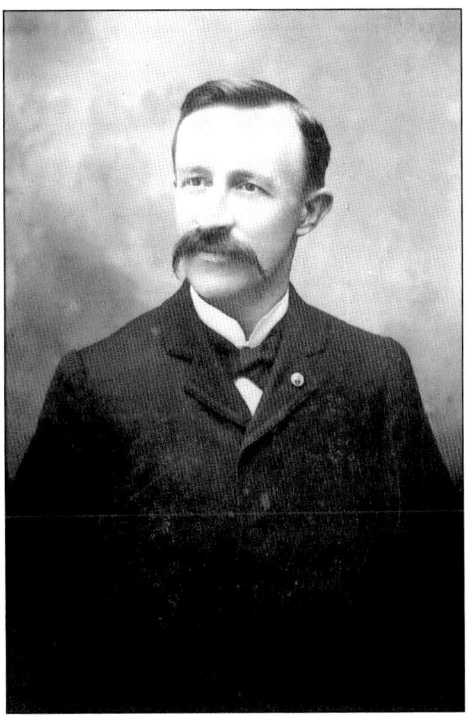

Christian W. Johnson is shown here in this c. 1900 photograph. He was the patriarch of another one of Nappanee's most honored families. As a youth, he was a member of the team of workers who helped to lay the B & O railroad tracks. Johnson was also an employee of the town's first drug store, and by 1900, he entered into a partnership which allowed for the opening of a drug store at the intersection of Main and Market streets. His son Harold joined him in the business in 1909, from that day on known as C.W. Johnson & Son. Another son, Lloyd, entered into the fold in 1916, followed by Lloyd's son, William—three generations of fathers, brothers, and sons. Johnson, for his part, remained active in the workings of his business until a fall in 1950, in which he received a hip injury, caused him to scale back his work commitments. He was a prominent figure in many other civic affairs, and ended an extraordinary life in 1953, at the age of 93. At the time of his passing, he was the oldest man in Nappanee. (Photo courtesy of Mr. and Mrs. William Johnson.)

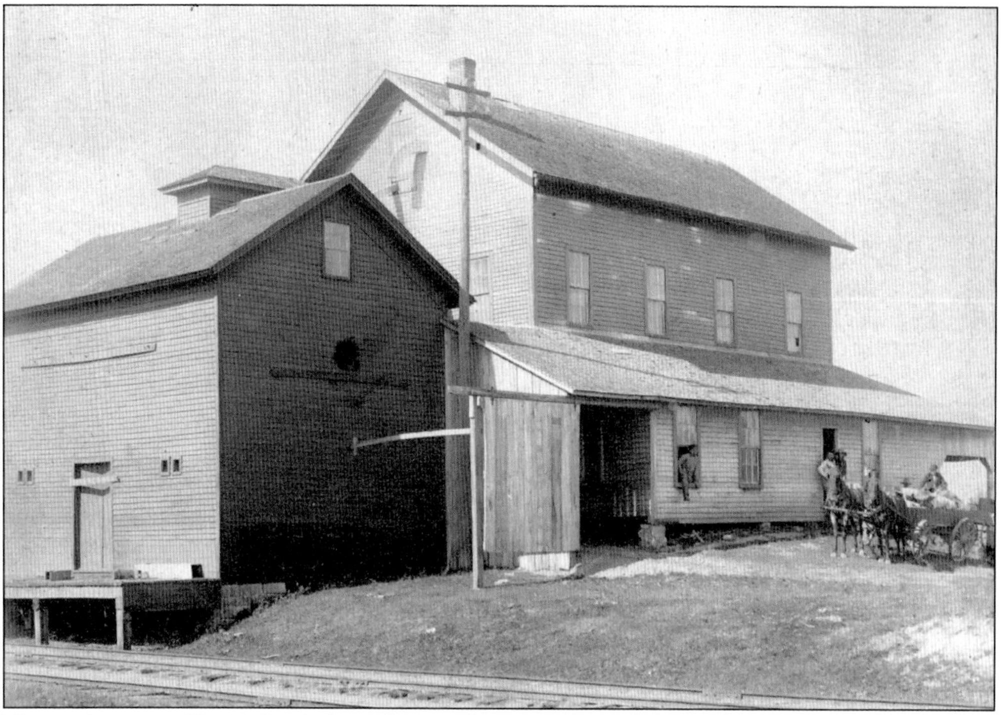

This early grist mill, which is believed to pre-date 1900, is shown somewhere near the downtown area—the name of the facility and its exact location is unknown. (Photo courtesy of Nappanee Public Library.)

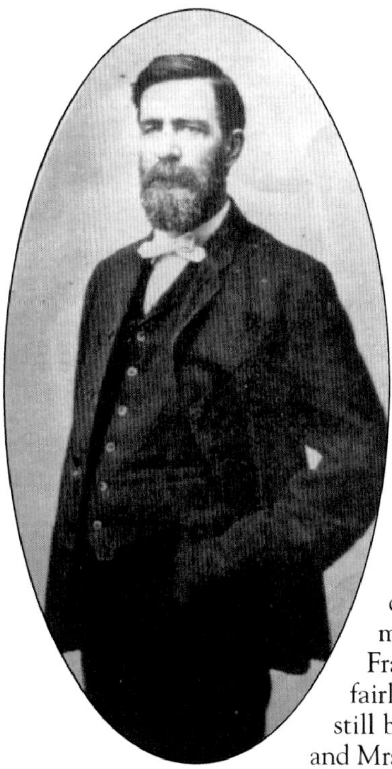

The great architect Henry Frazier, the man responsible for designing a number of structures and homes in Nappanee, appears as he looked at the time of the early 1900s. Born in Stark County, Ohio, in 1849, Frazier was just three years old when he and his grandfather came to live in Elkhart County. After attending "common schools" in the region, he studied at the State Normal School in Terre Haute. He then spent twenty years as an educator, spending five of those years teaching public school in Nappanee. He devoted a great deal of his free time to carpentry, and this may have fueled his desire to begin a career in architecture. Frazier's tenure with designing and crafting buildings was of fairly short duration—just 14 years, but his contributions can still be seen throughout the community. (Photo courtesy of Mr. and Mrs. William Johnson.)

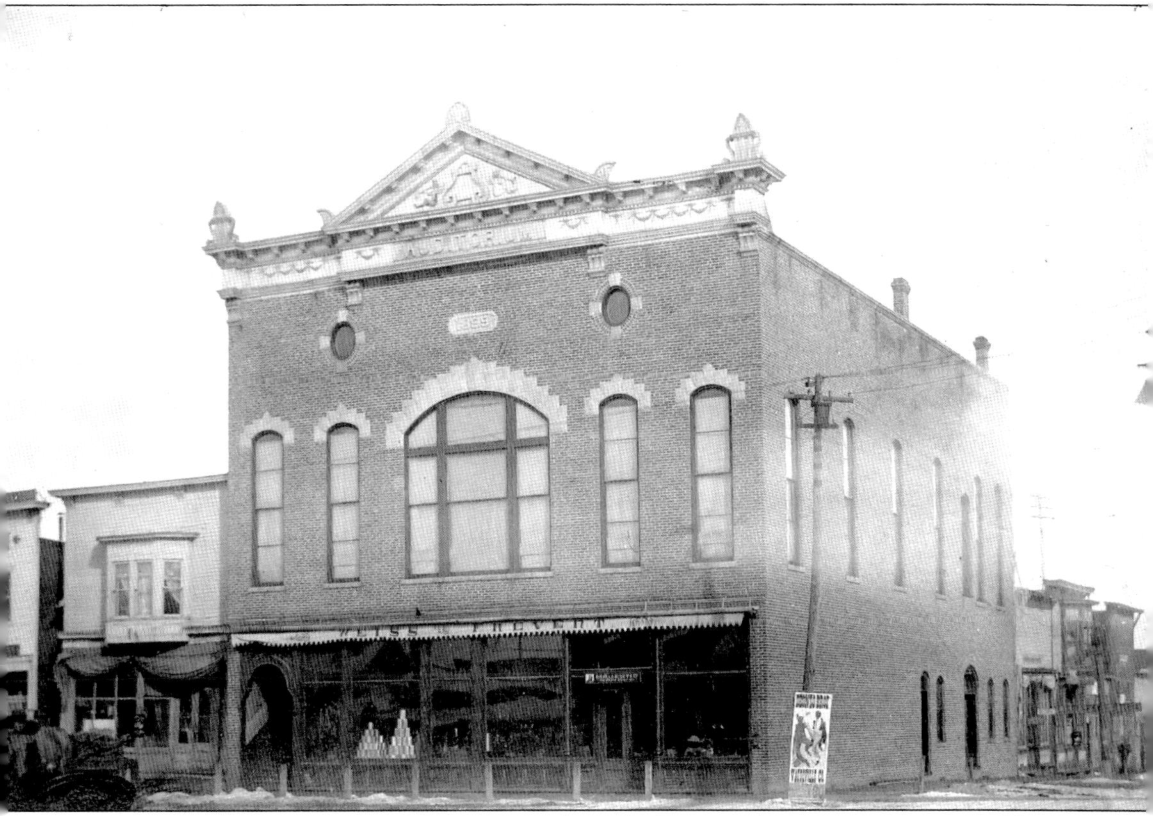

Its time spent gracing central Nappanee was a relatively short one, but what a time it was. This was the towering building known simply as the Auditorium. Built in 1899, and situated on the northwest corner of Main and Market streets, it was the perfect complement to a bustling downtown in a rapidly growing new city. Audiences from across the county would travel to Nappanee to see vaudevillians, comedians, musicians, and high school presentations. Admission charges ranged anywhere from a dime to 20¢. The Auditorium was also one of the first outlets in the region to offer "moving pictures" in the late 1910s. By 1923, patrons could view a movie by way of state-of-the-art projection equipment. In January of 1937, the Auditorium was a casualty of a massive inferno that began in the lower level of the building, in the Jet White store, and threatened to consume the entire city block. Reports began to circulate that "Nappanee was on fire," and extra manpower was summoned from the nearby towns of Bremen, Wakarusa, New Paris, Elkhart, and Warsaw. At the height of the event, as flames towered into the sky, it was estimated that some 5,000 onlookers cascaded into the area to watch the blaze. The building was rendered a total loss at $40,000 and was never rebuilt. There were no known accounts of serious injury. (Photo courtesy of Nappanee Public Library.)

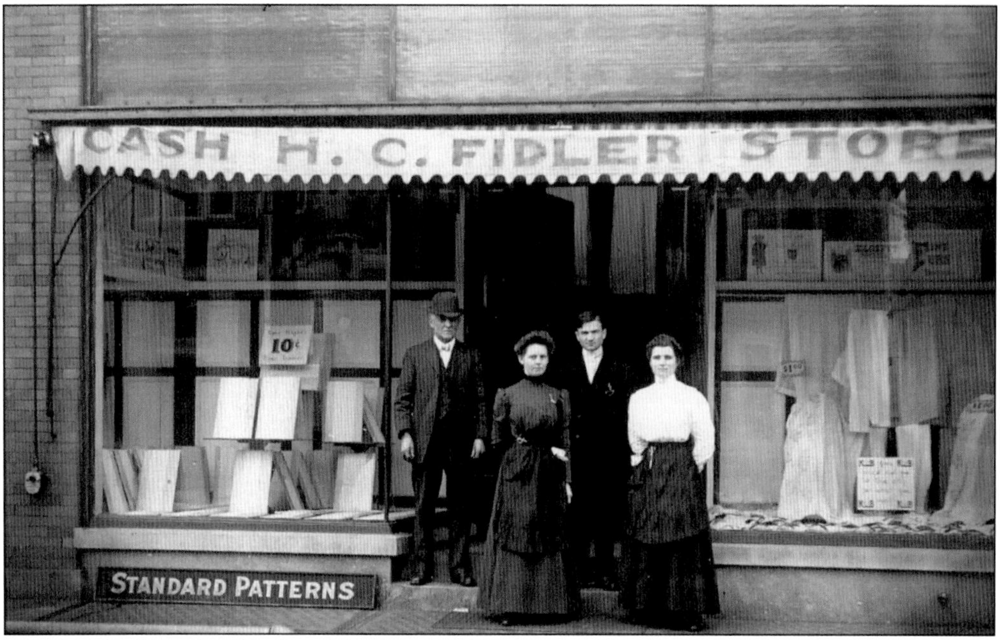

This is a look at the facade of the H.C. Fidler Store, which later became Fidler & Rickert's Dry Goods. The picture is c. 1900. A sign in the window reads "Standard Patterns—10¢. None higher, none lower." The woman wearing a white blouse is Fanny Miller. The business was adjacent to Kaufman's Department Store, in the 100 block of East Market Street. (Photo courtesy of Mr. and Mrs. Dean Henry.)

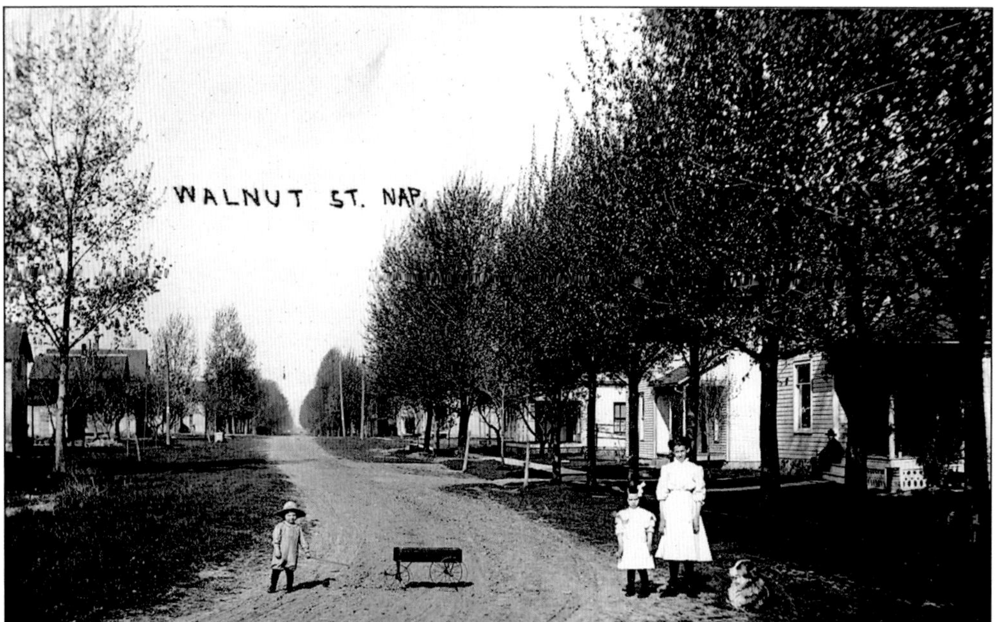

A gently winding dirt road weaves its way through a peaceful neighborhood, in this undated look at what was then, and still is today, Walnut Street. (Photo courtesy of Nappanee Public Library.)

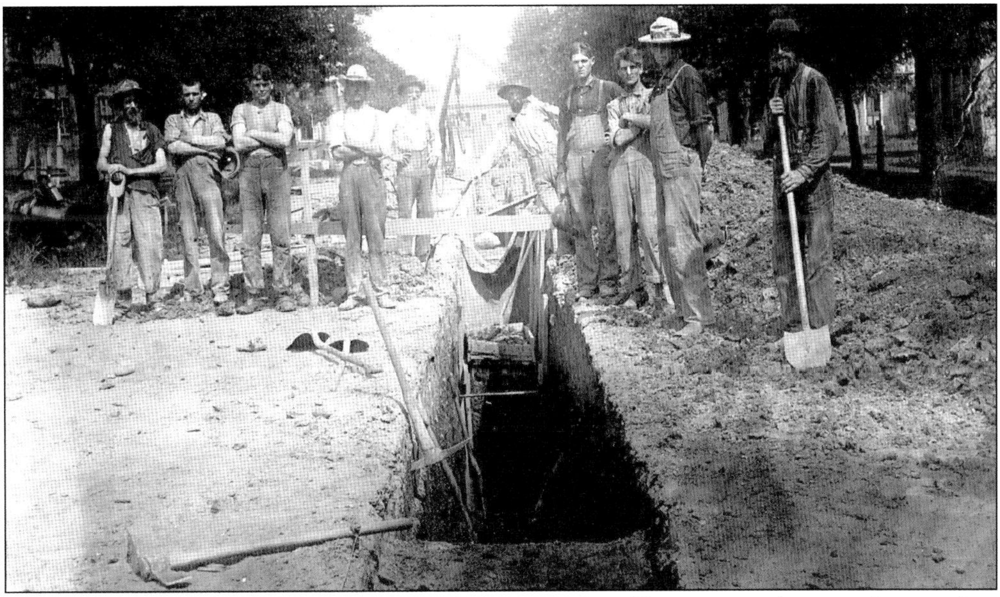

These men pause for a moment on this ambitious project of laying sewer lines in the city. It is not known for certain exactly where this particular pipeline was being installed, or when, but it was reported by the Nappanee News that in 1904, the city received bids for the completion of a north-south sewer line. Prior to that, there were other lines, presumably in and near the downtown square. The best news brief to acknowledge that fact came in the form of an 1892 story where the city had to deal with the nuisance of ridding the sewer system of catfish. (Photo courtesy of Nappanee Public Library.)

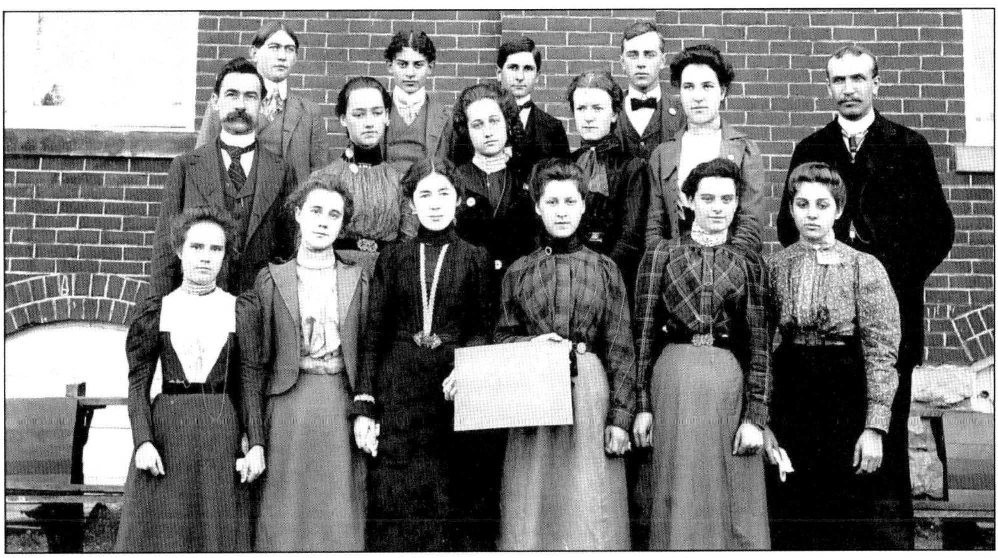

Students of the senior class of '02 pose for a class photo outside the city's first brick school building. Pictured from left to right are: (front row) Nora Stahly, Beulah Tillman, two unidentified, Ida Blessing, and Maude Walters; (second row) unidentified, Dinah Frazier, unidentified, Clara Gray, and unidentified. The last gentleman in the second row is Dr. S.W. Baer, the superintendent, and the last fellow in the third row is Otto Basye—other classmates in the third row are not identified. (Photo courtesy of Nappanee Public Library.)

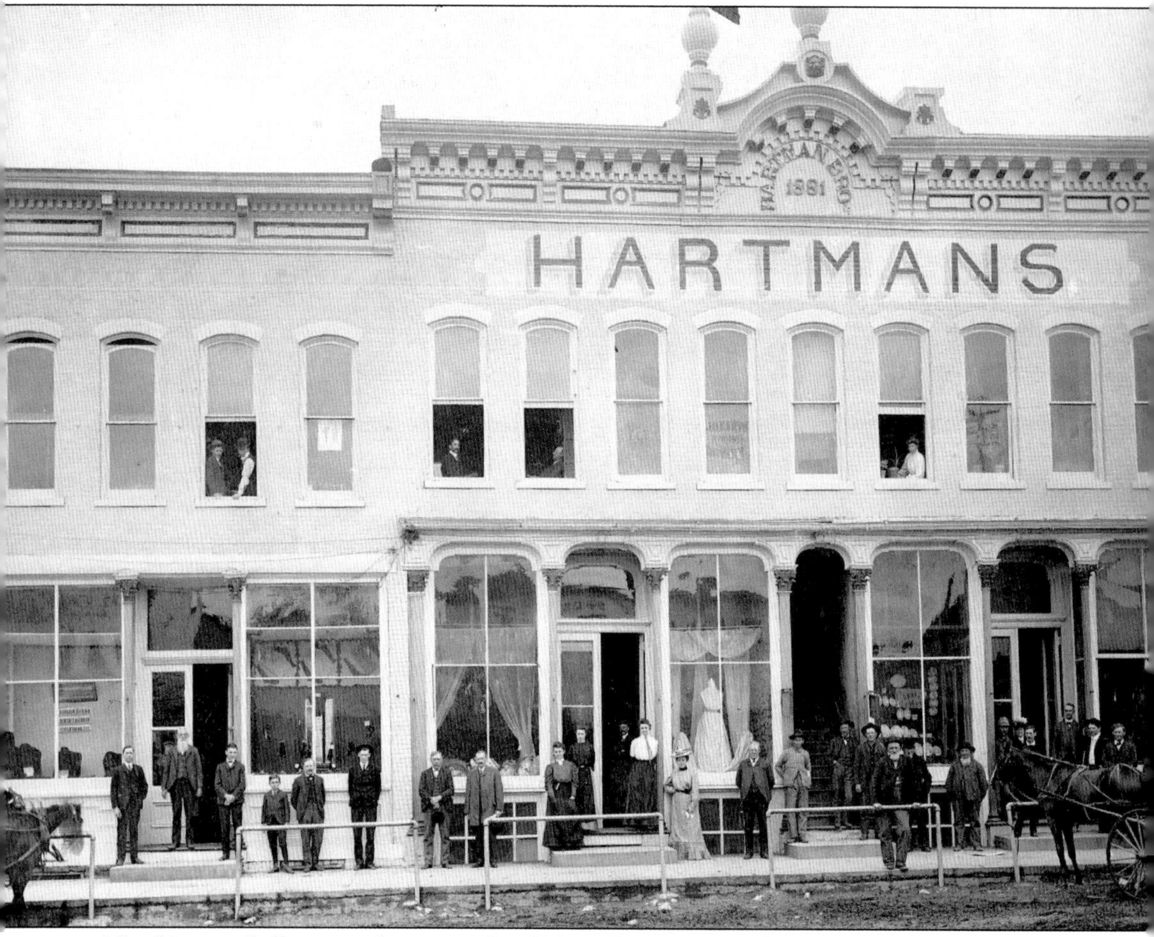

The Hartman's Store on the west side of Main Street, is seen here in the early 1900s. Owned by Samuel Hartman, it was the largest store of its kind in the area. Advertisements billed this business as a "triple store," as it encompassed the length of three storefronts. There was an entertainment venue in the back portion of the top floor, which was called Hartman Hall, once known as Stahly Hall. The brothers of the Hartman family had quite an enterprise in their day, also owning a sawmill and a charcoal manufacturing plant. Samuel Hartman also owned the Napanee Hotel, later called the Napanee House, which was right across the street from the store, on East Main Street. An 1888 article offered an explanation as to why there was just one "p" in the name—supposedly, the sign company charged $1 per letter, so Hartman dropped one "p" in an effort to save some money. When the Hartman brothers passed away, the store was broken up into three separate businesses—a grocery store, a dry goods store, and a clothing store. Pictured, though not listed in order, are Edward Lape, John Hartman, Edgar Ringenberg, Horace Hartman, Jesse Ringenberg, Jacob Hartman, Ivy Hartman, Dinah Hartman Slabaugh, Tobias Hartman, Frank Walters, and Lillie Geyer. (Photo courtesy of Nappanee Public Library.)

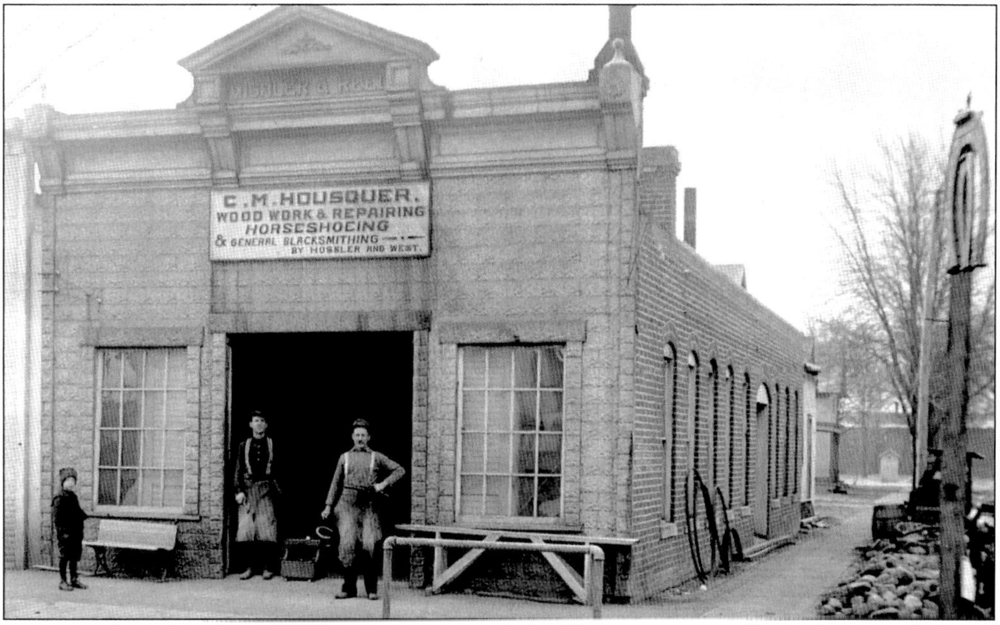

This might well be an establishment with one of the longest names in the history of Nappanee business. Located in the Mishler and Reed building, this was the C.M. Housour Wood Work & Repairing, Horseshoeing, and General Blacksmithing, by Hossler and West. The photo is undated. (Photo courtesy of Mr. and Mrs. Dean Henry.)

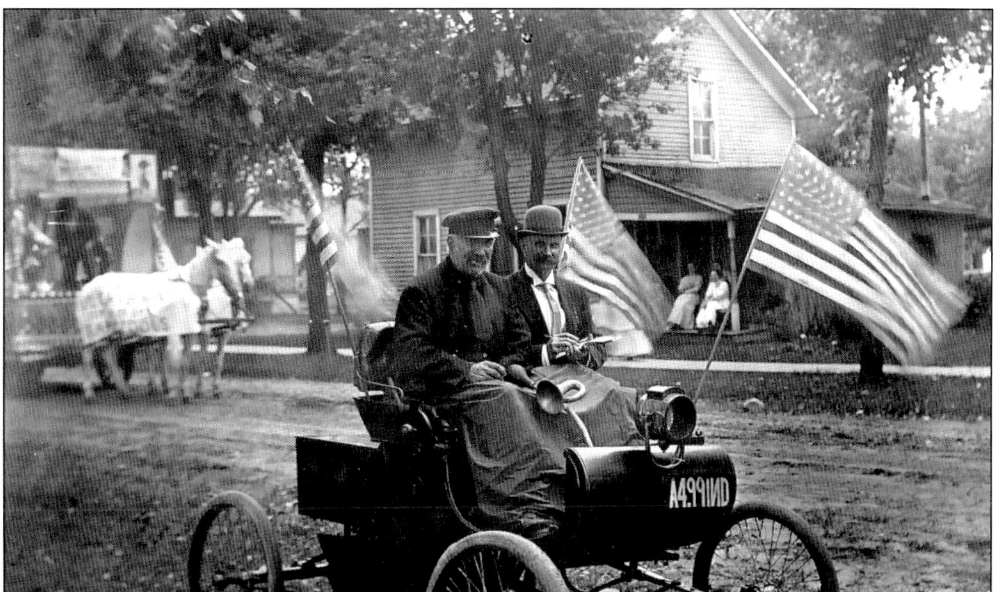

Nappanee's first automobile, an Oldsmobile, was owned by Charles "Connie" Volkmann. Volkmann was the founder of Nappanee's first industry, the Globe and Iron Works. His passenger is Gordon H. Murray, editor of the Nappanee News. (Photo courtesy of Nappanee Public Library.)

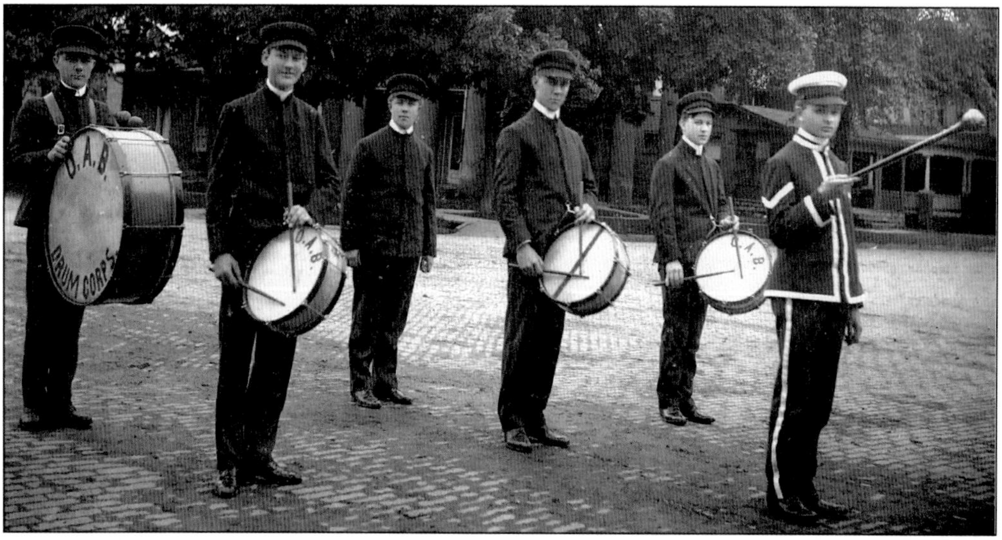

The local drum corps, known as the OAB boys, are pictured here in 1904. From left to right are Harry Price, Bill Bechtel, Burton Uline, Arthur Price, Ed Wilson, and Edgar Ringenberg. Ringenberg was the group president, and Wilson served as secretary-treasurer. (Photo courtesy of Nappanee Public Library.)

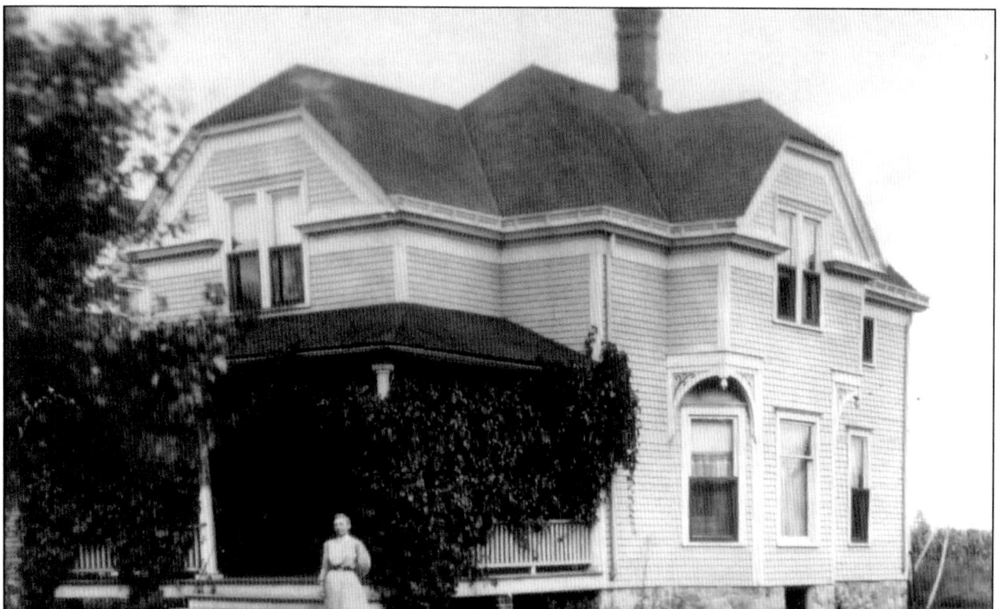

In 1905, a grouping of six homes was built in the 301-350 block of North Hartman Street. The homes were created as an investment venture for Frank Coppes, one of the founders of the Coppes line of businesses. Each house was available for rent at a cost of $10 a month. Five of the six original houses are still standing, although their appearances have been altered somewhat over the years. They were all inspired by a popular design from that era, called a basic gable-ell shape. Some touches of elegance were added to the exterior, such as cornice returns at the gables, bay windows with decorative brackets, and jerkin-head roofs. (Photo courtesy of Mr. and Mrs. William Johnson.)

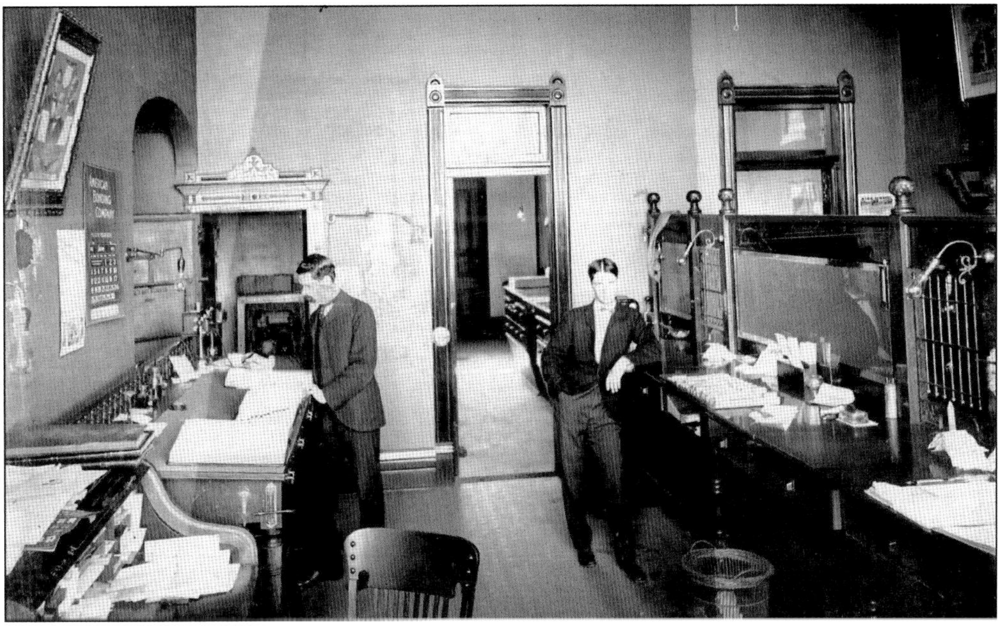

Harry Greene and Fred Coppes are shown in the interior of the Farmers and Traders Bank, which was located at 104 South Main Street. The stately structure, formed from Bedford limestone, still exists in the heart of the city, and presently houses Justus Property Management. It was erected to carry particular features of colossal columns with Ionic order capitals, and a recessed pediment entry. It was believed that this specific type of construction presented an aura of justice. (Photo courtesy of Nappanee Public Library.)

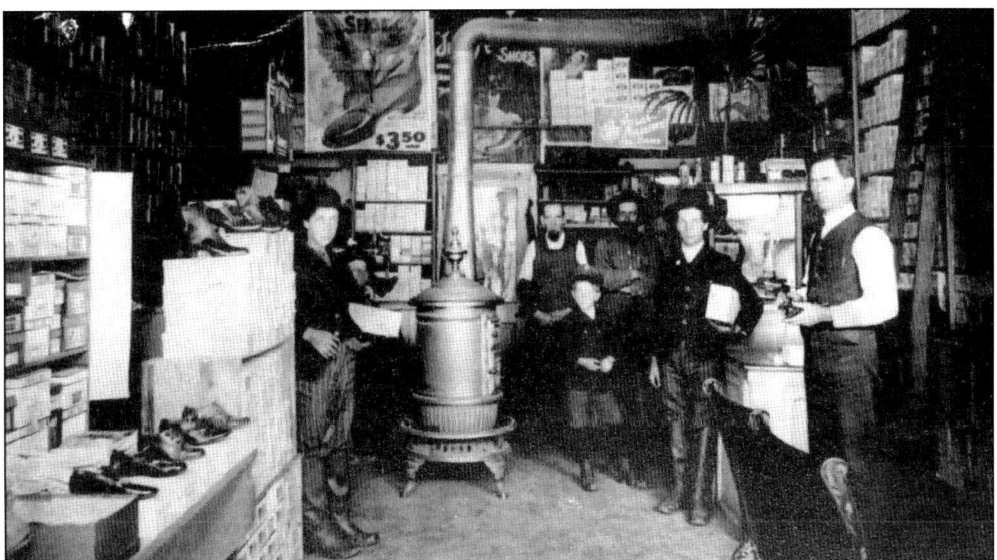

Blosser's Shoe Store, located at 104 East Market Street, was housed in Nappanee's first brick building. Pictured, but not identified in order are Elias Blosser, Dan Waterman, and William Wagner. The little boy is Lowell Blosser, age seven and the gentleman seated in the back is identified as Mr. Felty, the father of Mrs. Frank Coppes. (Photo courtesy of Nappanee Public Library.)

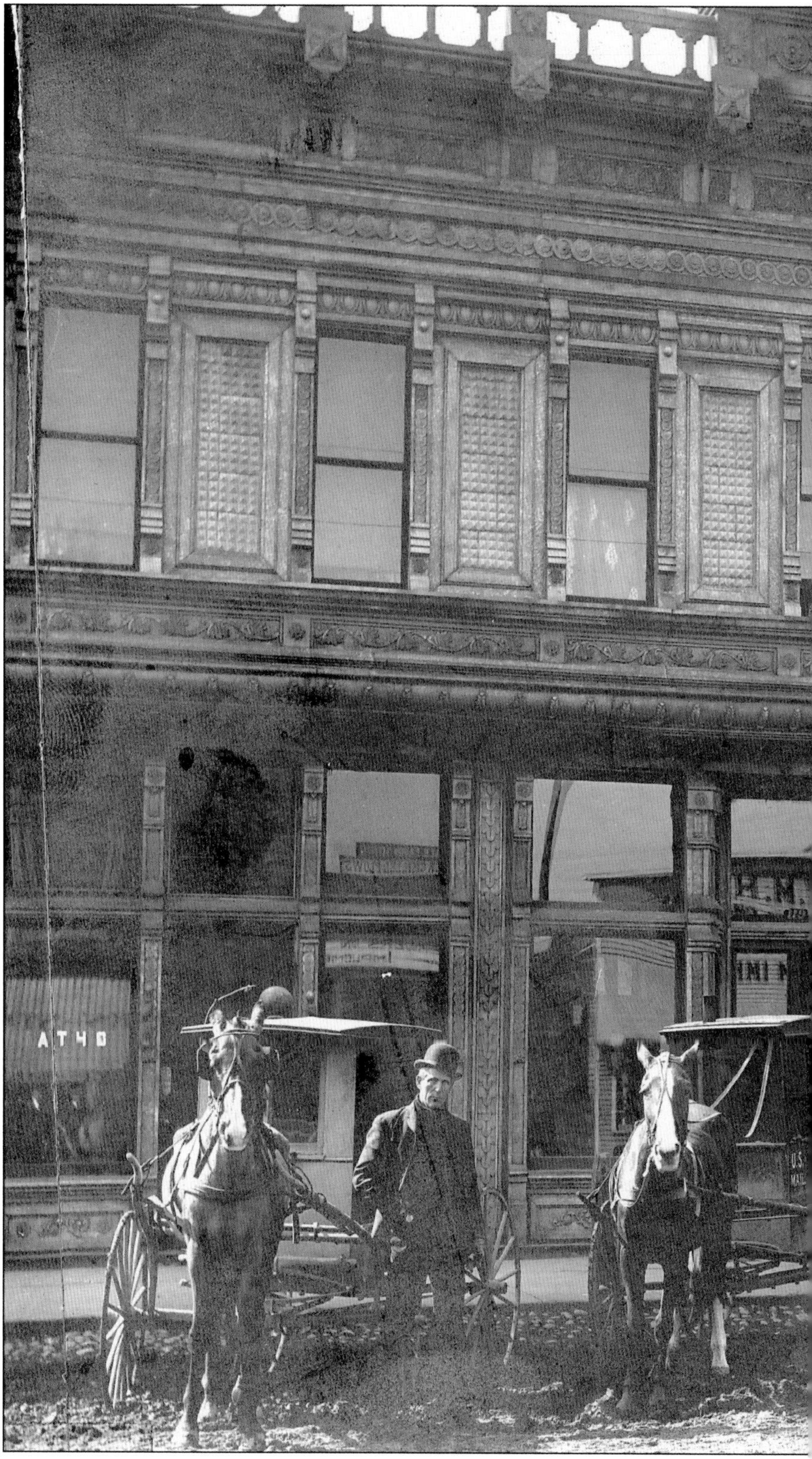

This impressive looking fleet constituted Nappanee's first mail carriers, in a photo taken in 1905. They are standing in front of the former Coppes Hotel, at the corner of East Market and South Elm streets. From left to right, are: (front row) Warren Terwilliger, Hal Brown, Jake Hemminger, and Ed Arch; (back row) Mike Hoover, Grace Miller, Alma Hossler, Freed Miller, William Miller, and Irvin Duker. (Photo courtesy of Nappanee Public Library.)

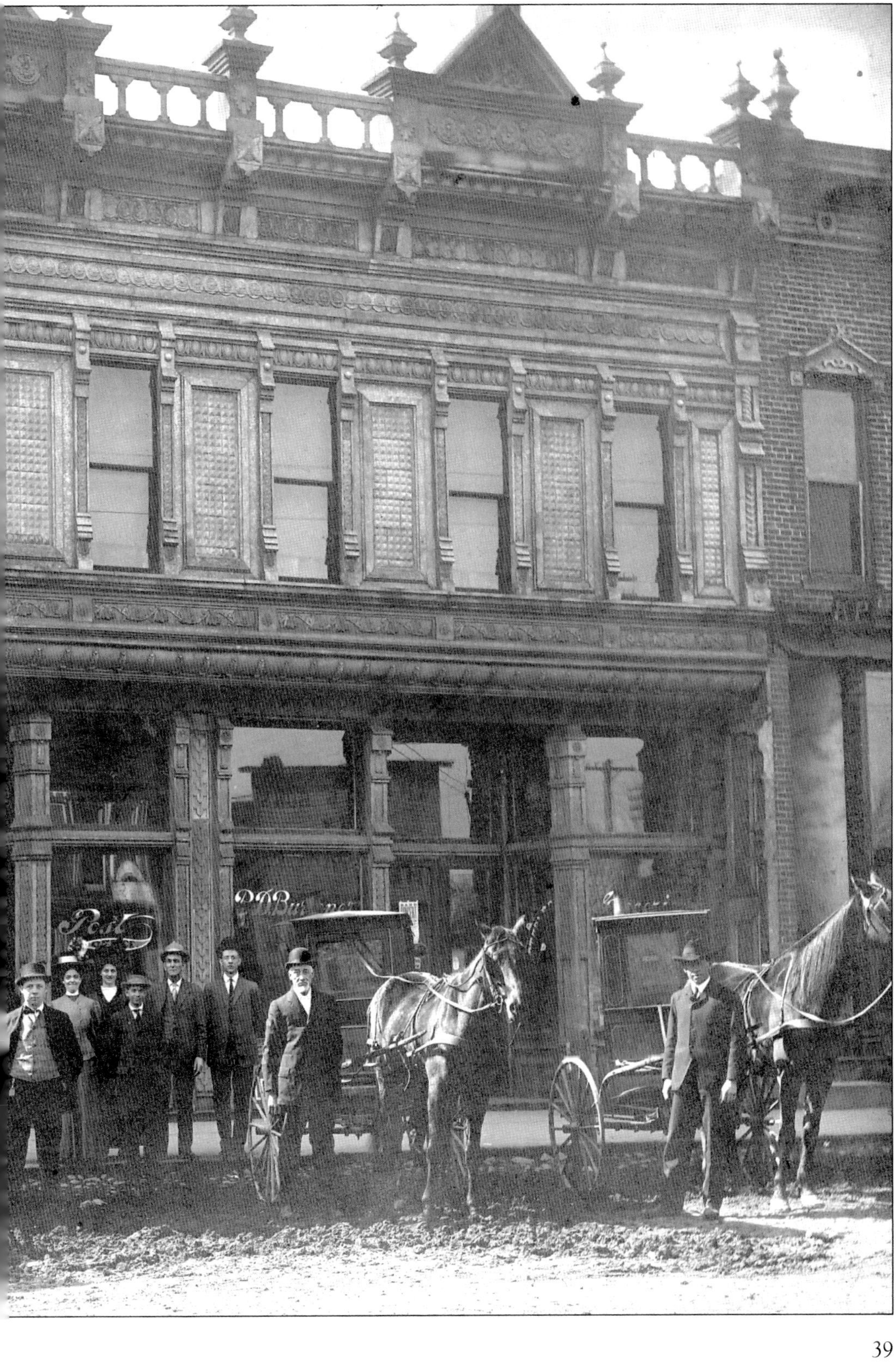

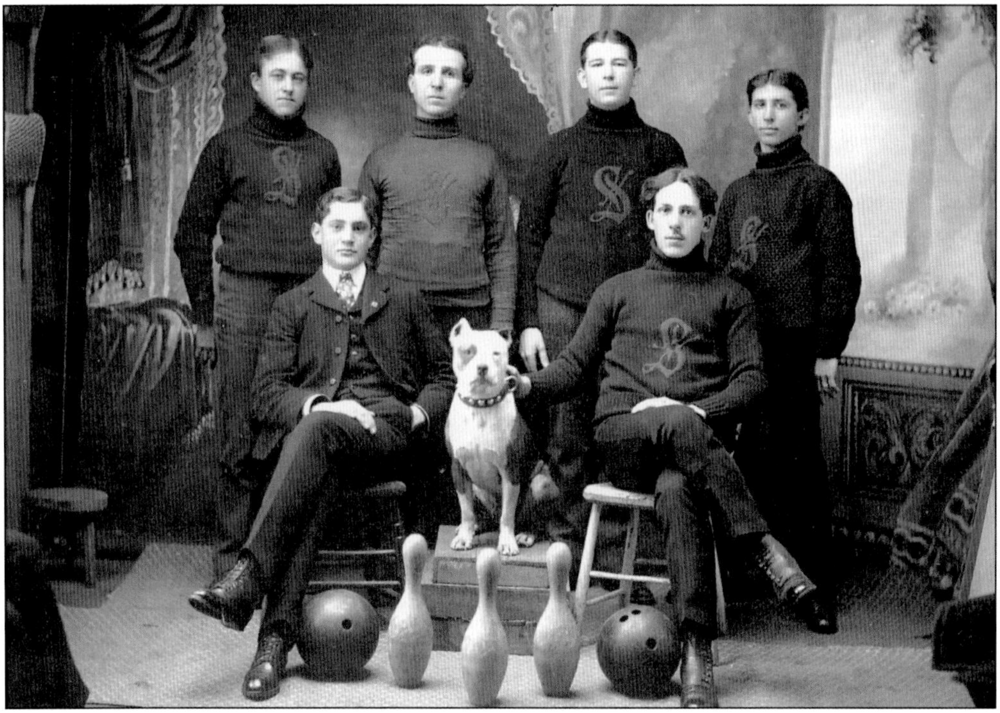

These are the young lads of the Nappanee High School bowling team from 1907. The only members whose names are known are the last two boys in the back row—Willis Wilson and Morton Reinoehl. (Photo courtesy of Nappanee Public Library.)

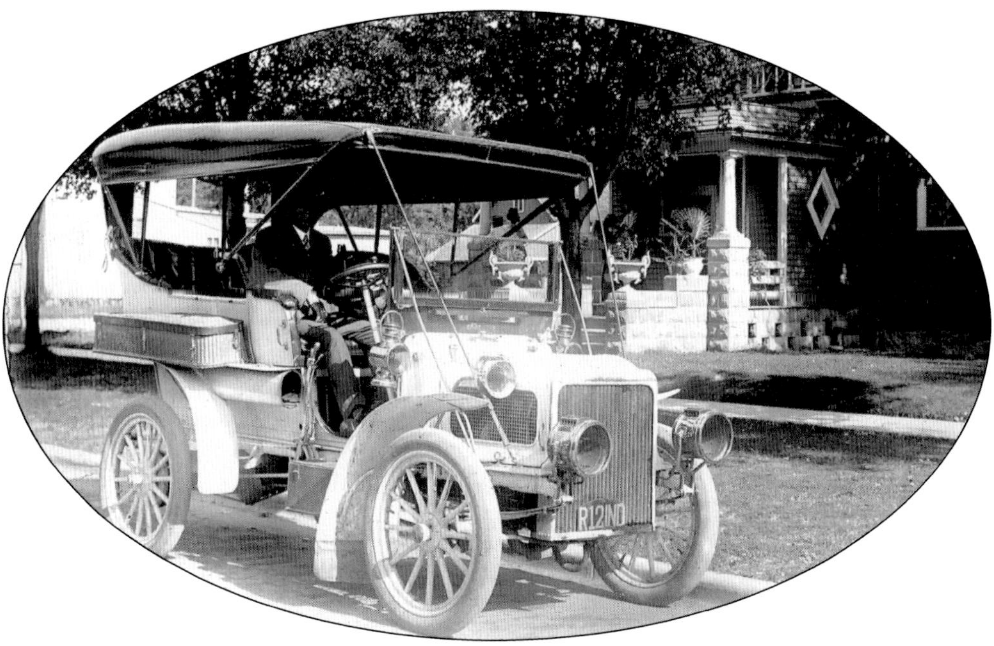

Shown here is another one of Nappanee's first automobiles. This one is a 1907 "White Steamer," which is being driven by William Miller. He is the father of Freed Miller, who was one of the first mail carriers in the city. (Photo courtesy of Nappanee Public Library.)

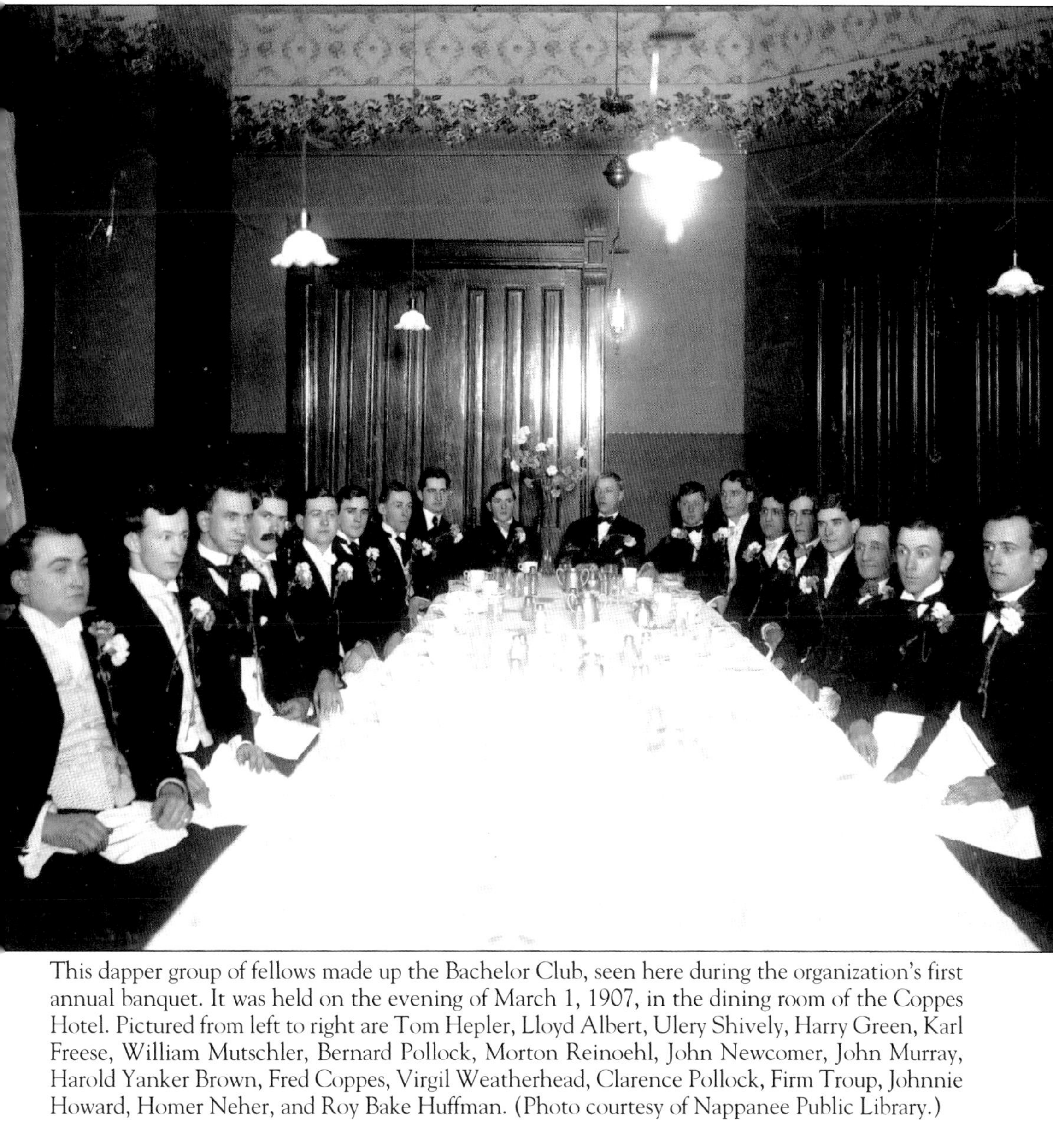

This dapper group of fellows made up the Bachelor Club, seen here during the organization's first annual banquet. It was held on the evening of March 1, 1907, in the dining room of the Coppes Hotel. Pictured from left to right are Tom Hepler, Lloyd Albert, Ulery Shively, Harry Green, Karl Freese, William Mutschler, Bernard Pollock, Morton Reinoehl, John Newcomer, John Murray, Harold Yanker Brown, Fred Coppes, Virgil Weatherhead, Clarence Pollock, Firm Troup, Johnnie Howard, Homer Neher, and Roy Bake Huffman. (Photo courtesy of Nappanee Public Library.)

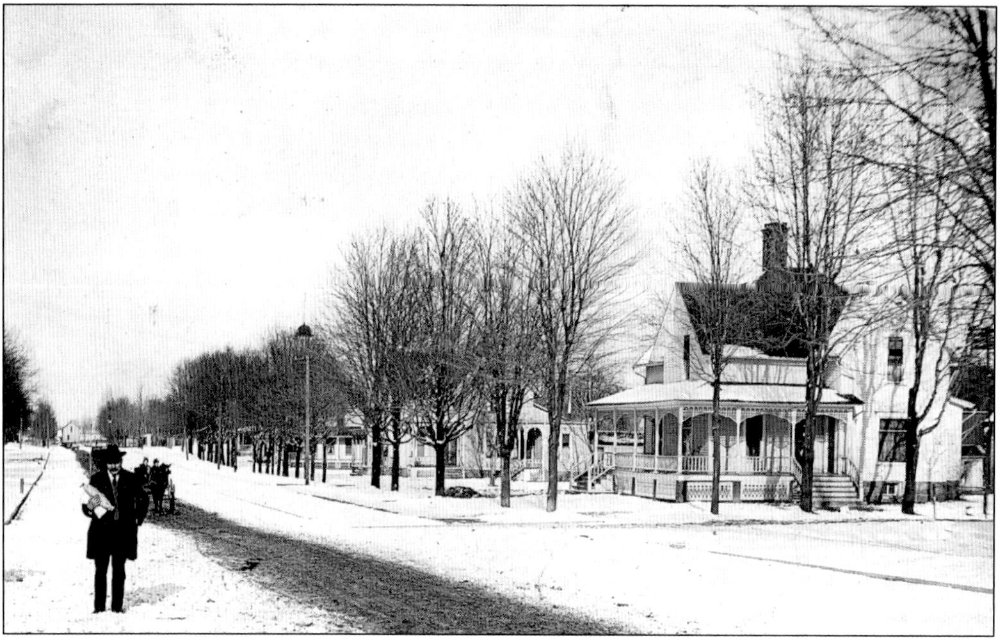

This 1908 photo shows a winter's day along North Main Street. (Photo courtesy of Nappanee Public Library.)

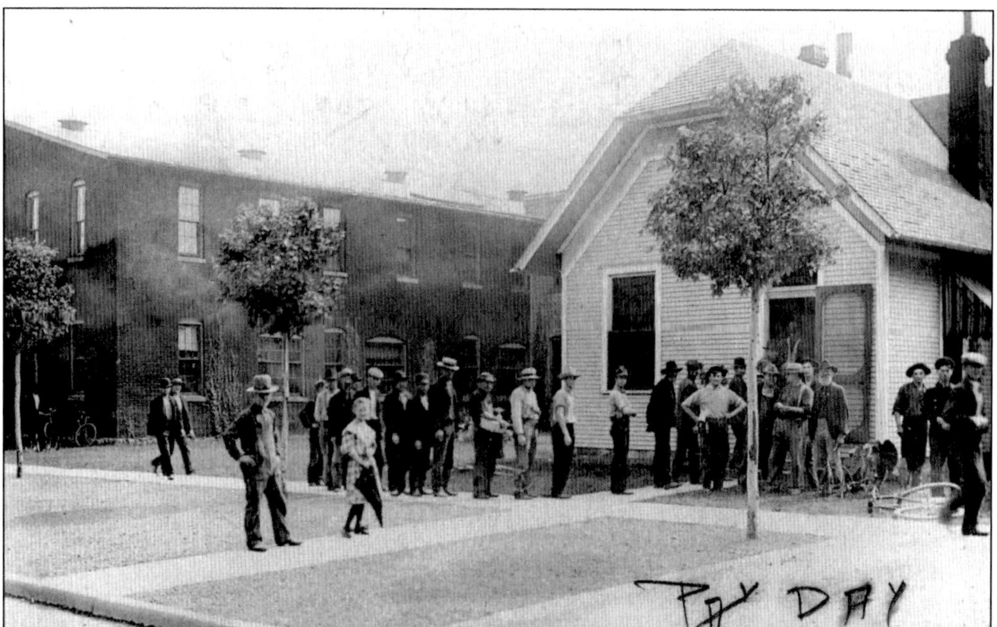

Men line the sidewalks in this 1908 scene, waiting to collect their wages as employees of the Coppes, Zook, and Mutschler factory. The plant is visible at left, and the building where the men are seen entering is still standing, but is vacant. (I.B. Miller photo, courtesy of Mr. and Mrs. Dean Henry.)

The former First National Bank, which was Nappanee's second financial institution, was built in 1908 and located at 151 South Main Street. The architectural style was Neo-Classical, and the building was raised using Bedford limestone and pressed brick. The original lobby of the bank featured mahogany ceiling beams and mission-style electric light brass chandeliers set inside panels. During the John Dillinger crime wave, a new copper burglar alarm was installed, in the hopes that the bank would not become a scene of the spree. (Photo courtesy of Mr. and Mrs. William Johnson.)

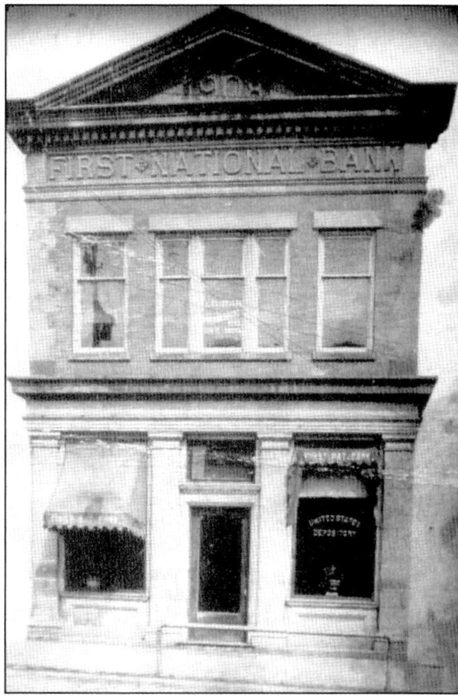

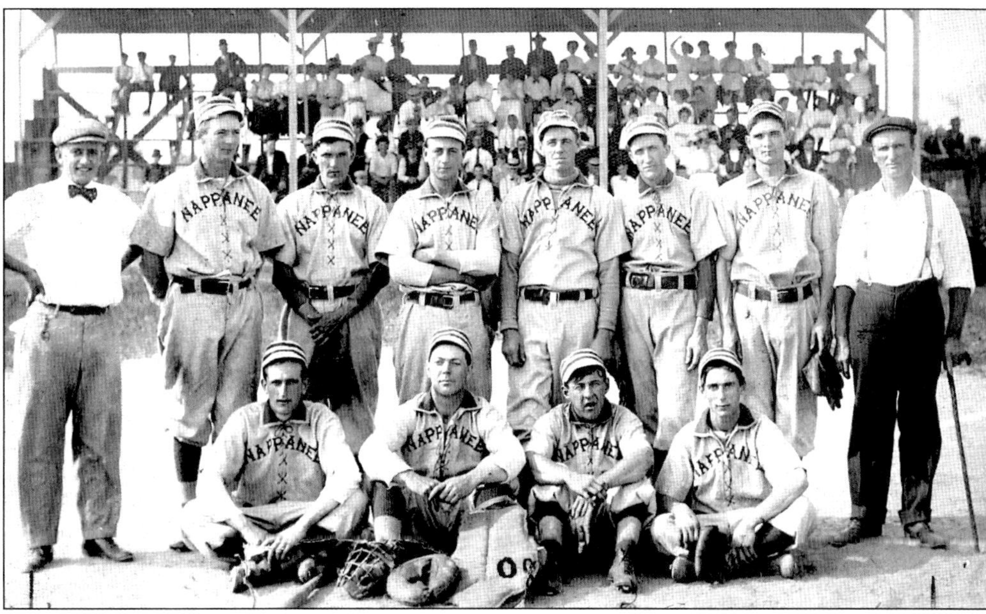

Nappanee's softball team from the 1908 season made for such an impressive photograph that postcards were fashioned of its likeness. One such card, dated September 10 of that year, went right to the point while describing one particular sports contest. "Saw the games. It was fine. Nappanee won." The signature was equally brief—"R.D." Team members were, from left to right: (seated) Harmon Tobias, Ora Geyer, Harry Biehl, and Tony Jones; (standing) Roy Huffman, Charles Wyson, Charles Tobias, Ed Geyer, Gible Austin (from Milford), Art Tobias, Firm Troup, and Charles Volkmann. Not shown is the team's bookkeeper, John Richmond. (Photo courtesy of Mr. and Mrs. Dean Henry.)

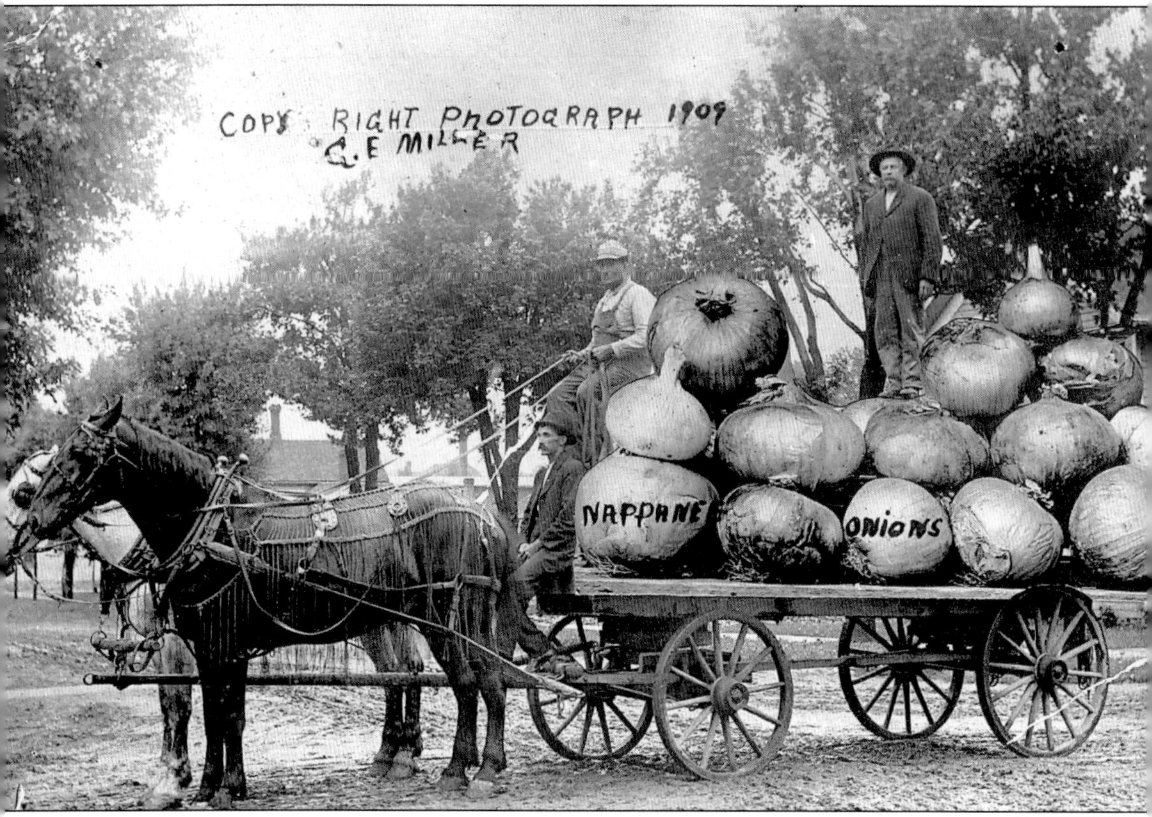

This wagonload of produce, seen in a 1909 image, is carrying a crop of enormous onions—a very profitable and abundant crop around the Nappanee area in the early part of the 20th century. The reaping of the onions was such a celebrated event in the town that there was at one time a festival devoted to the harvest. (G.E. Miller photo, courtesy of Nappanee Public Library.)

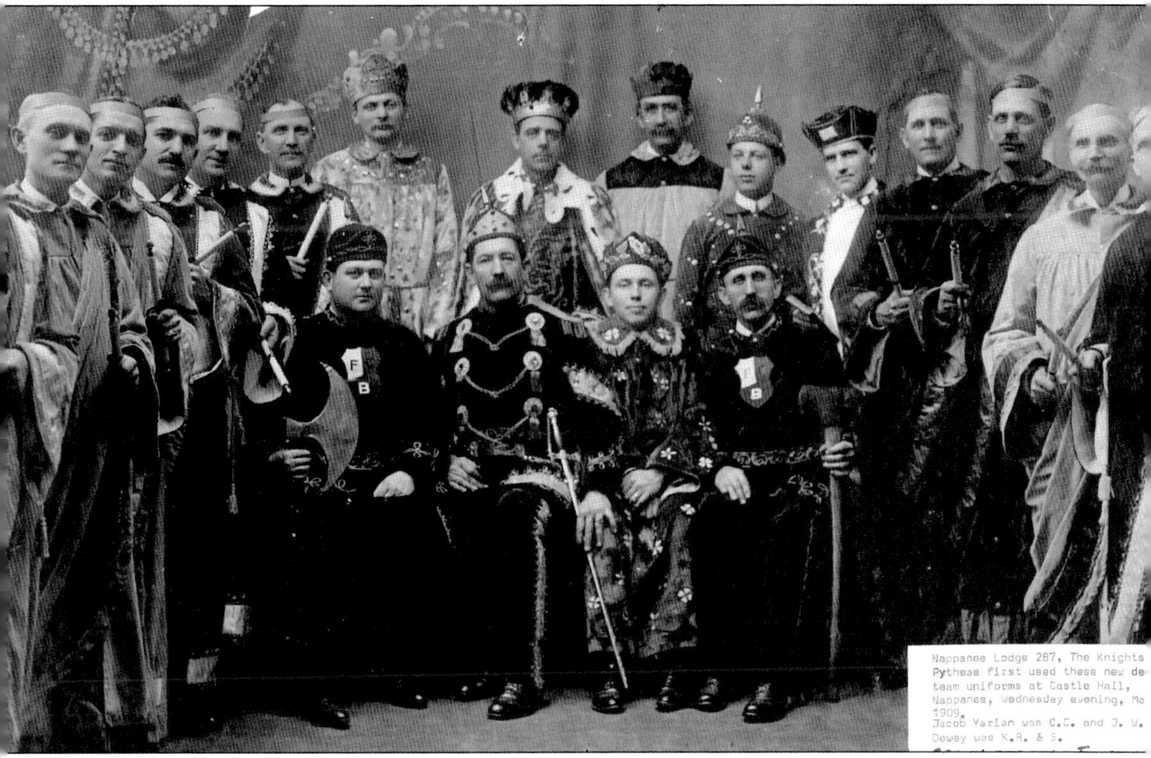

Taken on the evening of May 5, 1909, these are the members of the Knights of Pythias Degree Team, Castle Hall, at Nappanee Lodge #287. The men are sporting new degree uniforms, worn for the very first time on the occasion of this picture. From left to right are: (seated) Karl Freese, George Miller, Jacob Yarian, and Sam Frevert; (standing) Nathan Craig, James Tillman, Fred Coppes, Harvey Coppes, Alex Wilson, Sam Craig, Karl Knobel, Albert Farrington, Michael Hoover, Bert (Penny) Yarian, Harry Greene, Fred Freese, Charles Gentzhorn, Gordon Murry, and Peter D. Burgner. (Photo courtesy of Nappanee Public Library.)

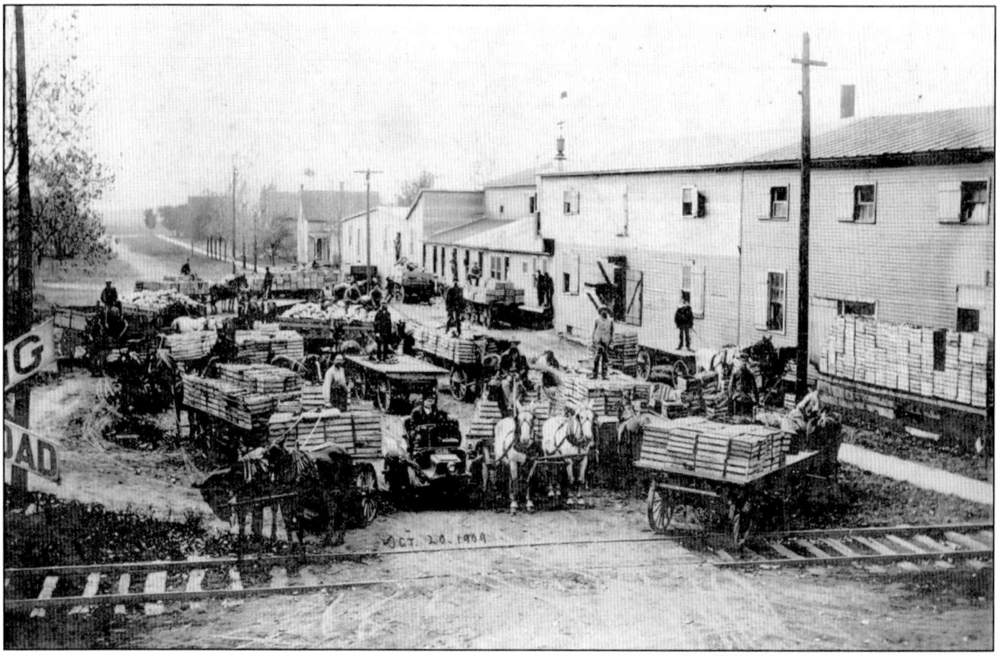

The Laughlin Bros. Co., an onion storage facility, is seen in this picture, dated October 20, 1909. The vast business was located one mile east of Nappanee, on land that is now the site of Fairmont Homes, Inc. The area was comically referred to at the time as "Onionville." (Photo courtesy of Nappanee Public Library.)

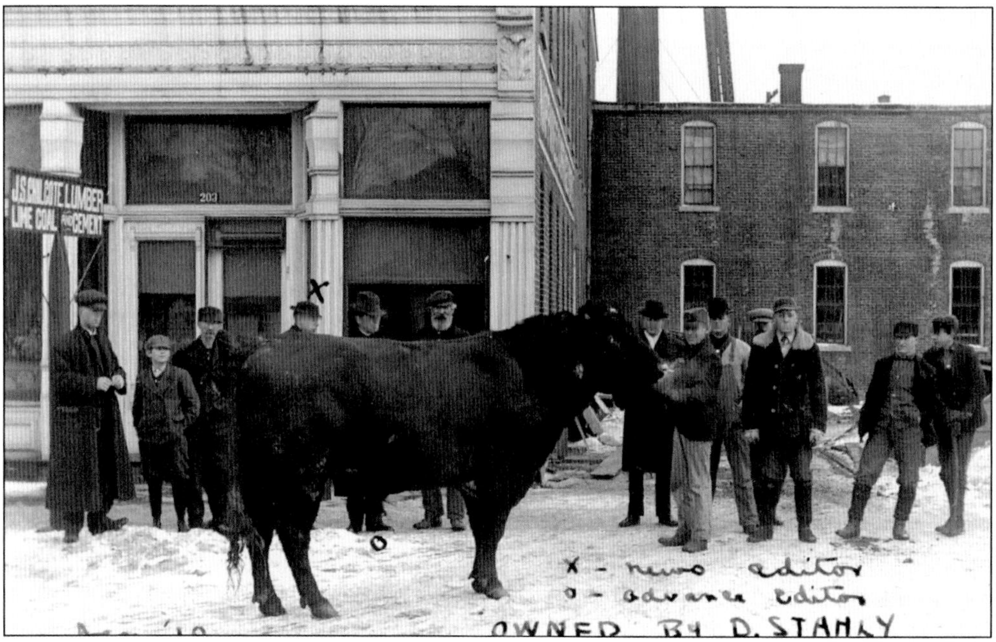

The arrival of Daniel Stahly's bull into the city made for interesting news, as this picture found its way into the January 26, 1909 edition of the Nappanee news. The caption read, "Daniel Stahly, living north of town, brought his four-year old short horn Durban bull in town Monday. It weighed 2000 pounds." (Photo courtesy of Mr. and Mrs. Dean Henry.)

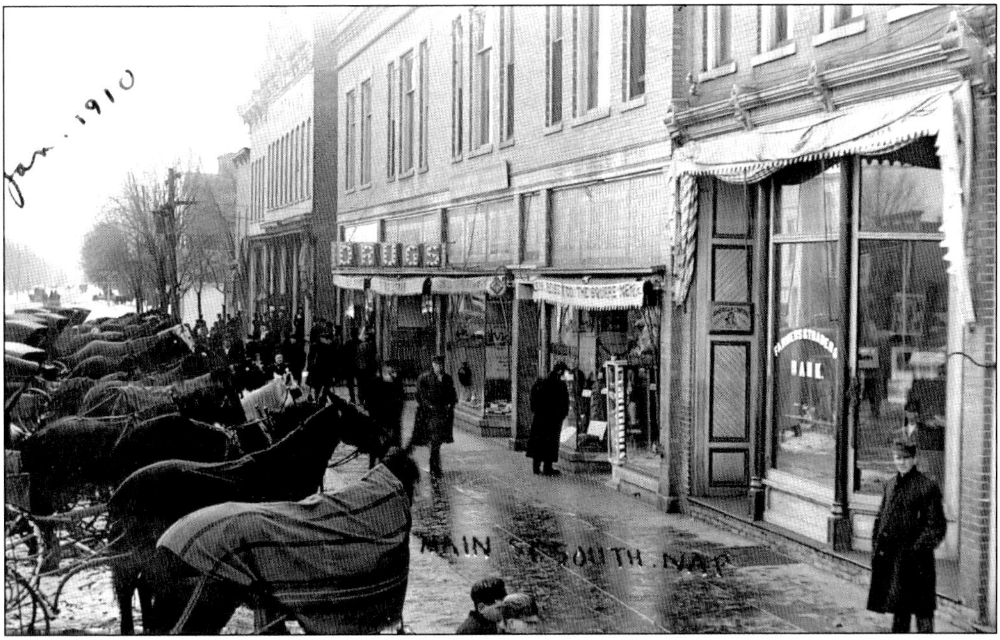

It looked like a busy day for the merchants of South Main Street, in this westward view, dated January, 1910. (Photo courtesy of Mr. and Mrs. Dean Henry.)

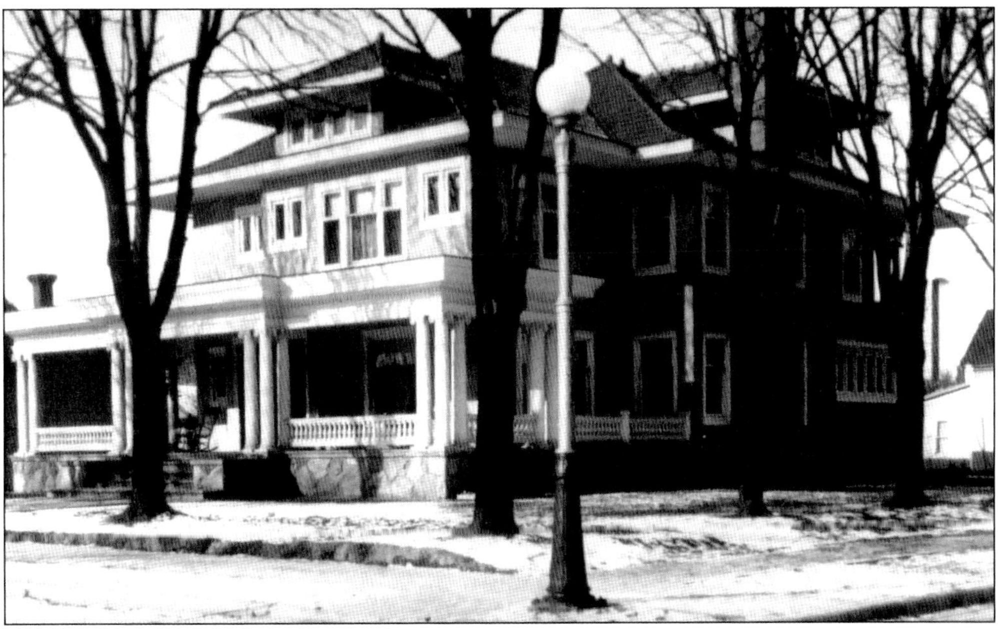

The address of this house is 258 East Walnut Street. Its first owner was Albert Mutschler. He was the father of Lamar and Carlyle Mutschler, and the owner of Mutschler Brothers Cabinets and Furniture. The look reflects a mix of both Colonial Revival and Prairie School stylings, and offered 3 stories and 18 rooms. Many of the rooms were adorned in tooled leather wallpaper, Honduras mahogany, oak woodwork, and pocket doors. Even the interior of the home's garage was finished with wild cherry wood. The original pale green wood siding that was part of the home in its 1910 construction was replaced by stucco in 1924. (Photo courtesy of Mr. and Mrs. William Johnson.)

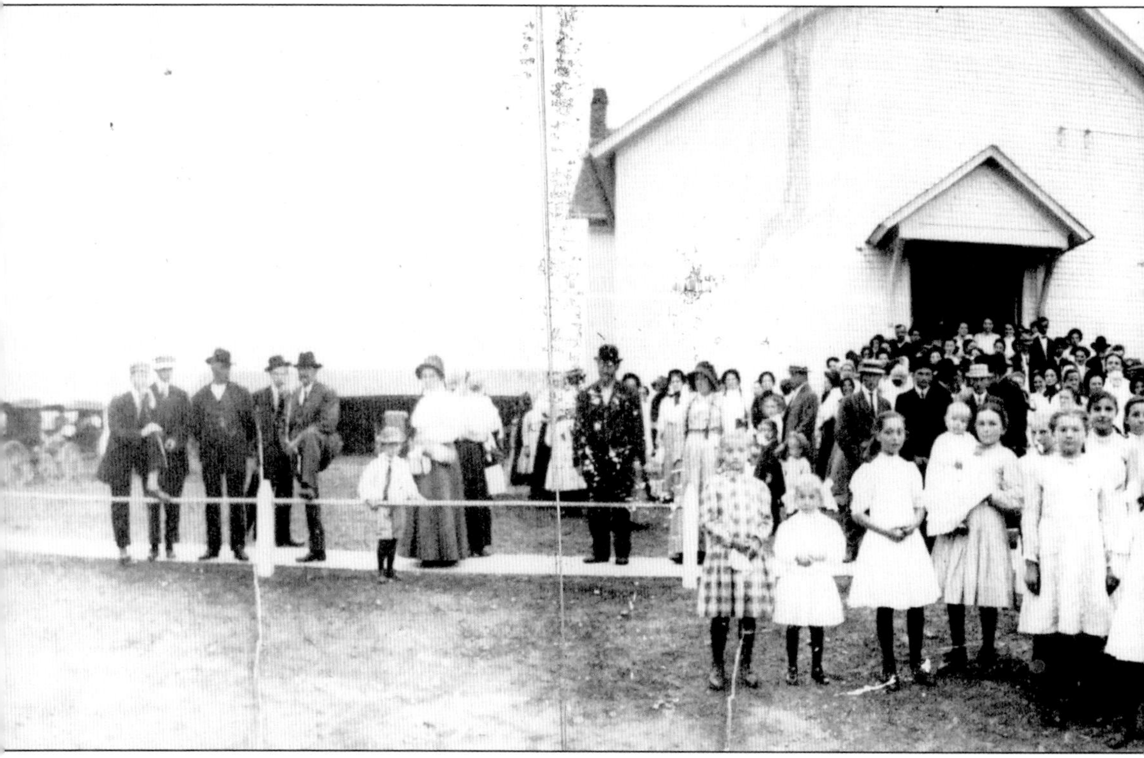

A panoramic view of the congregation of the First Mennonite Church, in a photo from 1910. The church went through various name changes over the years, such as the Amish-Mennonite Church, then the West Market Street Mennonite Church. In 1926, the church became affiliated

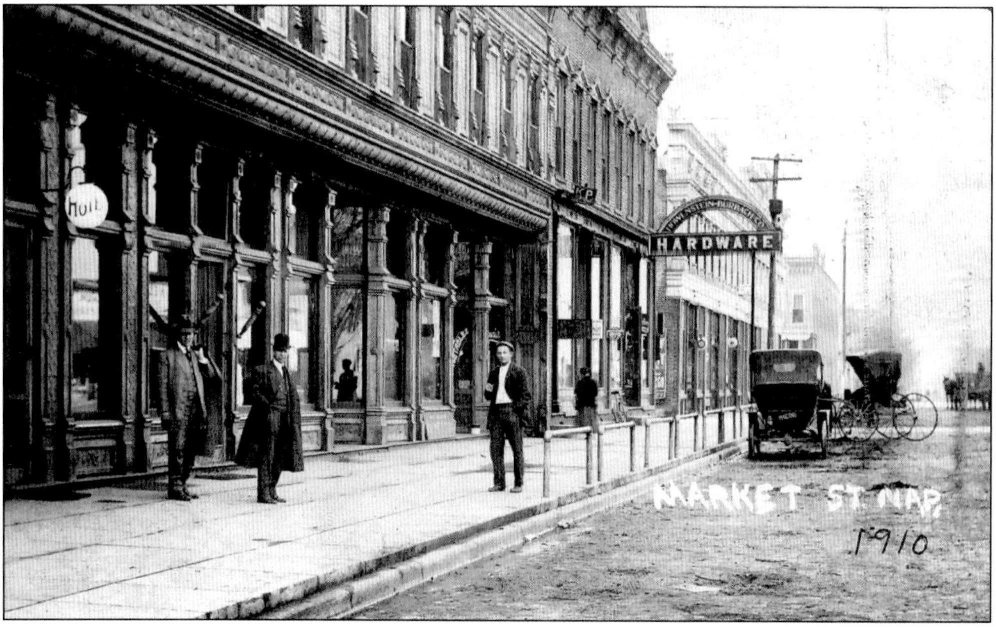

This is a 1910 glimpse of a day along the south side of East Market Street. (Photo courtesy of Nappanee Public Library.)

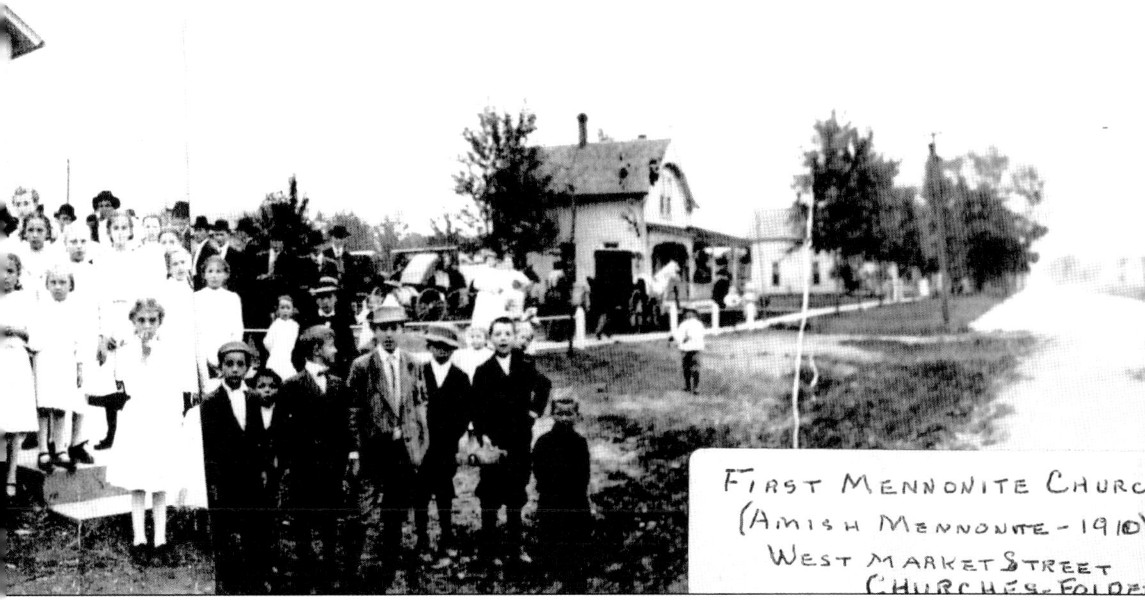

with the General Conference of the Mennonite Church of North America, and finally was given the name of First Mennonite Church of Nappanee. Worshippers still gather at 900 West Market Street. (Photo courtesy of Nappanee Public Library.)

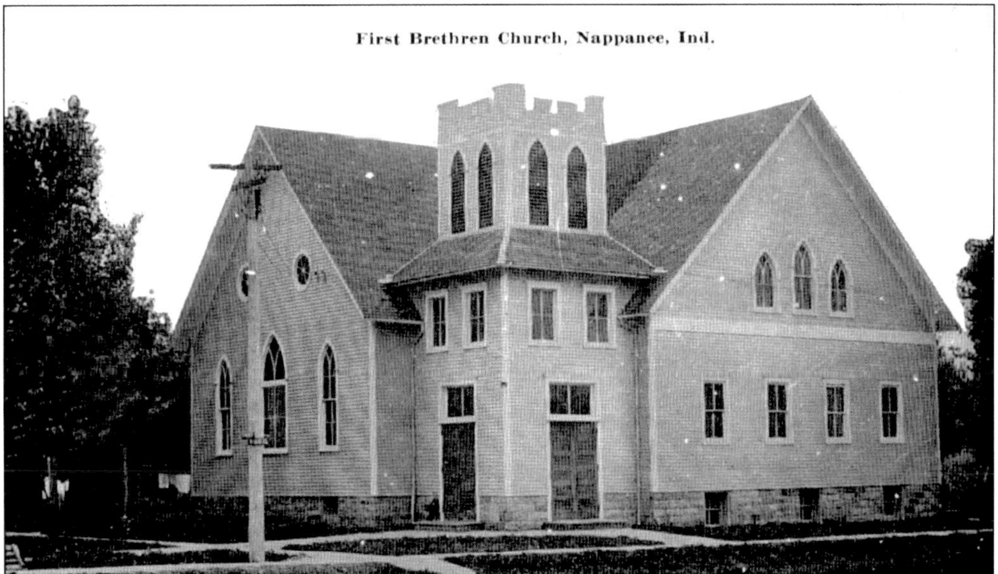

Nappanee's First Brethren Church, in its original incarnation. The facility was destroyed by a fire in February 1945, and was quickly replaced with a new church home, which is still in use at 1600 North Main Street in Nappanee. (Photo courtesy of Nappanee Public Library.)

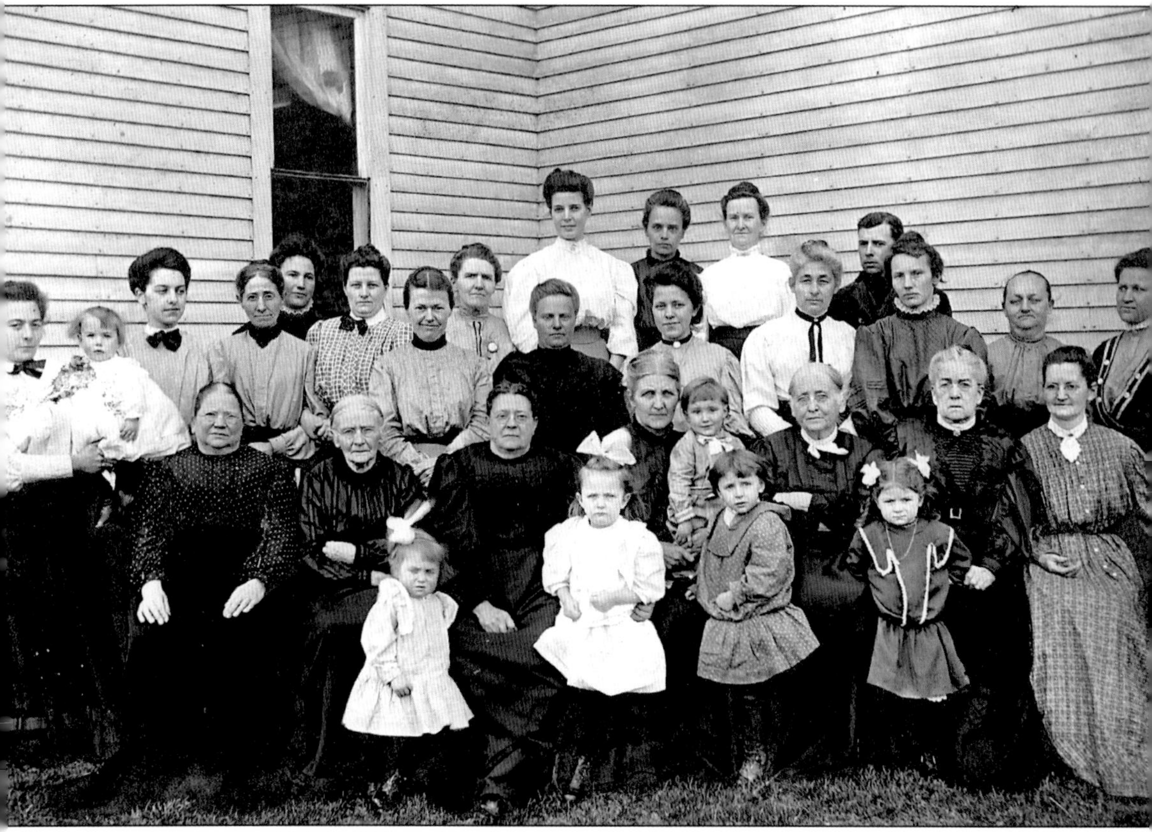

It certainly would have been interesting to know what transpired during the meetings of the Ladies' Rural Club, shown here in this 1910 picture. From left to right are: (front row) Mrs. Barbara Stahly, Mrs. George Walker, Cynthia Mays (little girl), Mrs. Ab Michael, unknown child, Mrs. John Ulery, Walter Ulery, Esther Coppes, "Grandma" Vickers, Gertrude Stoudnour, Mrs. John Stouder, and Mrs. Emma Hudson; (second row, standing) Clara Mays and son, Mrs. Maurice Roose, Mrs. Katie Troyer, two unidentified, Mrs. Lulu Stoudnour, Irena Culp, two unidentified, Mrs. Katie Geyer, two unidentified, Anna Snyder, Mrs. Lucy Ulery, Mrs. Ellen Roose, and Mrs. Susan Coppes; (third row) Mabel Hudson, Mrs. Sarah Geyer, two unidentified, and Milo Hudson. (Photo courtesy of Nappanee Public Library.)

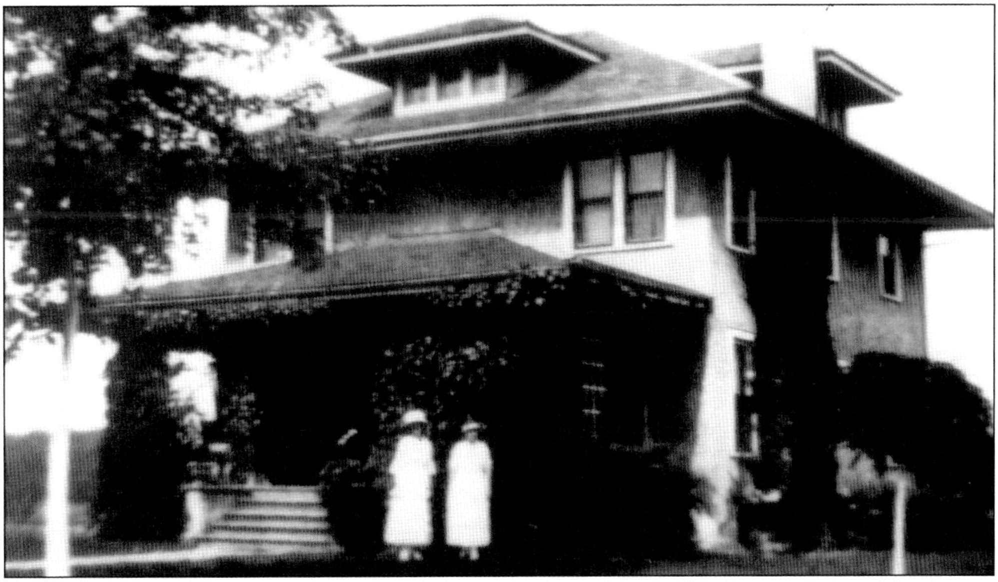

The owner of the Freese Brothers Creamery, Karl Freese Sr., was the first resident of this home, which was designed by Henry Frazier and built in 1910. Located at 401 North Hartman Street and patterned after the American Foursquare dimension, it had a hip-style roof with dormers and a front porch. There were some touches of Prairie School workings as well, as seen in the wide roof overhangs and the stucco. (Photo courtesy of Mr. and Mrs. William Johnson.)

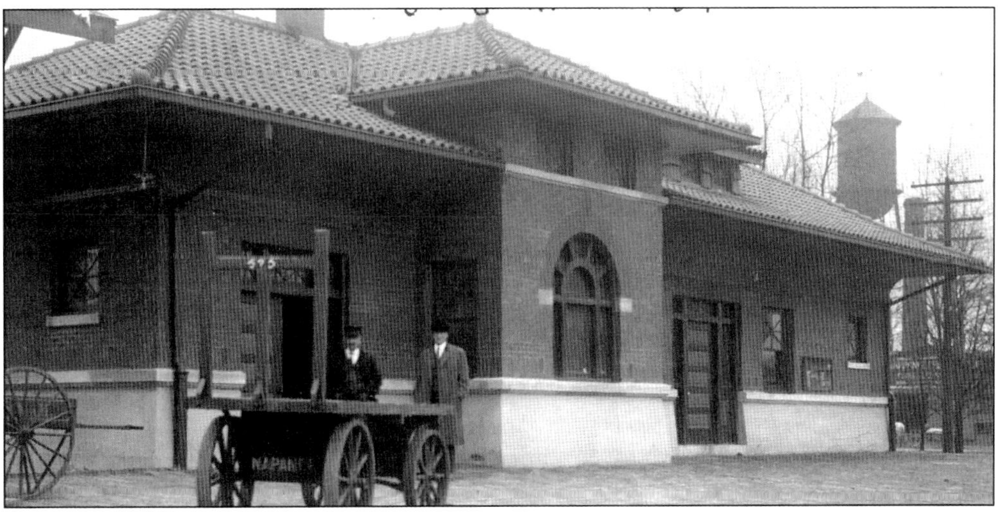

After the premier B & O station was relocated to a private lot in 1911, this new structure was introduced to take its place. Having served the community in some fashion for more than 90 years, it has been heralded as the most architecturally significant structure still remaining on the B & O line. The look of this depot is most unusual in that it was modeled after the Prairie School architectural style, which was quite common for homes during this era, but very unique and rare for commercial buildings. The depot sports a low-pitched hip roof, broad overhanging eaves, decorative window patterns, and brick bands. It is located on the west side of South Main Street, where it functions as an arrival and departure point of Amtrak service. A massive remodeling project, many years in the making, is slated for completion in May of 2003, to restore the depot to its historic integrity. (Photo courtesy of Mr. and Mrs. Dean Henry.)

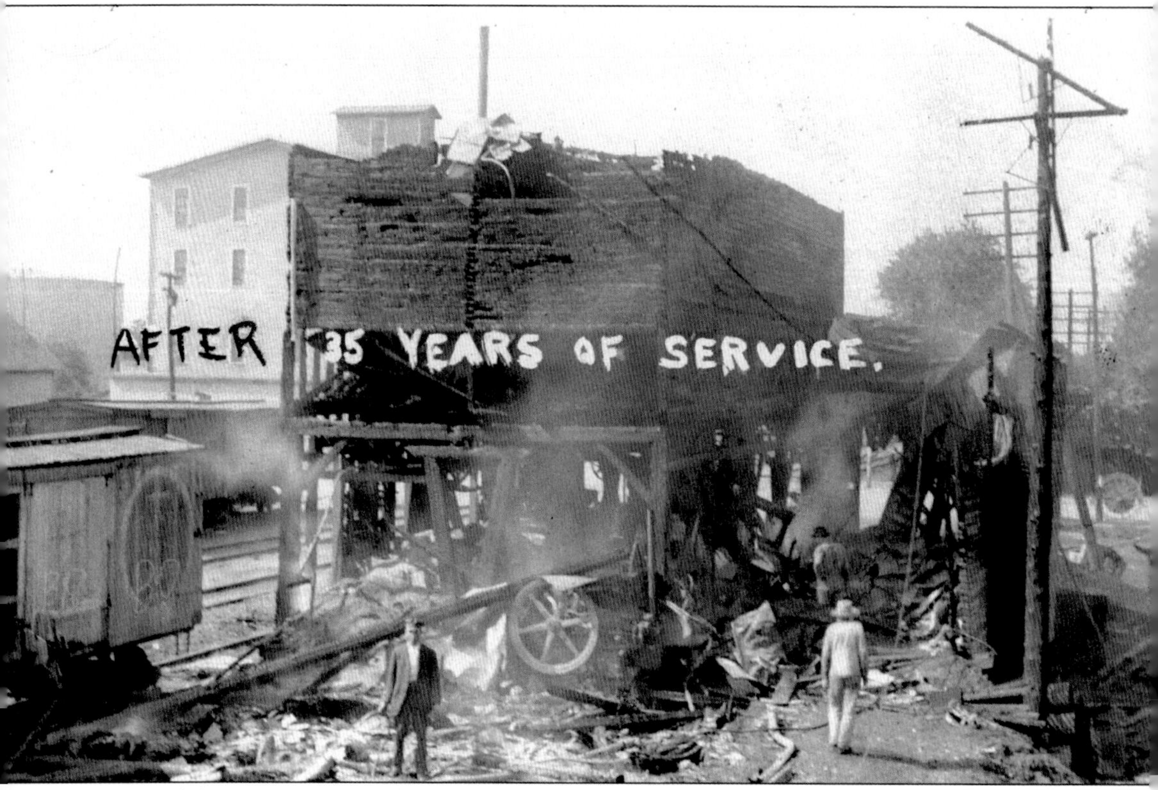

One of the most sensational events of the year 1910 was the blaze that left the Hartman Bros. Elevator a smoldering, wretched disaster. The somber but simple inscription on the photo perhaps captures the sentiment best—"after 35 years of service." The business was one of the city's firsts, dating back to 1875. The fire occurred on September 30, 1910, and the rubble was cleared away in November of that year. The clean-up effort was just as newsworthy as the fire itself—the headline was splashed across the front page of the November 16, 1910 edition of the Nappanee News. (Photo courtesy of Mr. and Mrs. Dean Henry.)

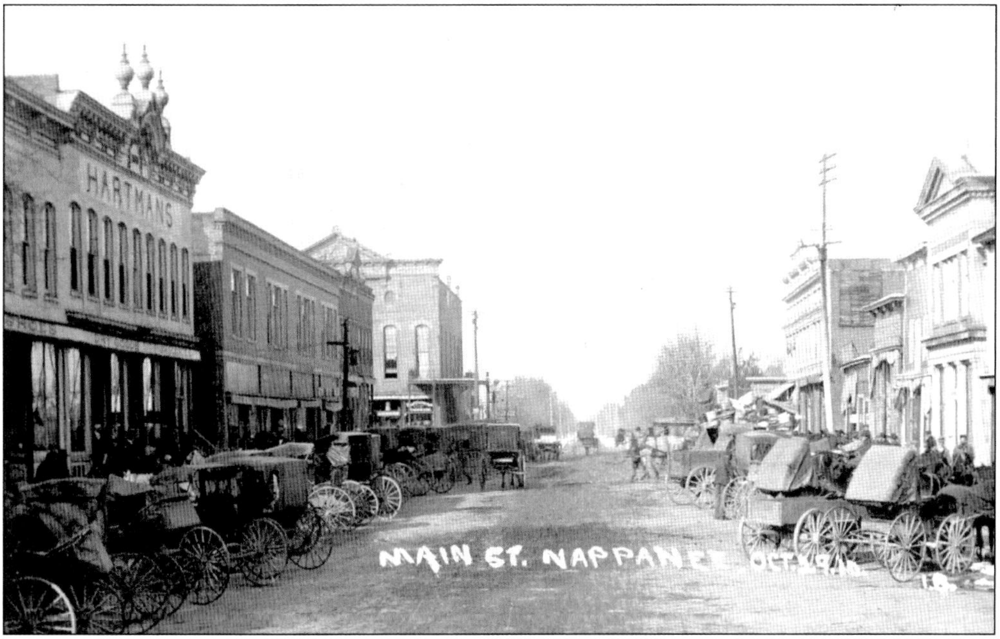

This is South Main Street, looking north, in a photo dated October 29, 1910. Near the left center of the picture, in the distance, the Auditorium can be seen. (Photo courtesy of Mr. and Mrs. Dean Henry.)

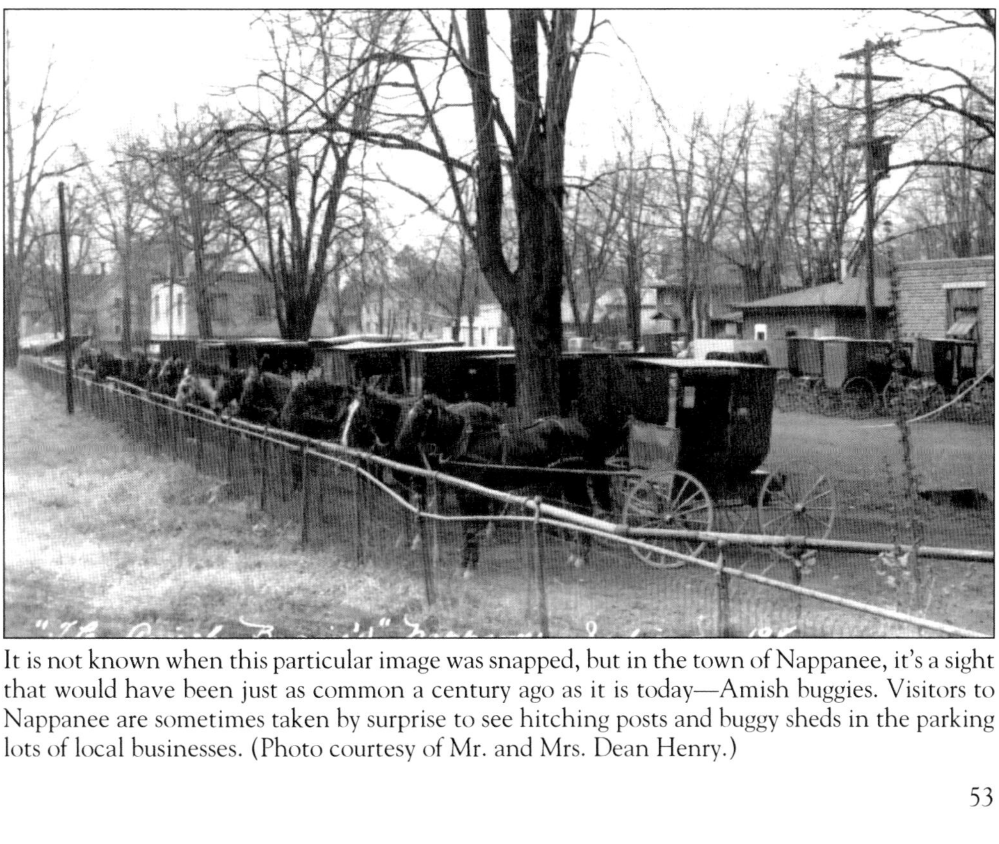

It is not known when this particular image was snapped, but in the town of Nappanee, it's a sight that would have been just as common a century ago as it is today—Amish buggies. Visitors to Nappanee are sometimes taken by surprise to see hitching posts and buggy sheds in the parking lots of local businesses. (Photo courtesy of Mr. and Mrs. Dean Henry.)

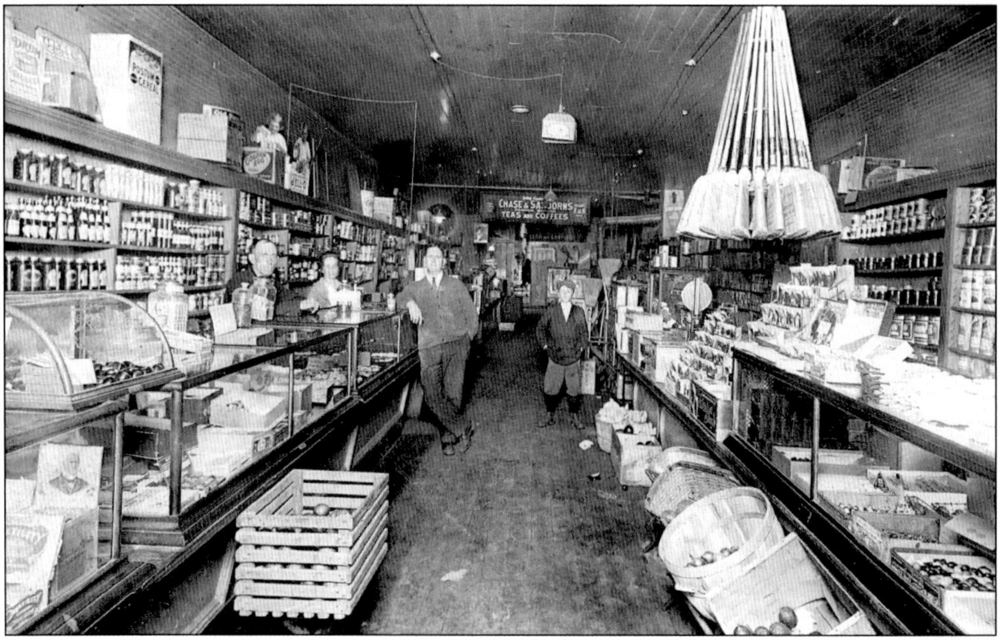

The former Best's Grocery Store, once situated at 152 East Market Street. Irvin and Bessie Best are standing behind the counter, while Wilbur and Jesse Best are seen in the aisle. The best estimate as to when this photograph might have been taken is sometime during the 1910s. (Photo courtesy of Nappanee Public Library.)

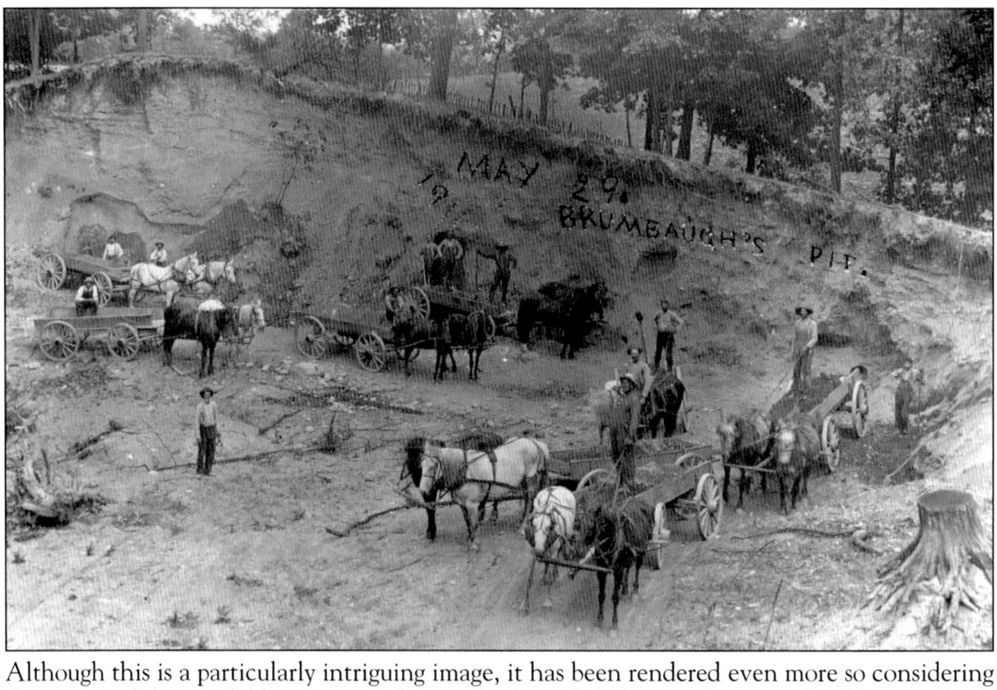

Although this is a particularly intriguing image, it has been rendered even more so considering that most of the available resources do not shed much light on what exactly this must have been. The picture bears only the name of Brumbaugh's Pit, and is inscribed with the date of May 29, 1911. (Photo courtesy of Nappanee Public Library.)

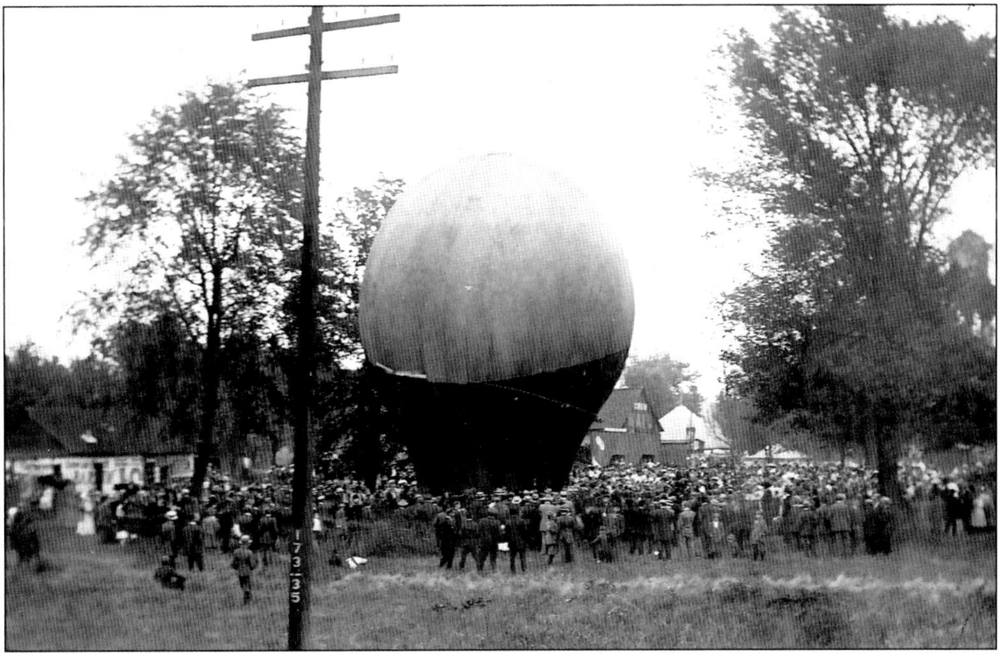

This 1911 hot air balloon launch must have been quite a spectacle. (Photo courtesy of Nappanee Public Library.)

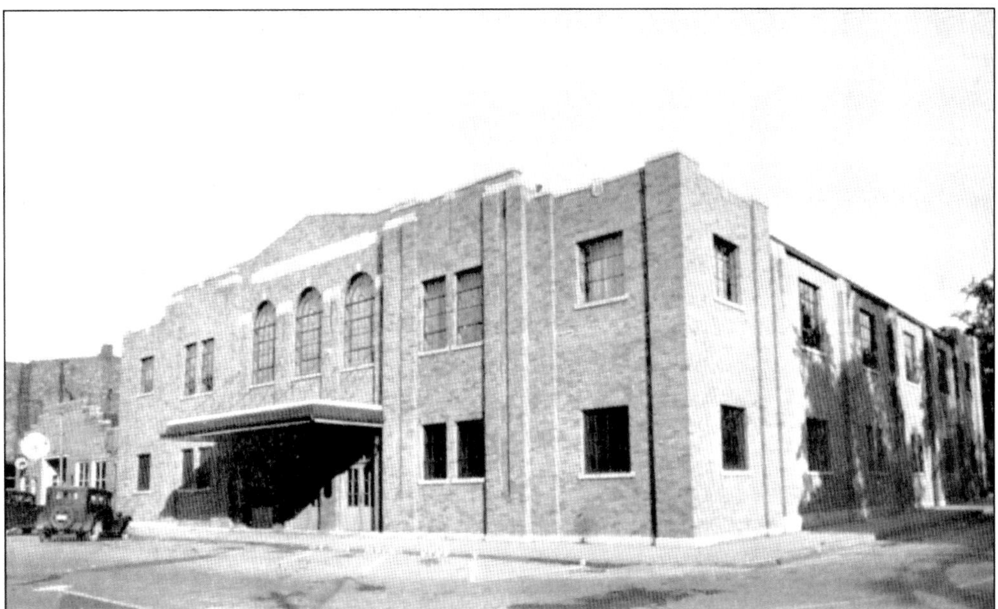
Once located on East Lincoln Street, this undated postcard depicts the former landmark known as the Community Building. It was a gymnasium, and the gathering place for a number of school functions, until the "new" high school was opened in 1958. This building was demolished in August of 1972. (Photo courtesy of Mr. and Mrs. Dean Henry.)

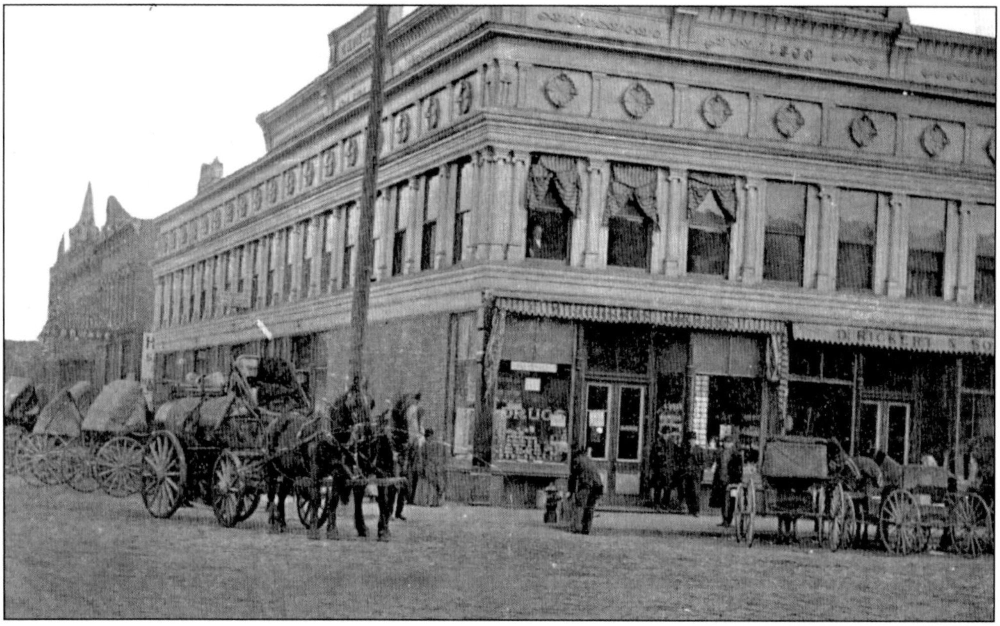

The southeast corner of Main and Market streets, spanning eastward, was known as the Deitrick, or Dietrich, block. This is how it looked during the 1910s. (Photo courtesy of Mr. and Mrs. Dean Henry.)

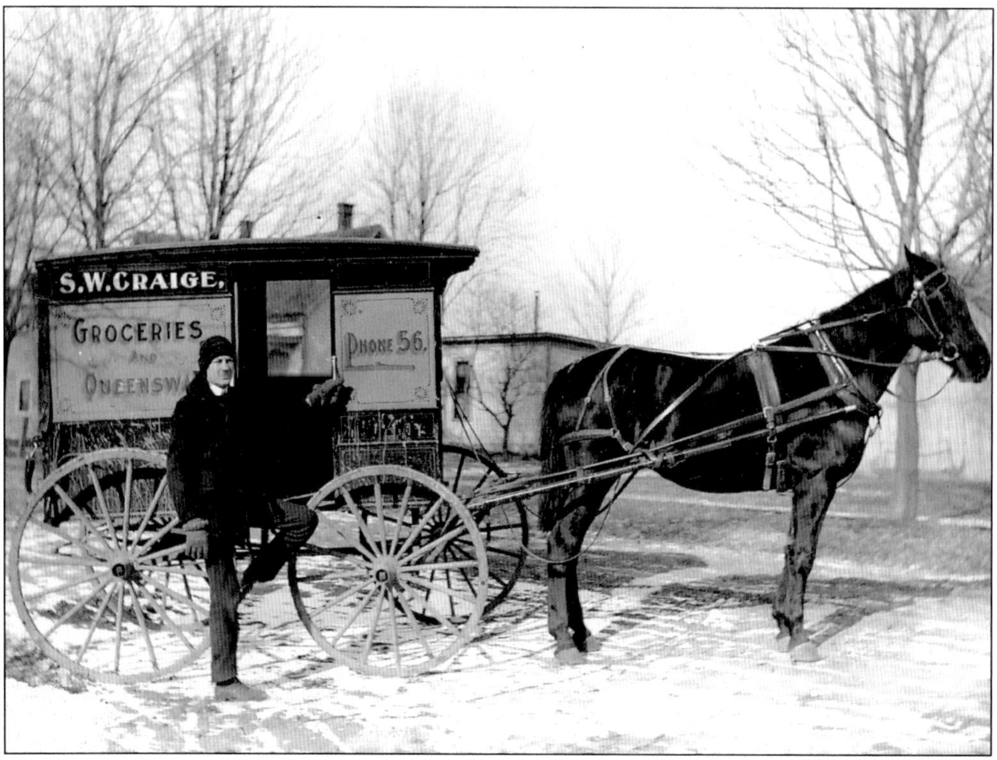

S.W. Craige, grocer, was the owner of this delivery cart. The gentleman driving is Ralph Bechtel. (Photo courtesy of Nappanee Public Library.)

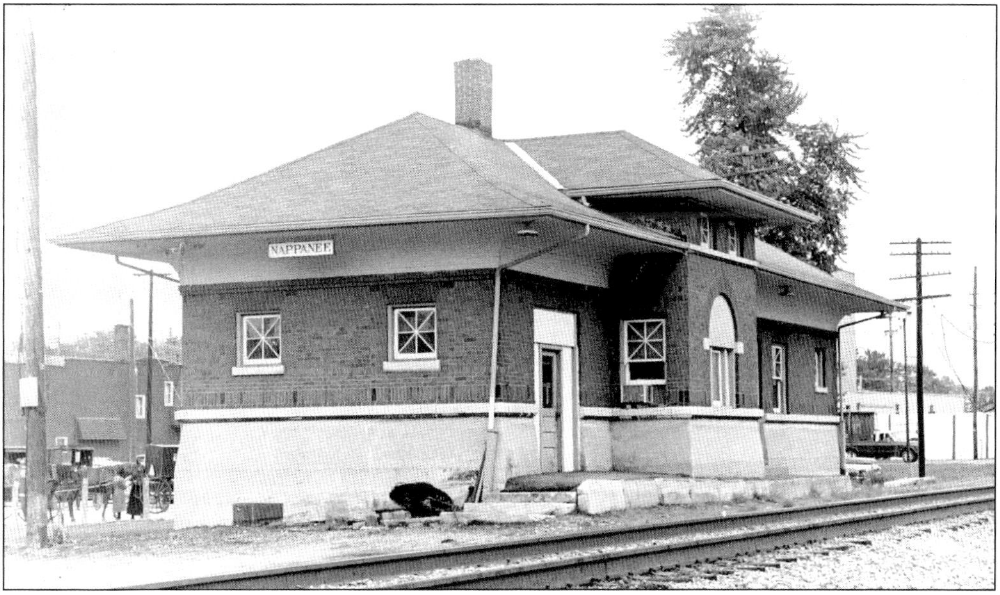

Here is another perspective of the train depot, in this undated photo. (Photo courtesy of Nappanee Public Library.)

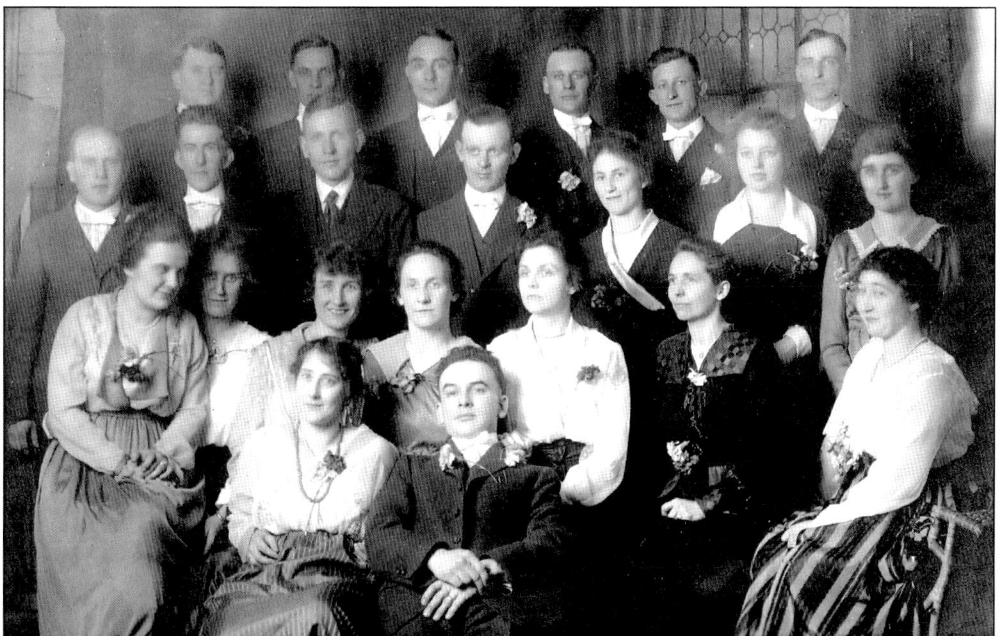
These are the distinguished members of Nappanee's Social Club, from around the 1910s. Pictured from left to right are: (front row) Hattie Eby and Wallace Lape; (second row) Ruth Hartman, Mabel Dunham, Joy Howenstein, Mrs. Carl Clemmer, Grace Neff, Bernetha Price, and Vivian Lape; (third row) Harry Eby, Warren Howenstein, Carl Clemmer, Lemuel Neff, Mabel Johnson, Mrs. Forrest DeFreese, and Beulah Guiss; (fourth row) Ira Dunham, Horace Hartman, Harry Price, Forrest DeFreese, Harold Johnson, and Ora Geyer. (Photo courtesy of Nappanee Public Library.)

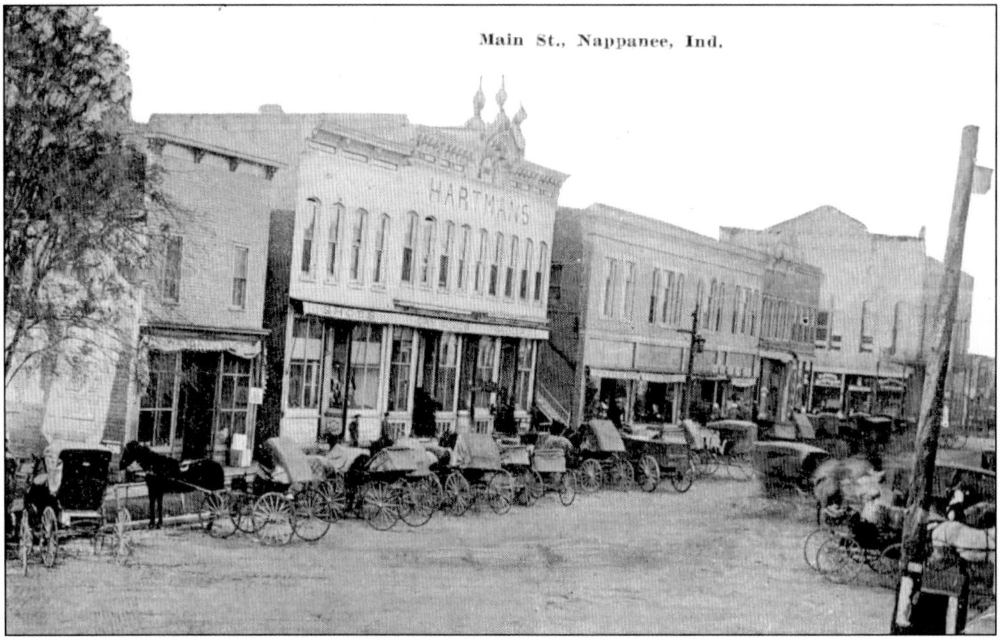

The west side of South Main Street, the way it was in 1914. Hartman's is plainly visible near the left. (Photo courtesy of Mr. and Mrs. Dean Henry.)

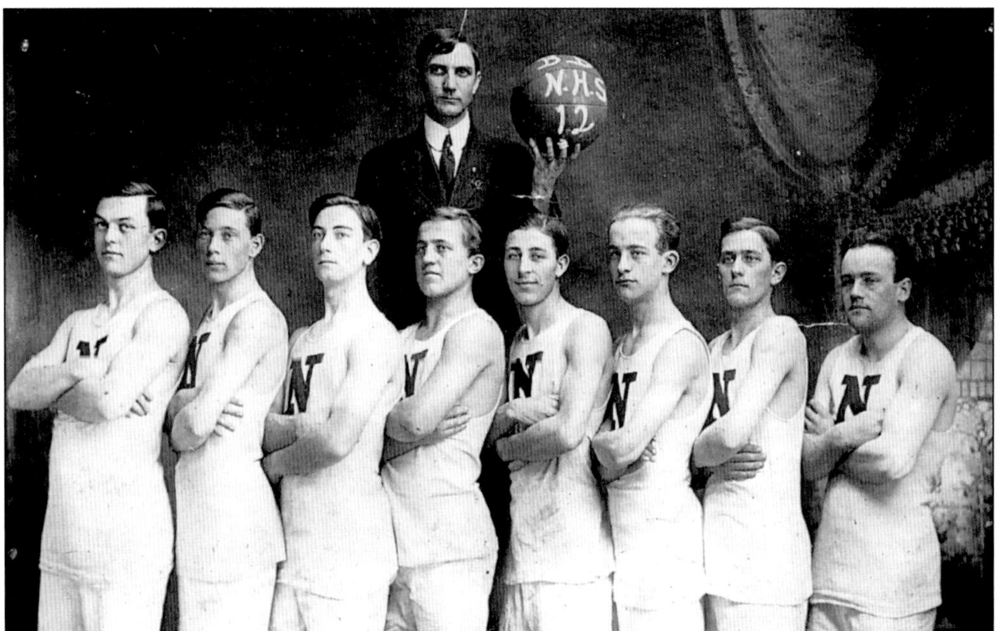

Teammates of the Nappanee High School basketball team pose for this photograph taken during their 1912 season. From left to right are Harry Iffert, Sam Sharp, George Warner, Noble Hollar, Lowell Terwilliger, Lloyd Johnson, Harve Frederick, and Galen Roose. The gentleman in back, holding the basketball, is coach O.E. Fisher. (Photo courtesy of Nappanee Public Library.)

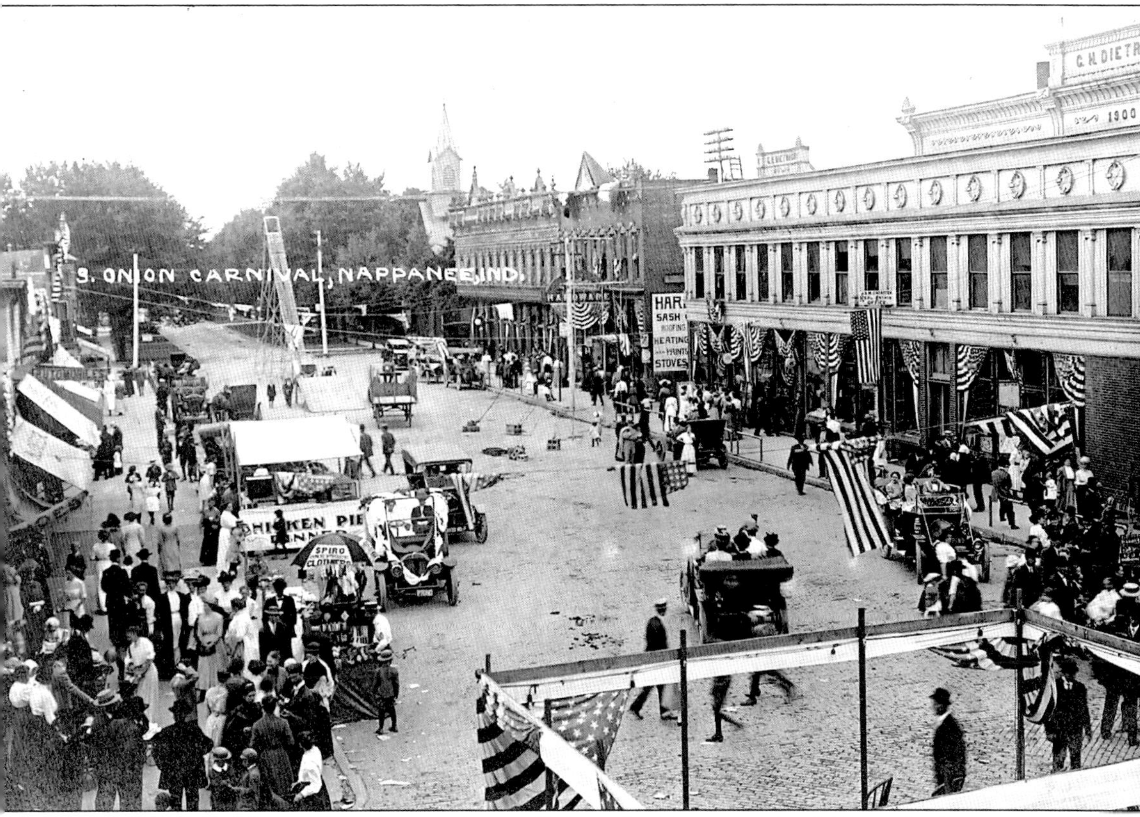

Many of the folks who reside in this area know all about the Nappanee Apple Festival, a homespun yet festive event held each fall in downtown Nappanee. But it may well be only the true locals who know about the story of Nappanee's "Onion Days." From 1909 through 1912, there was time set aside for a couple of days in August to celebrate the harvest of the onion, which at the time was one of Nappanee's most lucrative crops. The downtown sector was bustling with activities and entertainment, from tight wire showcases to hot air balloon rides to high divers. The music of minstrel bands filled the atmosphere, and the sight of decorated automobiles parading through the streets made for a spectacle. (Photo courtesy of Nappanee Public Library.)

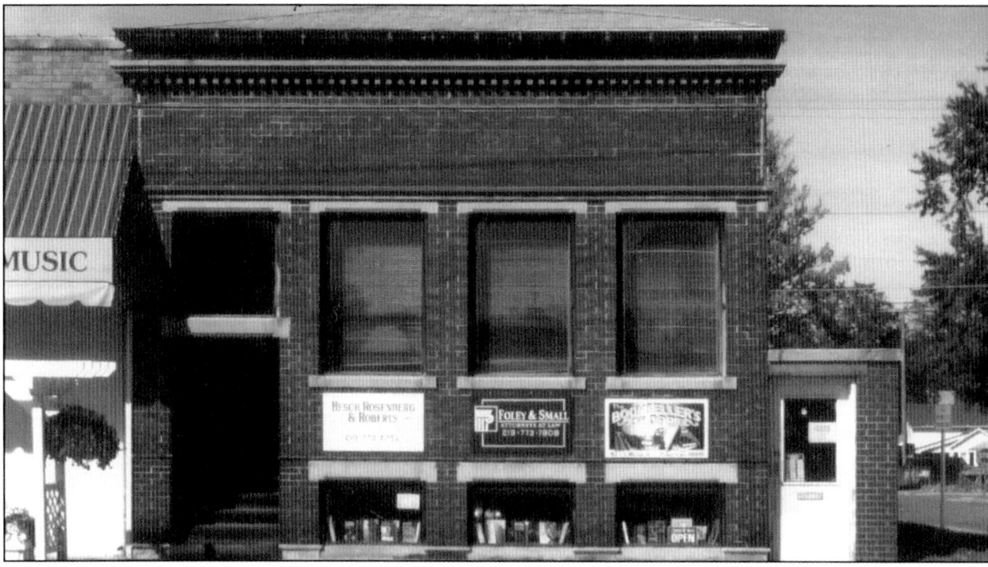

This is the exterior of what was once the Price Hospital, located at 160 East Market Street. Henry Frazier was the mastermind behind the one-story structure, which offered a raised basement, and was inspired by the Arts and Crafts design. Upon its opening in 1913, it was touted as one of the most advanced medical facilities in the region. There was a waiting area, preparatory and operating rooms, and a ward which could accommodate the needs of up to three patients. Additional rooms were used to store medicines, conduct examinations, and consult with patients. The Price Hospital was created for brothers Willard Price and M. Delbert Price, both physicians. It is worth noting that when Nappanee's status changed to a city some years later, in 1926, Dr. Willard Price served as the first mayor. (Photo courtesy of Mr. and Mrs. William Johnson.)

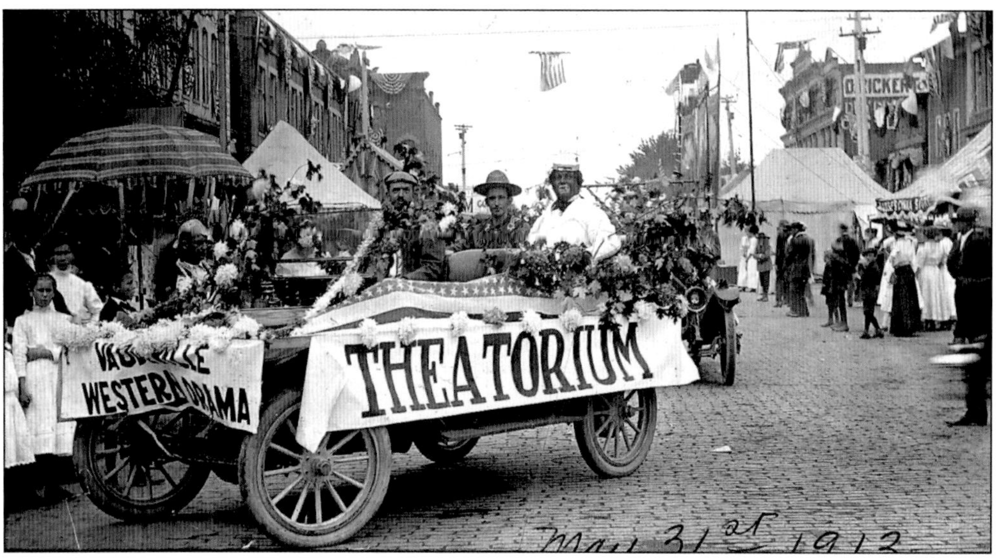

Nappanee's first movie theatre was known as the Theatorium, and it is being represented by an elaborate float in a city parade from May 31, 1913. Tom Greene was the theatre's proprietor, and he is seen driving the float. Gail Best, in the rear, was the projectionist. The admission fee to see a motion picture in that era was 5¢. (Photo courtesy of Nappanee Public Library.)

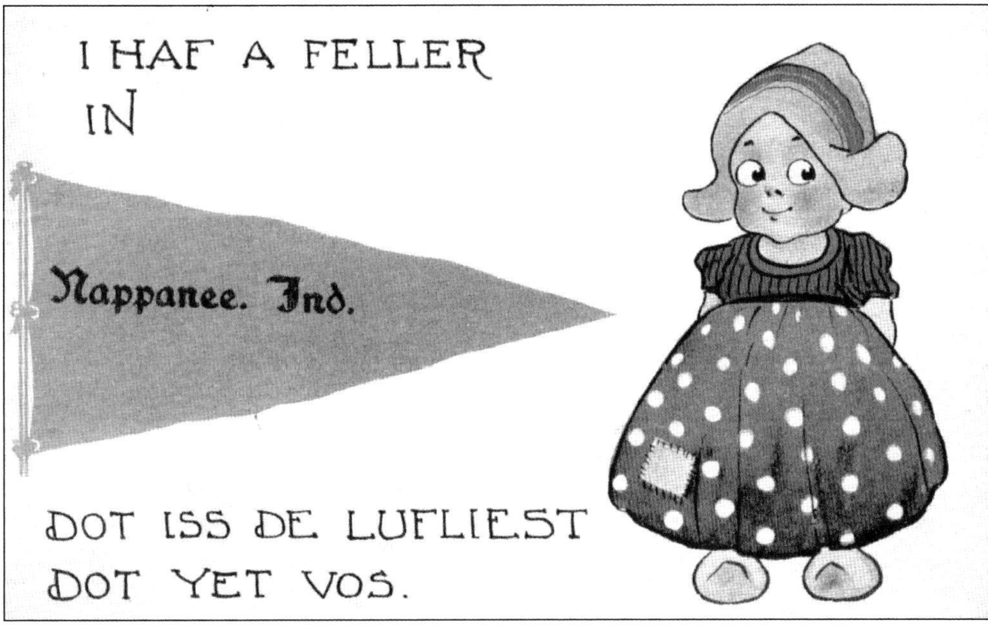

A charmingly drawn postcard, featuring a little Dutch girl, boasts a comment in this precise English translation, "I Have a Fellow in Nappanee—That Is The Loveliest That Yet Was." The card carried a 1914 postmark. (Photo courtesy of Mr. and Mrs. Dean Henry.)

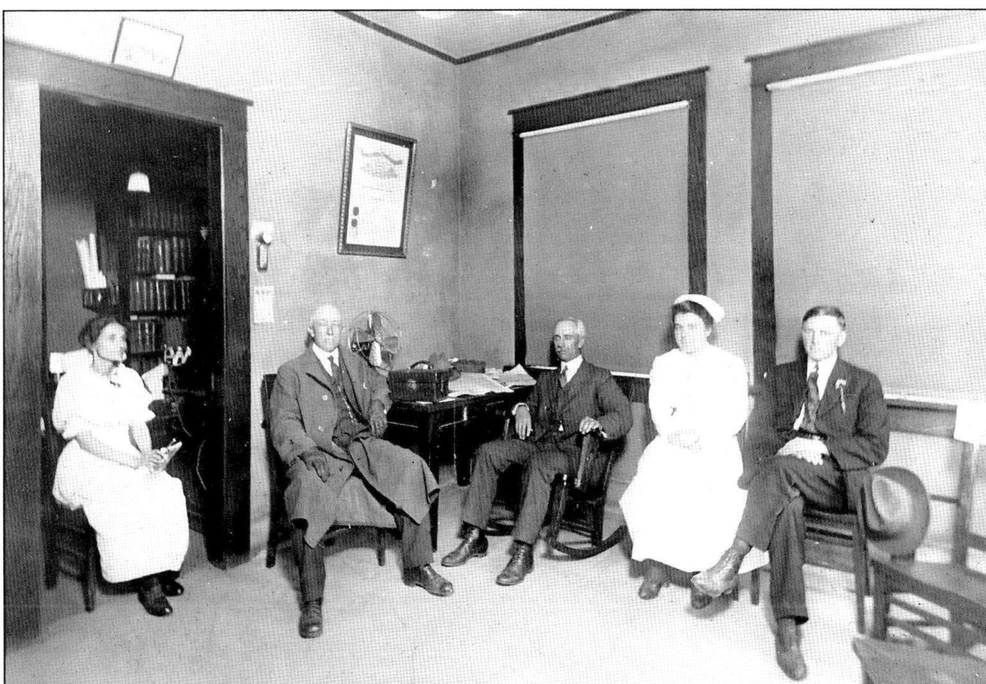

The staff of the Price Hospital is seen in a photograph dated 1915. At far left is Bessie Culp, the office girl, who died in 1916. Beside her is Dr. Willard Price, M.D., followed by Dr. M. Delbert Price, M.D., Nurse Melinda "Lynn" Yoder Foley, and an unidentified gent, thought to have been a pharmaceutical salesman. (Photo courtesy of Nappanee Public Library.)

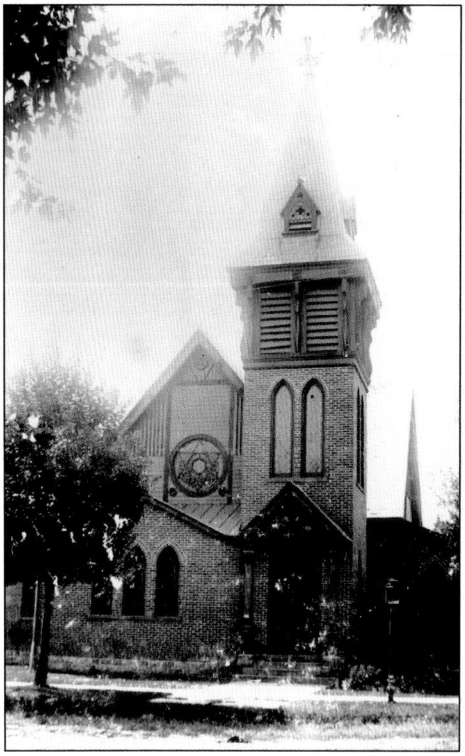

The Methodist Episcopal Church is pictured as it appeared prior to 1916. Methodism was one of the city's first actively practiced religions, first convening regular membership in 1880. Meetings were held in various public outlets, such as the school building and the Hartman Brothers Hall, before the church was organized in 1886. This church was built in 1887 on a lot located at 301 East Market Street, at a cost of just over $5,000. By 1915, the church was deemed too small for its purpose, and a new, Renaissance-style church would be open for services in just one year. (Photo courtesy of Nappanee Public Library.)

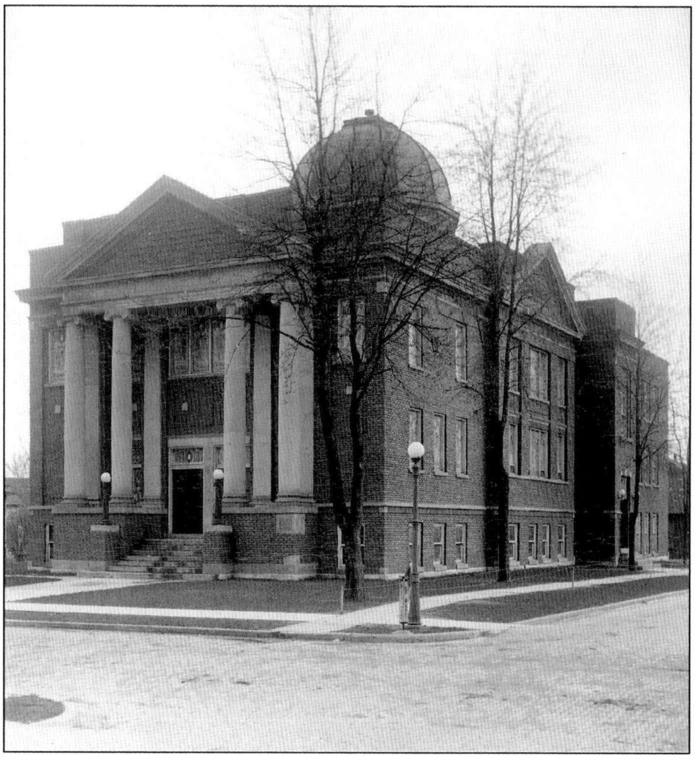

The new Methodist Church premiered in June of 1916 at the same location as the former church, 301 East Market Street. The spacious, magnificent facility with its delicately ornate dome was almost double the space of the previous building, and was built using lumber and brick from the old structure. The majority of the church was razed in March of 1988, with only the sanctuary preserved for future use. (Photo courtesy of Nappanee Public Library.)

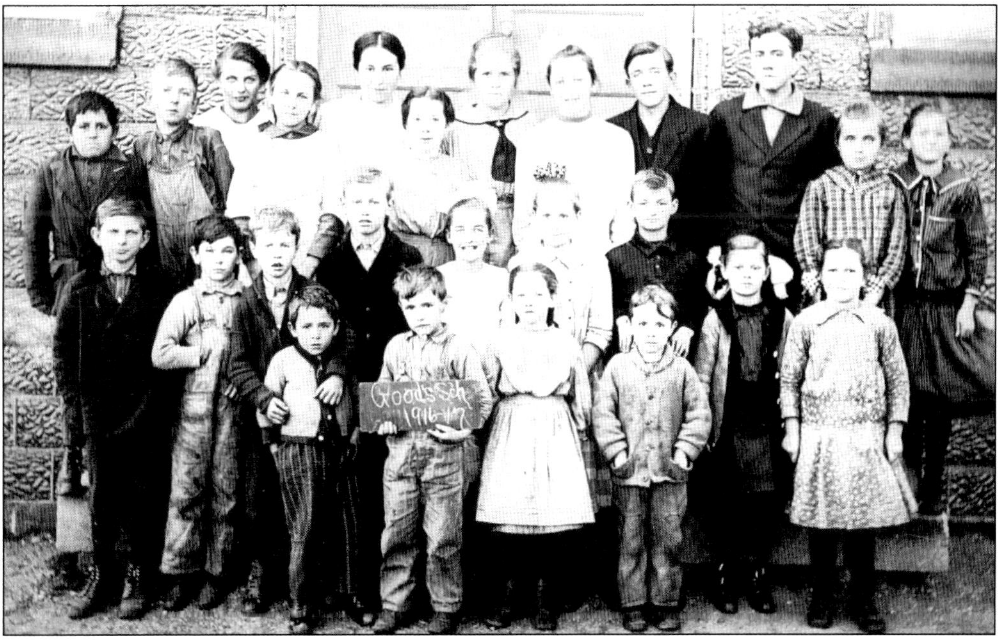

This was one of the one-room schoolhouses of the region, rather fittingly called the Good School. Students are shown here in a class photograph from 1916. The school was one under the Union Township administration, and the building still stands at the northeast corner of County Road 44 and County Road 7—it is used as a private residence. (Photo courtesy of Mr. and Mrs. Dean Henry.)

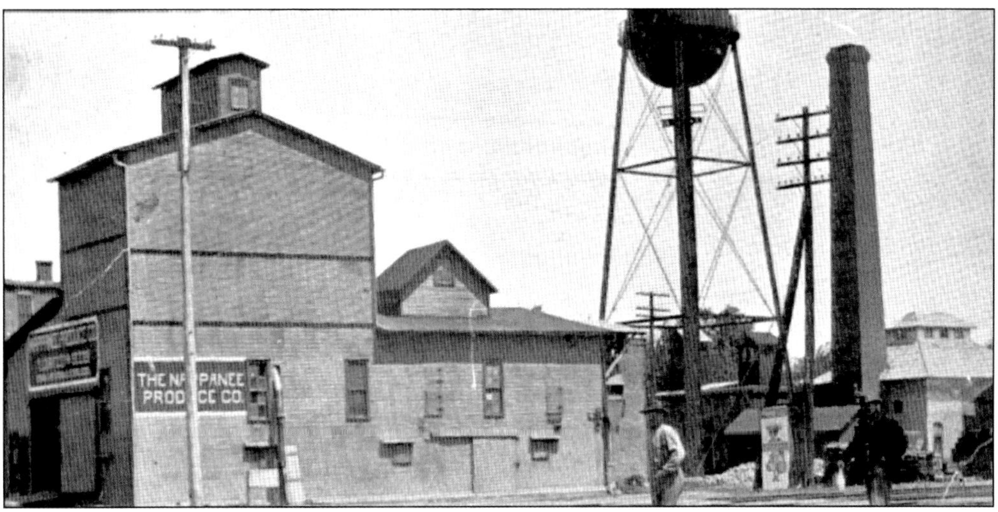

An article from the August 17, 1904 edition of the Nappanee News sheds some light on the events surrounding this, the Nappanee Produce Co. The story tells of a new 40 by 60-foot storage warehouse being built near the South Main Street railroad crossing. The business was managed by G.D. Stauffer and partnered by W.W. Stauffer and H.R. Stauffer. By 1914, the company was able to expand further by adding more room for crib capacity and hay storage. They also added a large elevator to accommodate 12,000 bushels. The Nappanee Produce Company was located on South Madison Street in a building known as the Brown Tank Factory. (Photo courtesy of Nappanee Public Library.)

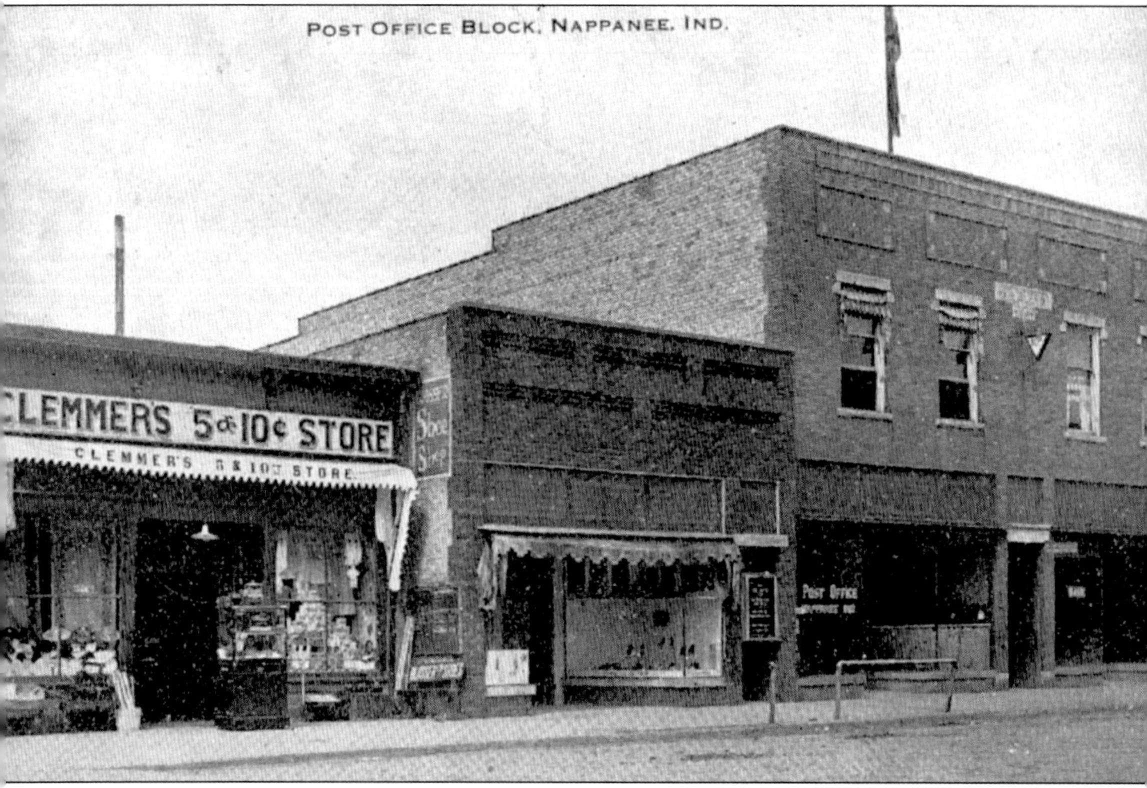

The north side of East Market Street was often referred to then as the "Post Office block." The storefronts belong to Clemmer's 5 and 10¢ Store, Blosser's Shoe Store, and the Post Office. (Photo courtesy of Nappanee Public Library.)

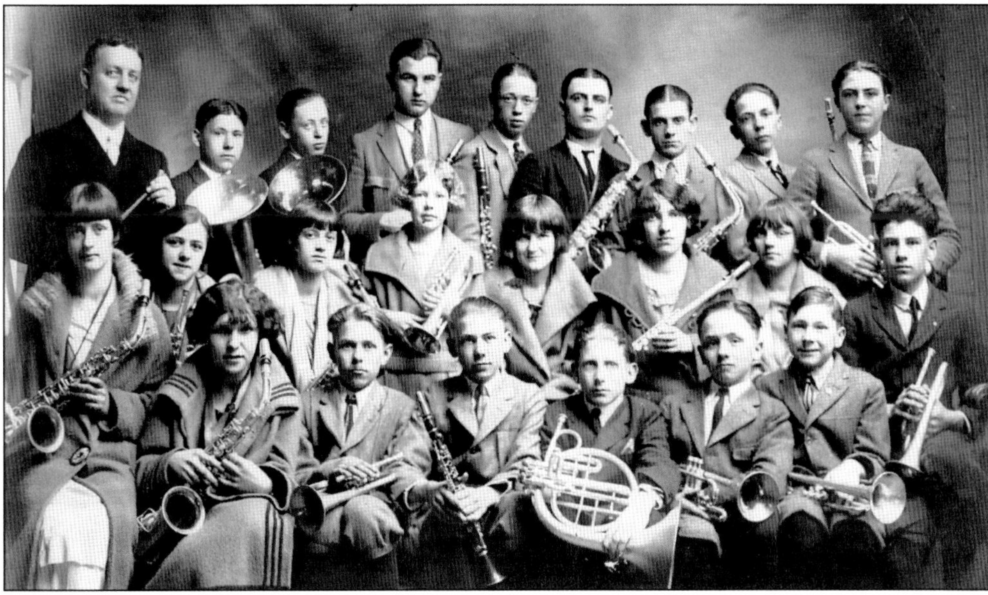

The young musicians of the First Brethren Sunday School band are shown in this 1920 photo. From left to right are: (front row) Isabelle Widmoyer, Ione Best, Charles Nixon, Fred Culp, Harrison Hossler, and an unknown boy; (second row) Dorothy Price, Marjorie Tobias, Edna Miller, Evelyn Miller, Myrtle Roose, Charlotte Pippen, and Maynard Lehman; (back row) Pastor E.L. Miller (director), Harry Sechrist, Bunk Widmoyer, Harold Myers, Mack Widmoyer, Kenton Mellinger, Dale Culp, John Price, and LaVon Mellinger. (Photo courtesy of Nappanee Public Library.)

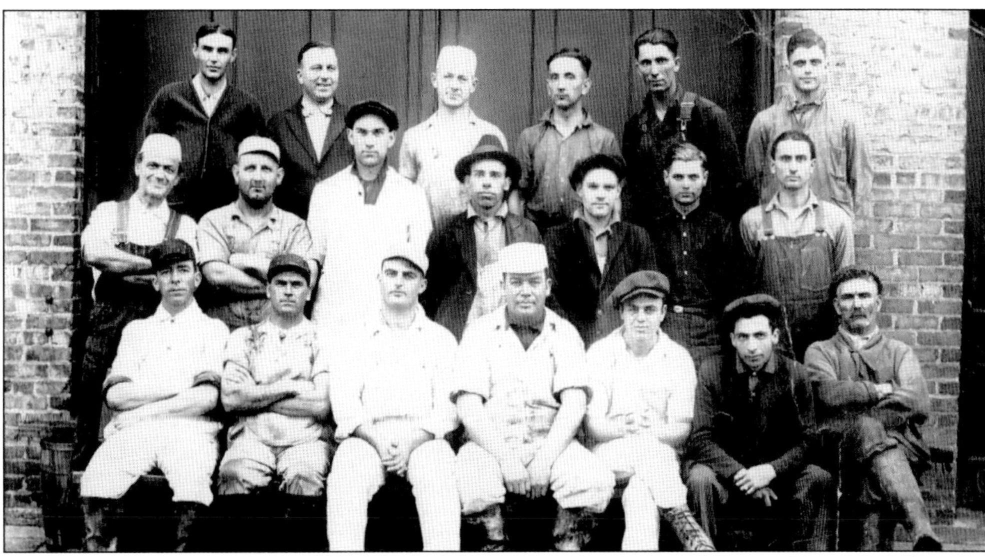

The men employed by the Freese Bros. Creamery take a moment to be photographed in this 1920s image. From left to right are: (front row) two unidentified, Kenton Mellinger, Bill Rupert, two unidentified, and John Mellinger; (second row) three unidentified, Walter Sechrist, John Hoover, and two unidentified, (third row) unidentified, Carl Miller, William Wagner, Oscar Haney, and Jack Gardner. The creamery was once situated on South Main Street. (Photo courtesy of Nappanee Public Library.)

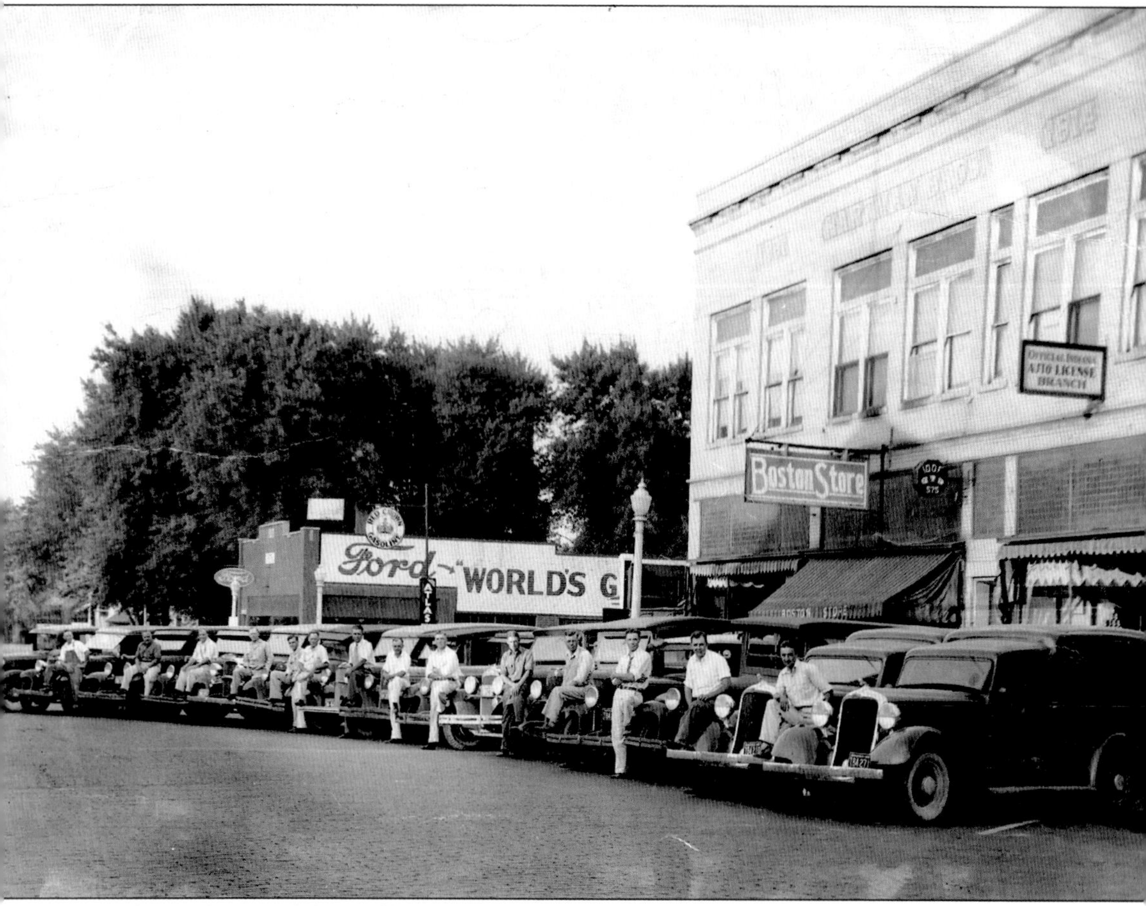

Delivery drivers of the Huffman Bakery show off their Ford trucks in front of the Ford Agency along South Main Street in the 1920s. The Huffman Bakery, which was located on West Market Street, had its origins in 1892 when Ogden Huffman took over the Stoops Bakery. In its earliest days, a "good day" was when the bakery turned out over 60 loaves of bread. By the late 1940s, thousands of loaves were being baked, as well as such treats as cakes, cookies, and other pastry items. Various family members would assume ownership of the bakery over the years, until its closing in 1961. (Photo courtesy of Nappanee Public Library.)

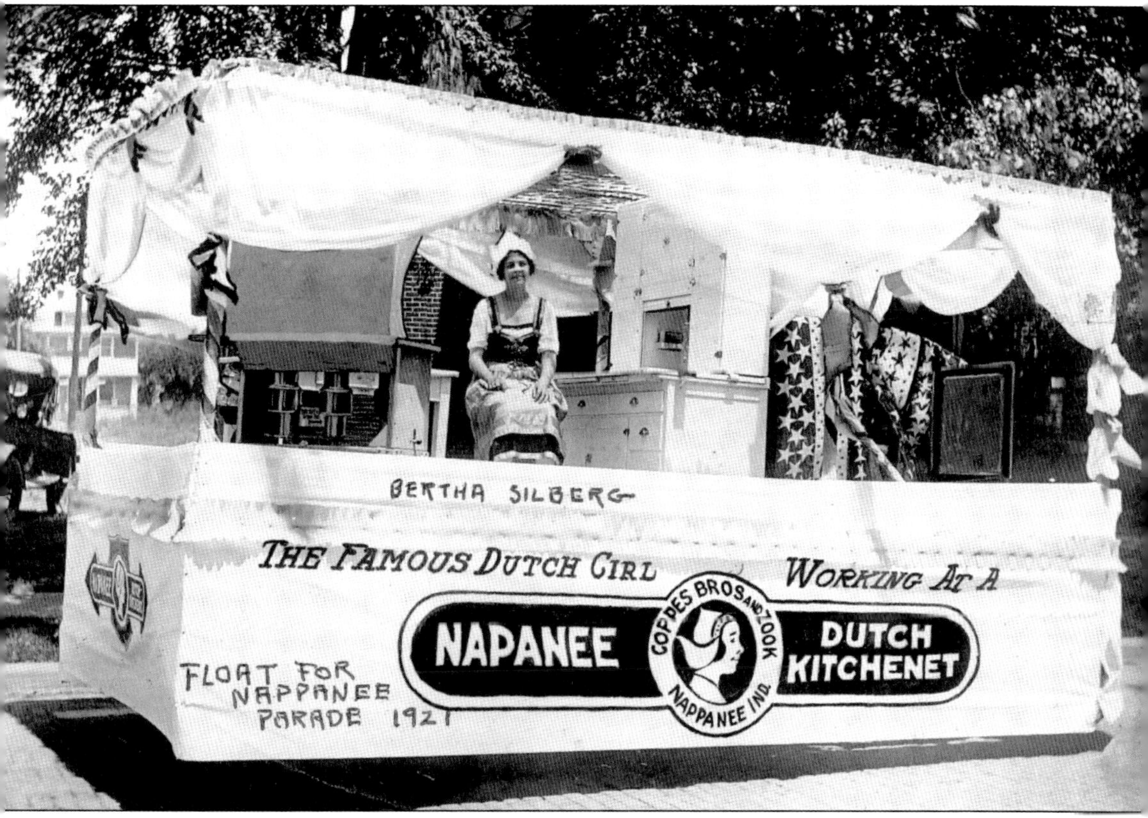

Bertha Silberg rides atop a Coppes Bros. and Zook float, which offers a look at a Nappanee Dutch Kitchenet, in a 1921 parade. (Photo courtesy of Nappanee Public Library.)

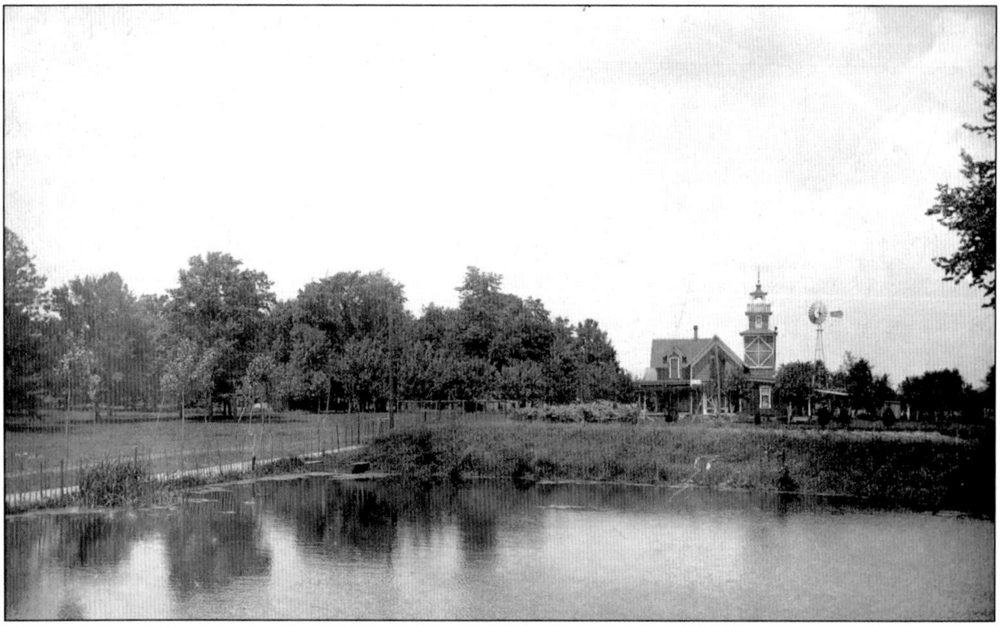

This is the predecessor to the West Side Park, which lies on the west side of north Nappanee Street. It was known as Frevert's Pond and Grove. (Photo courtesy of Nappanee Public Library.)

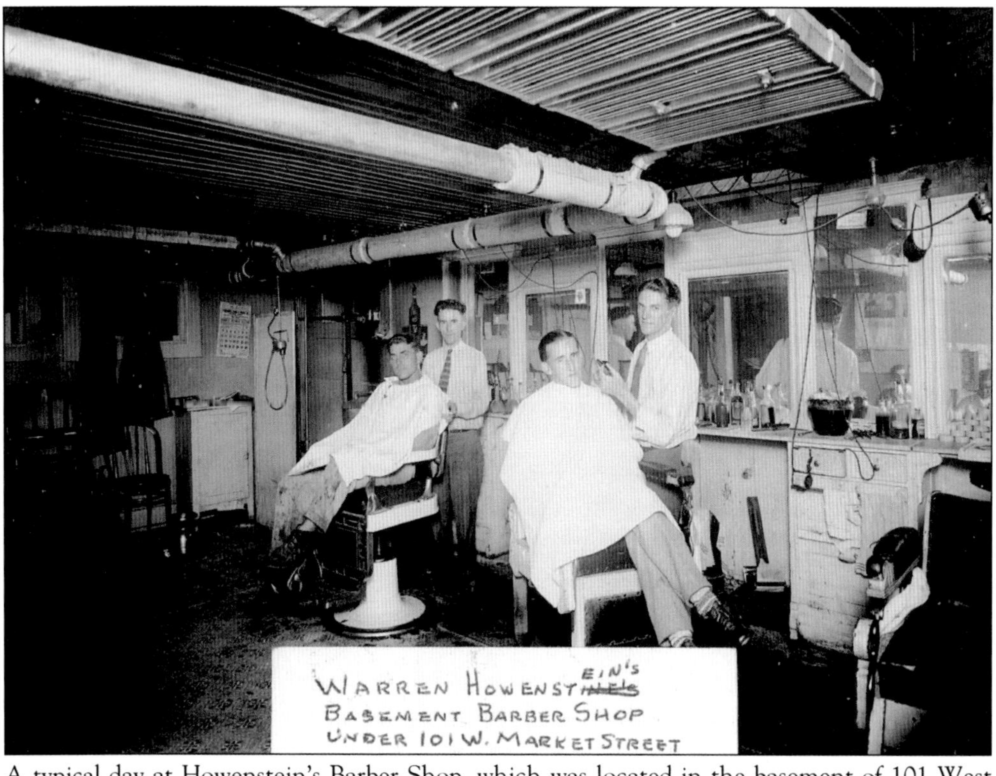

A typical day at Howenstein's Barber Shop, which was located in the basement of 101 West Market Street. From left to right are Willard Reed, Warren Howenstein, Farrel Arch, and an unknown barber. (Photo courtesy of Nappanee Public Library.)

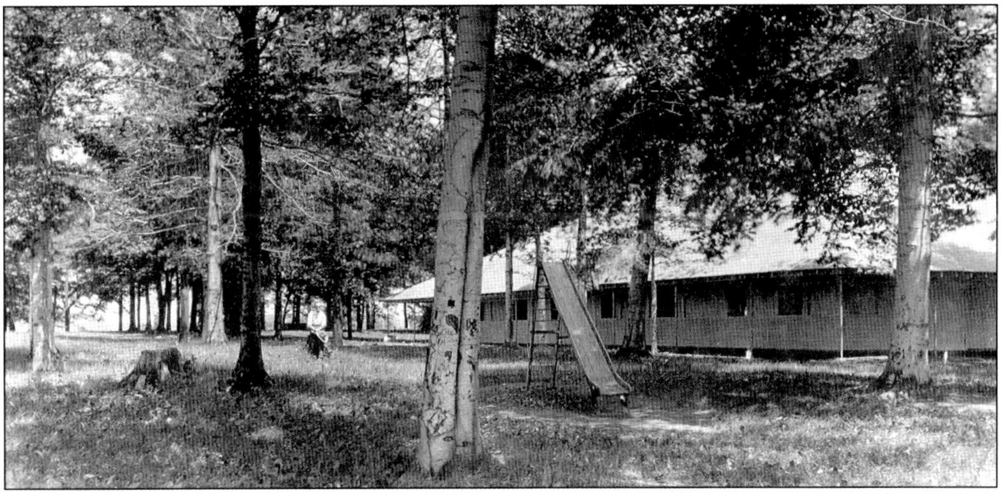

This is a look at the Community Park Pavilion, also referred to as the West Park Pavilion. It was built in 1923, on land that was donated to the city for the purpose of raising a suitable entertainment venue. At the time, "chautauquas" were in vogue, with performers traveling from across the nation to present "educational and recreational assemblies." In its first season, which debuted in July of 1924, the Croatian Tamburica Orchestra and DeMarco Symphony Harp Ensemble were headliners. Later that year, the Chautauqua gatherings dwindled, and after operating for two seasons, a $400 debt mired further functions. The original guarantors were forced to pay the funds directly from their own pockets. (Photo courtesy of Mr. and Mrs. Dean Henry.)

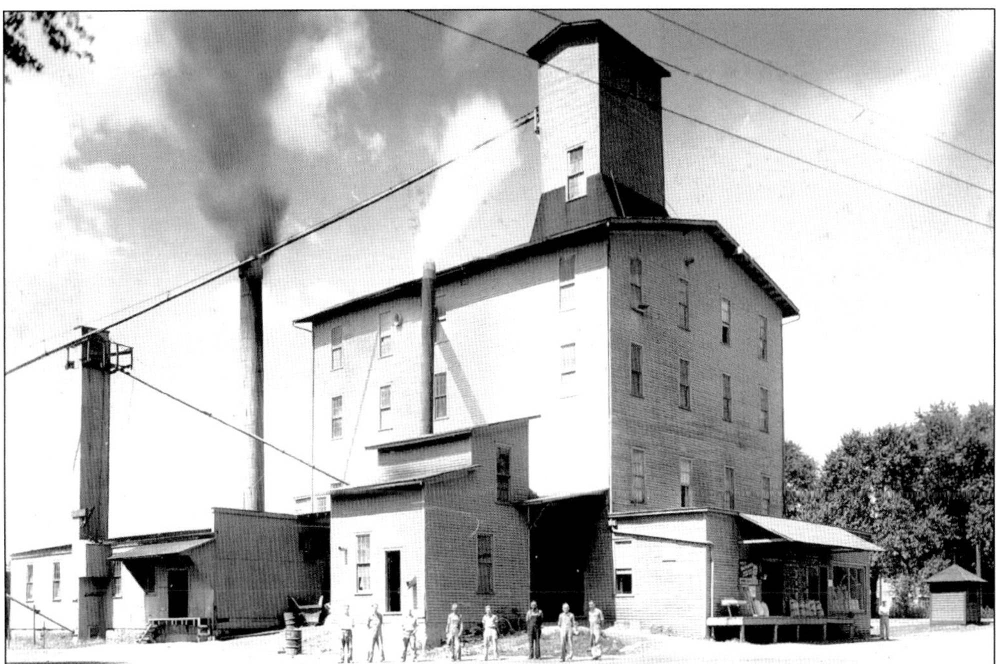

A small group of gentlemen comprised the employees of the Nappanee Milling Company, which was located at 301 South Main. The photo is dated 1925. Seen from left to right are Glenn Oswald, Glenn Bliele, Bill Freet, Dave Shaum, Jesse Hepler, Jesse Bliele, Roy Robison, and W.E. Johnson. (Photo courtesy of Nappanee Public Library.)

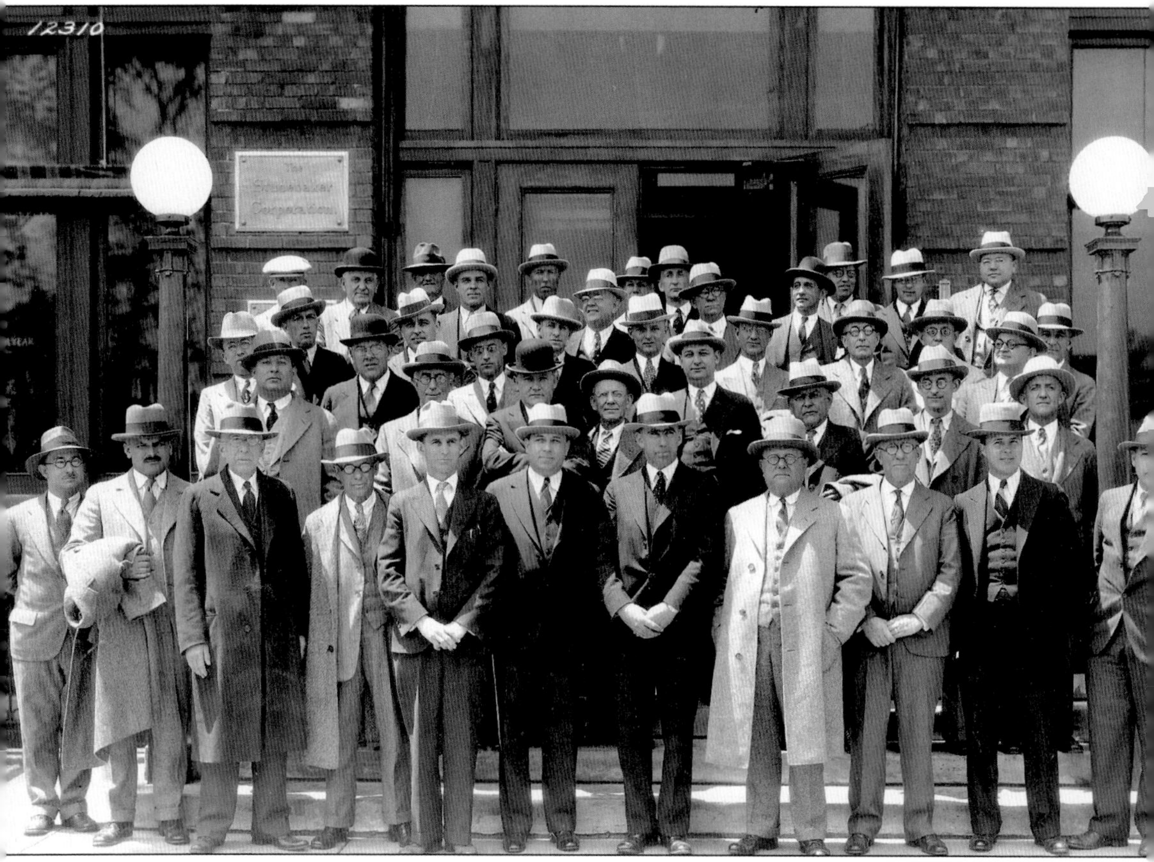

Members of the Nappanee Kiwanis Club have an adventure touring the Studebaker Automobile Factory in South Bend. The year was 1928. From left to right are: (first row) Frank Rehrer, Roy Berlin, Harry R. Stauffer, Dr. H.J. DeFreese, Bert Brundage, unidentified, Menno Pletcher, Frank Coppes, Dr. Willard Price, LaMar Mutschler, and Claude Coppes; (second row) George Fales, unidentified, Noah Lehman, Ralph Metzler, Rev. R.L. Burns, Claude Stoops, Fred Coppes, unidentified, Lloyd Johnson, and Harvey Bechtel; (third row) Orris Mishler, Howard Prickett, Henry W. Eastman, Morton Long, Ralph Arnott, Dr. Owen Lentz, Roy Ruckman, Harold Gray, Lee Mullett, and Guy Loudermilk; (fourth row) unidentified, George Freese, Jasper Abel, unidentified, Clem Brown, Mart Mullett, Arthur Miller, unidentified, Dr. Delbert Price, Marvin Coppes, Harvey Fields, Carlyle A. Mutschler, and Dr. G.L. Oyler. (Photo courtesy of Nappanee Public Library.)

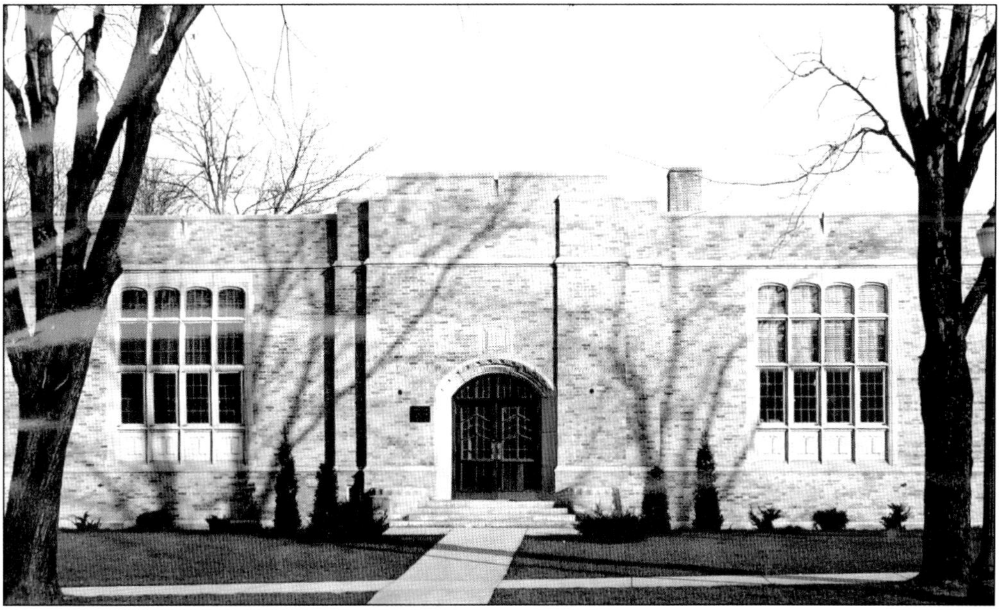

The Nappanee Public Library is seen here in the 1930s. In the 70-plus years since this image was captured, the library has undergone vast renovations, but perhaps none more intriguing than the 1985 venture in which new sections of the library were built around the existing facade—something of a library within a library. Today, patrons who are browsing the adult section of the library can still walk through the 1930s entryway, as it is now a unique and historical focal point. More recently, the library underwent another major renovation in 2001. (Photo courtesy of Nappanee Public Library.)

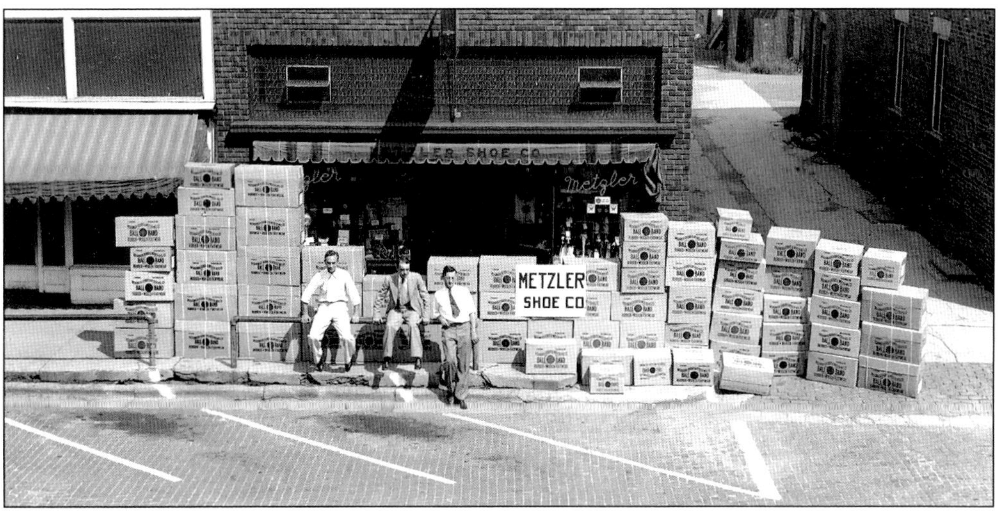

This photo is a testimony to one of the most creative ways to advertise a business—the men of the Metzler Shoe Company, surrounded by a shipment from Ball Band Rubber Goods in 1933. The employees are Everett "Bag" Pippen, Virgil Stuckman, and Ralph Metzler. Metzler Shoes dates back to 1924, and has consistently been under the helm of several generations of Metzler family members since that time. Dan Metzler is the present owner, and is a descendant of Daniel Metzler, one of the first settlers of Nappanee. The business can be found at 111 South Main Street. (Photo courtesy of Nappanee Public Library.)

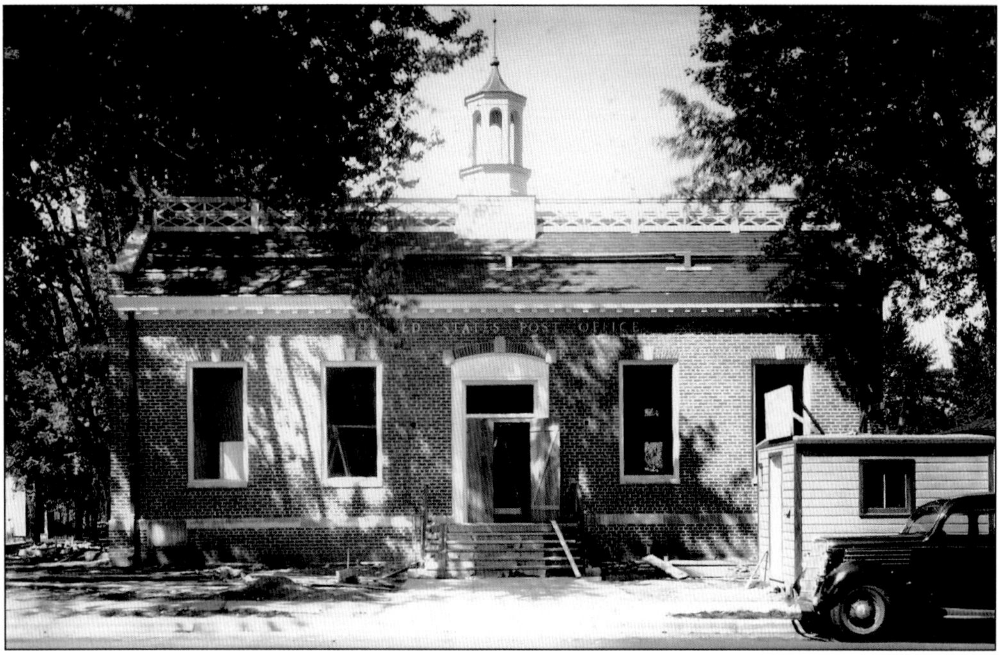

The present Nappanee Post Office, located at 202 East Market Street, just one month before it opened for business in September of 1935. The lobby of the building is bedecked with a hand-painted mural, a result of President Franklin Roosevelt's "New Deal" program, which provided unemployment relief. The artist, Grant C. Christian, used his future wife as the model for the young girl in the picture. She can be seen standing by a fence, awaiting the arrival of the postman. The 11 by 4 foot artwork is fittingly titled, *Waiting for the Mail.* (Photo courtesy of Nappanee Public Library.)

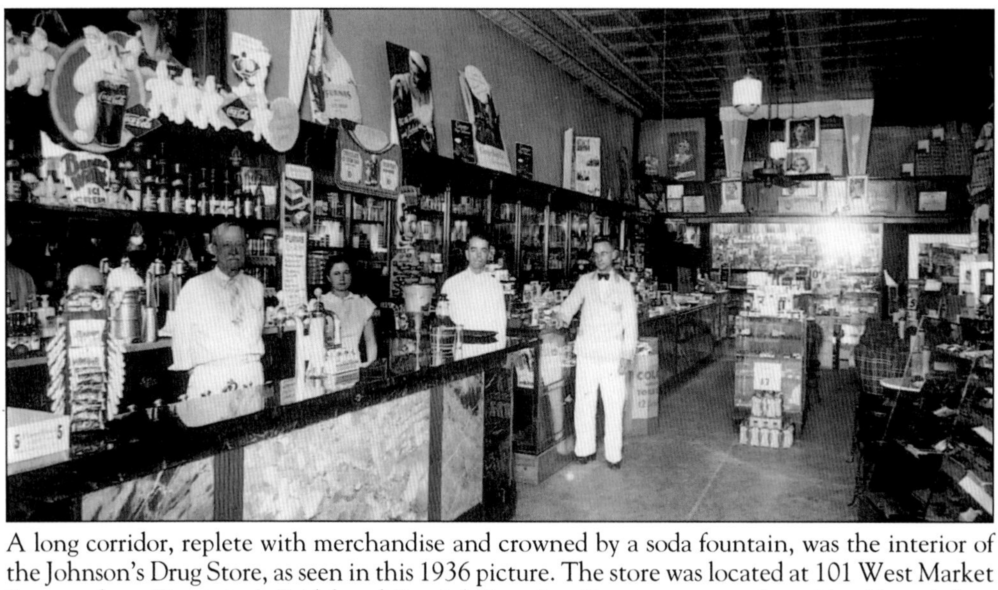

A long corridor, replete with merchandise and crowned by a soda fountain, was the interior of the Johnson's Drug Store, as seen in this 1936 picture. The store was located at 101 West Market Street, where Dominica's Bridal and Special Occasion Boutique currently resides. From left to right are Christian W. Johnson (founder), Jeanette Richmond Hockert, Lloyd Farrington, and Lloyd Johnson. (Photo courtesy of Mr. and Mrs. William Johnson.)

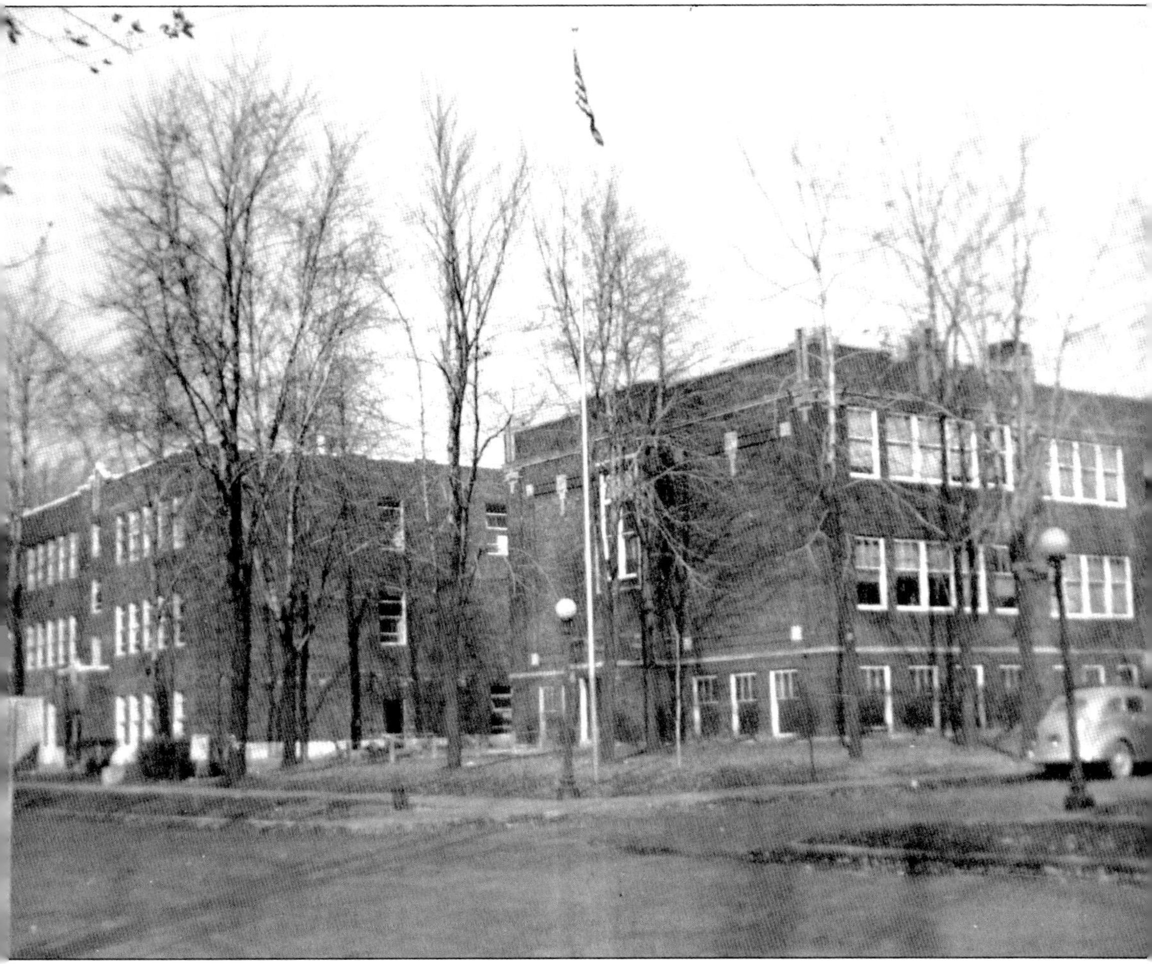

These are the buildings which graced the Central School complex as it appeared around 1937. The two brick schoolhouses were created some 20 years apart, in the hopes of remedying a common problem among a fast-growing city—too many students and not enough space. The building to the right was constructed first, in 1918, and was then the Nappanee High School. By 1937, it was decided to build a newer, somewhat identical facility just to the north, and that building became the new high school. The older structure was demolished that same year. For another 20 years, the Nappanee High School served at that location until the completion of a spacious, single-story campus in 1958 on South Jackson Street. It was known as the East Side School, and it was the final era of Nappanee High School until the 1960s. In 1962, the school systems of Wakarusa and Nappanee consolidated to create the Wa-Nee School Corporation, and in 1970, the new NorthWood High School bowed just north of Nappanee. The former East Side School now houses the students of the Nappanee Elementary School. After the East Side project, Central School was a haven for elementary school students, and remained in that capacity until the conclusion of the 1991–92 school year. After a period of vacancy, the building is now home to the Main Street Suites, which features the Nappanee Area Chamber of Commerce, the Boys and Girls Club, the Nappanee Redevelopment Commission, Lee Anne Stewart Dance School, and the Revival Tabernacle. Construction and renovation efforts are now underway to convert the second floor into 22 units of housing for senior citizens, with one wing ready to welcome tenants in May of 2003, and an additional wing slated for opening in November of 2003. (Photo courtesy of Nappanee Public Library.)

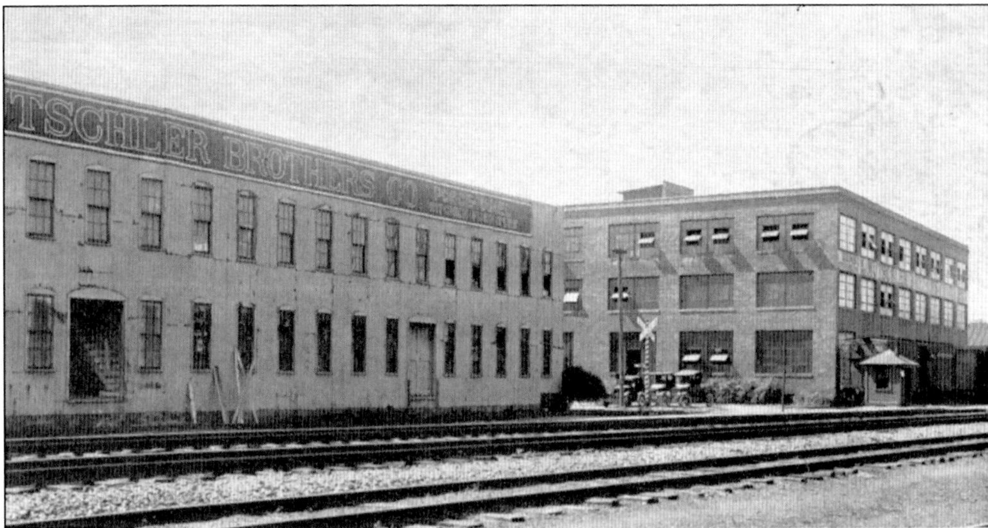

Mutschler Brothers Company, Nappanee, Ind.

In 1913, the Mutschler Bros. Company was founded, after breaking away from the Coppes and Zook partnership. This postcard of the complex is dated 1946. Continuing in its earliest traditions, the company flourished on its own merits, by serving a national market through its dealer organization and four additional assembly plants located in Boston, Miami, New Orleans, and Easton, Maryland. The number of local employees varied from 150 to 340 people, and annual sales often exceeded $5 million. The family ownership of Mutschler Bros. ended in 1969, when the company was purchased by American Standard. (Photo courtesy of Mr. and Mrs. Dean Henry.)

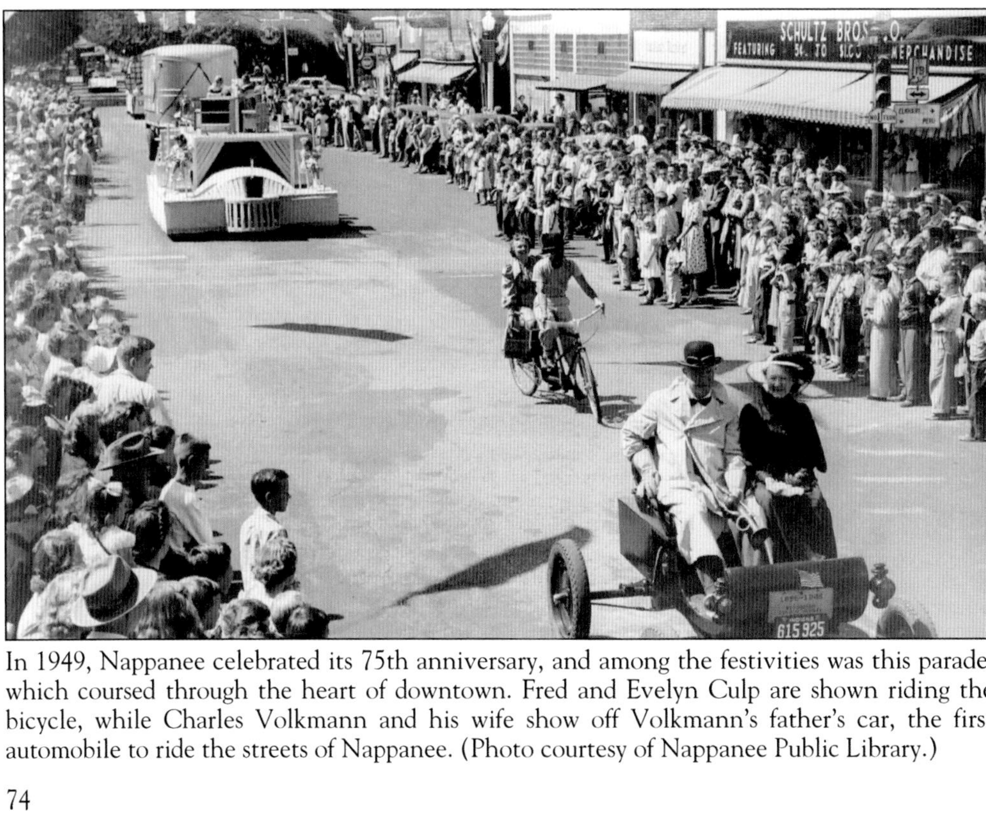

In 1949, Nappanee celebrated its 75th anniversary, and among the festivities was this parade, which coursed through the heart of downtown. Fred and Evelyn Culp are shown riding the bicycle, while Charles Volkmann and his wife show off Volkmann's father's car, the first automobile to ride the streets of Nappanee. (Photo courtesy of Nappanee Public Library.)

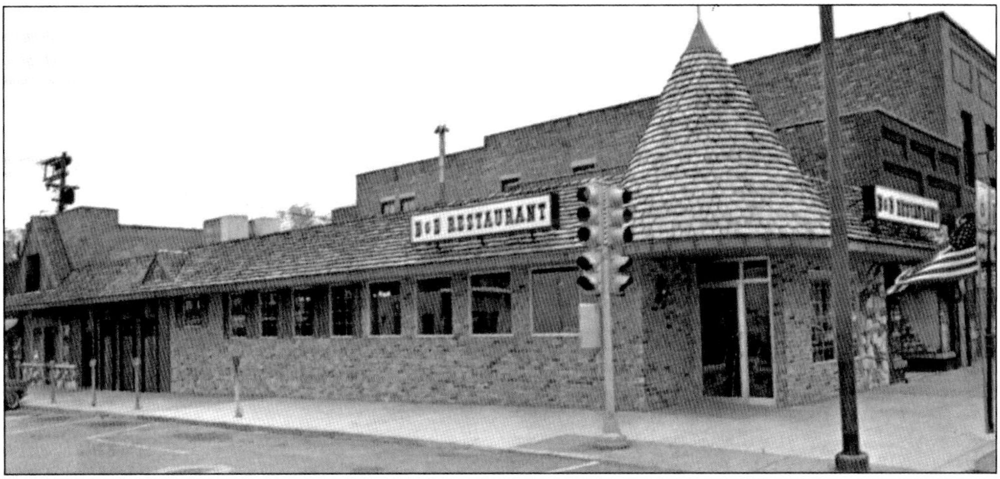

For almost 70 years, the B & B Restaurant was, literally and poetically, part of the heart of Nappanee. It was situated at the northeast corner of Main and Market Streets. The history of the restaurant actually includes a chapter from Locke lore, when Buck Widmoyer and Bus Hostetter relocated the building to Nappanee from Locke in 1925. The men opened up the new eatery under the title of "Bunk and Bus Cafe." Before the year was out, however, the men were at odds over whether to shift their sights to the Syracuse area—Bus wanted to go, while Bunk was content to stay. It was decided that they would flip a coin, with the winner buying out the loser's share. Bunk Widmoyer won that infamous coin toss, and the establishment became the B & B Restaurant—Bunk believing that the use of the term "cafe" might mislead patrons into thinking there were only beverages served. During the Depression era, the B & B offered such special entrees as the 1¢ egg sandwich, a bowl of soup for a nickel, or a slice of their scrumptious pie. In the 1930's the B & B was also the first restaurant in northern Indiana to offer air conditioning. The restaurant closed in 1993, and in 1994, several folks joined in an event called "The Last Coffee Break," where Bunk Widmoyer's son, David, who ran the restaurant for 42 years, reminisced about the good old days. (Photo courtesy of Mr. and Mrs. Dean Henry.)

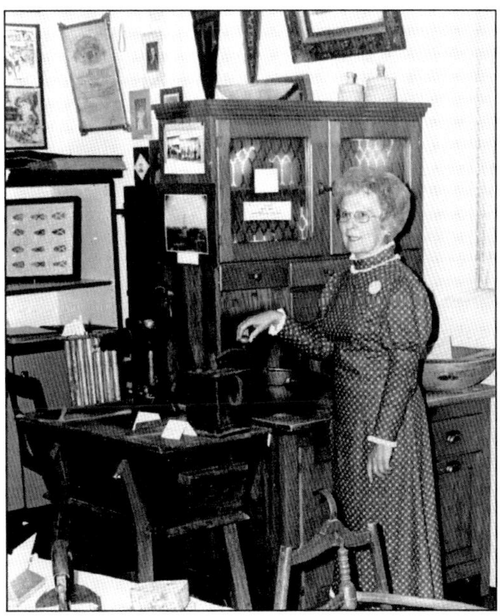

Evelyn Lehman Culp is seen here assuming a regal pose while presenting the artifacts of the Evelyn Lehman Culp Heritage Center. The museum was unveiled in 1974, to coincide with the 100th anniversary of the founding of Nappanee. Here, she offers a glimpse inside a kitchen of yesteryear, with a coffee grinder, dough tray, cradle ironing board, and double duty iron. Since its debut, the Heritage Center has welcomed visitors from around the country, and eventually grew to encompass almost the entire lower level of the Nappanee Public Library. When the Nappanee Public Library recently completed a renovation, an entire section of the library was dedicated to the continuing mission to preserve Nappanee's rich heritage, a mission that Evelyn Culp carried out until her passing in 2002. (Photo courtesy of the Nappanee Public Library.)

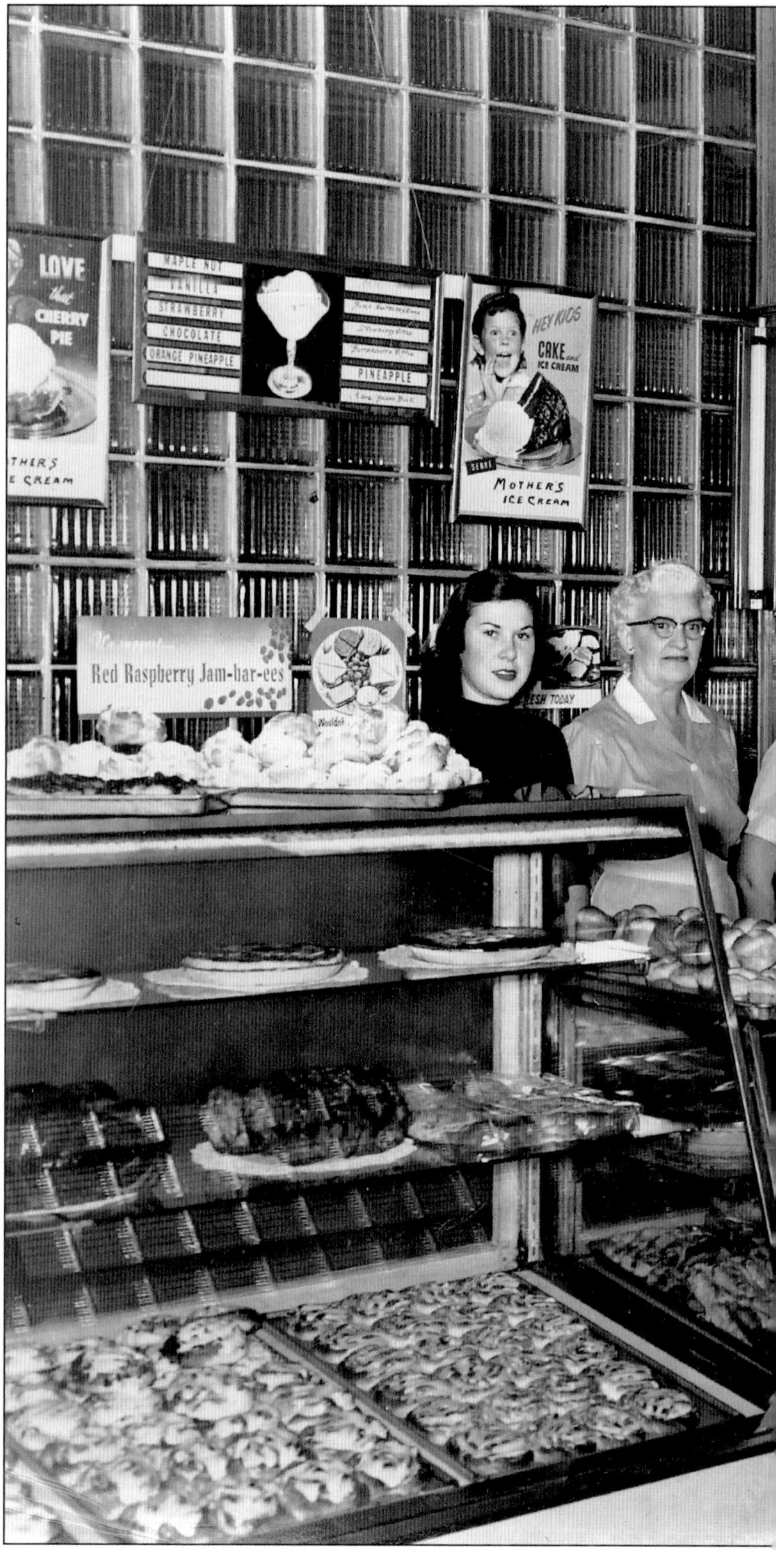

The ladies who kept things busy for the Huffman Bakery, in this 1954 photo are, from left to right, Nancy Coppes, Lydia Arnott, Becky Moore, Eloise Ganger Ogle, Opal Ruff Sponseller, and Norma Pippenger Hershberger. (Photo courtesy of Nappanee Public Library.)

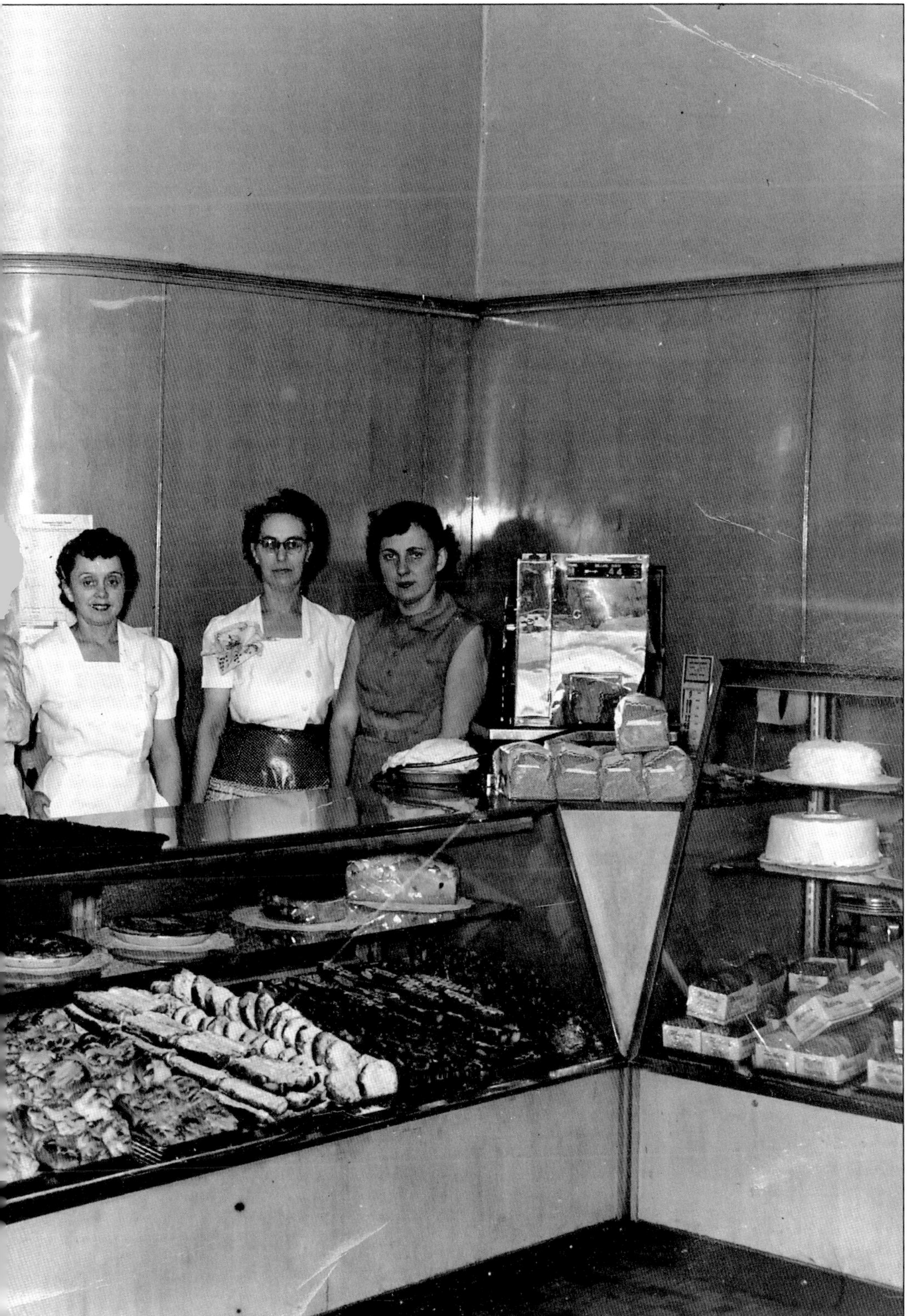

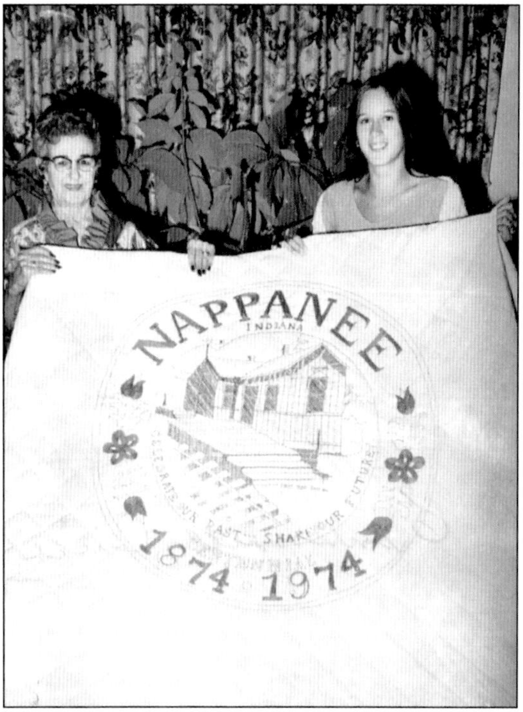

This work of art demonstrated the skill and imagination of Ranita Hopewell, right, who designed the logo, and Mrs. William C. Best, left, who sewed the quilt. The quilt was viewed for the first time during the 1974 centennial. (Photo courtesy of Nappanee Public Library.)

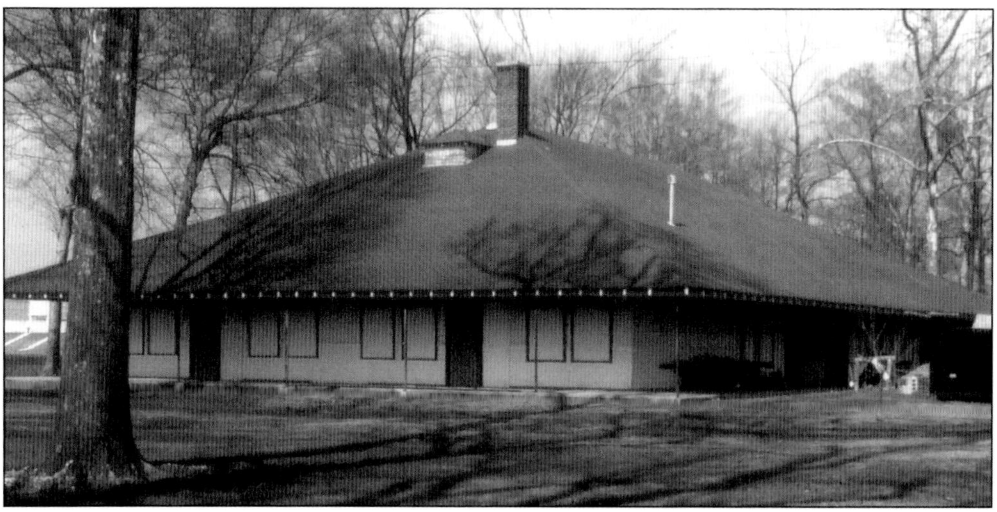

The Community Park (West Park) Pavilion is seen here around the time of its renovation phase in the mid 1990s. After the heyday of the traveling chautauquas came to an end in the 1920s, the pavilion was quiet for a time until the formation of Nappanee's "Pavilion Players," a local civic theatre group which premiered in 1958. The actors presented a number of theatrical showcases over the years, until a sad chain of events nearly silenced the pavilion forever. A massive fire in 1964, then another in 1977, caused a tremendous amount of interior and structural damage. In 1994, it was listed on the National Register of Historic Places. The local community theatre group, long since renamed the Nappanee Civic Theatre, hosted a ribbon-cutting ceremony in February of 1995 and the cast and crew chose to perform *You Can't Take It With You*, which was the first show presented by the Pavilion Players years before. The author and her husband both had roles in the 1995 production. (Photo courtesy of Mr. and Mrs. William Johnson.)

Two

WAKARUSA
From the Roots of Salem—
Extending the Olive Branch

Folks who are not entirely familiar with this enclave of Elkhart County are often bemused, and a bit befuddled, by the town's unique name. Invariably, the questions are raised, "Is that an Indian name?" followed by, "What does it mean?" Well, according to the best possible translations, and the most meticulously kept records of the community's early days, Wakarusa means, "knee deep in mud."

Not long before Wakarusa came into being, the region was mostly uninhabited. The first person to secure a homestead there was Frederick Morris, who arrived from Ohio in 1833. He set about building his own cabin and also saw to it that there would be a northbound road to the nearest neighboring settlement—that of Jamestown. By the spring of 1836, other families had come to live, and it seemed prudent that a township be established. It was through the workings of Cornelius Terwilliger, Jacob Sailor, Frederick Morris, David Allen, and Samuel and Levi Martin that their new homeland became Olive Township.

The next year, Isaac Martin opened his home to represent a makeshift polling place in the township's first election. Twelve people turned out to cast their votes, placing their ballots in a sugar bowl. Within a few more years, in 1845, the first township school was built, which not only served as a place of learning, but as a venue for revival meetings and other public functions. A fellow by the name of Harvey Bly helped to simplify the lives of his fellow homesteaders by allowing his log cabin to be used for the purposes of a post office in 1849. The primitive but effective facility was known as Mt. Olive.

In 1852, a gentleman named Henry Myers purchased 80 acres of land in the southwest section of Elkhart County with plans to create a town. The land was platted by a trio of men named Holdeman, Smeltzer, and Pletcher, and the post office at Mt. Olive was moved to the new location, called Salem.

Merchants were soon to follow. Thomas Inks had the first two-story house, which doubled as the first retail store, built on what is now North Elkhart Street. He operated a dry goods mercantile in the front portion of the home, while the family dwelled in the rear. The second floor was Inks Hall, which was a large public outlet for parties and holiday events. The local Lutheran fellowship erected the town's first church, while the first public school was erected in 1856. The school was a simple, one-room structure situated on the southwest corner of the town square, where Elkhart and Waterford streets now intersect.

For the next seven years, the area was referred to as Salem, until it was revealed that there was another city in Indiana called Salem. This explained why the mail was often subject to some carrier confusion. The people convened in a public forum to decide upon a new name, and Jackson Woolverton, another one of the first merchants, suggested the name of Wakarusa. He selected this name in honor of a place where he had once lived—Wakarusa, Kansas. When the origins of "Wakarusa" were deciphered from the Indian meaning of "knee deep in mud," the residents found this new name particularly apropos, given that the land had a rather boggy consistency. After a great deal of discussion from dissenters and supporters alike, the town eventually became Wakarusa in 1859.

The number of residents within the boundaries of the town limits topped 400 between 1860 and 1870, although when the Civil War erupted, more than 100 men were sent to join the Union Army.

In 1873, the Chicago and Canada Southern Railroad carried the first train service through Wakarusa. The first local newspaper, the *Wakarusa Weekly Sun*, debuted on June 18, 1874. One of the very first issues to spark spirited editorials included the matter of crumbling, rotted wood sidewalks, which were becoming a bitterly regarded hazard for the womenfolk. It seemed that their long garments were becoming ensnared on the boards. So the ladies took to the streets in a very public manner, which yielded almost immediate results. The story of the "boardwalk incident" can be found in the photo chronicles of this chapter.

With the surge in population, it became quite clear that there was an urgent need for a larger schoolhouse, and in 1878, a three-room brick schoolhouse was opened on the south side of Waterford Street, about two and a half blocks east of the center of town. It was later remodeled to allow for four rooms on each of the floors. By 1879, the *Wakarusa Weekly Sun* had folded, and there would be no local newspaper until D.A. Rheubottom founded the *Wakarusa Tribune* in 1890, a weekly newspaper still in existence today. The Wabash Railroad unveiled its new depot at the Wakarusa station in 1892, which is now a landmark on the grounds of the Wakarusa Historical Museums.

The most devastating and horrific moments in the last days of the 19th century involved the great fire which systematically devoured the better share of an entire city block in the early morning hours of October 29, 1899. The proprietor of Knisely and Burner's Hardware Store, who resided just above the store, awoke at around 5 a.m. to the furious barking of his dog. Upon investigating, he was driven back by a dense plume of smoke. Knisely's cries of "fire" caused the town to quickly rush to aid. By that time, however, the fury of flames had already consumed much of the Eshelman block. The "bucket brigade," a group of men who worked to pump water and douse what was within their reach and their manpower, became a local legend.

It was roughly estimated that the fire cost $60,000 in goods and structural damage. Fifteen businesses, along with the post office and the telephone exchange, were damaged. No cause for the fire was ever determined, and thankfully there was no loss of life or serious injury—with the lone exception of Knisely's dog, whose yelps awoke his master and saved his life.

The saga prompted expedient action within the community. On December 3, 1899, the town council arranged for the delivery of fire fighting equipment, and just weeks later Wakarusa's first volunteer fire brigade was activated.

By the dawn of the 1900s, life was fruitful, and good fortunes propelled the community into what was then documented as a place which "affords many attractions as a place of residence, and is a business center whose importance is growing every year." There were 917 inhabitants by this time, and the town had a splendid recreational facility in a sparkling pond that was a popular summer haven for swimming, fishing, and family gatherings. Wakarusa High School presented the school's first football team in 1907, and soon after, the first basketball team. Drama and other extracurricular activities were added by 1921. The Wabash Railroad was running at full operation, carrying four passenger trains within a 24-hour period, as well as providing a route for hauling mail.

A new school was opened during the spring of 1924. The Wakarusa High School remained an institution until the merging of the Wakarusa and Nappanee school systems in 1962. The former high school later converted to NorthWood Middle School, and was finally razed in 2003.

Wakarusa is a quaint and humble place, and a welcoming and inviting community in which to work and raise a family. The town is also a major contributor to the workforce of Elkhart County. The early settlers who founded the town more than 150 years ago would be proud of what has been taken place in their wake, and the townspeople in this day can be proud of the legacy their forefathers left behind.

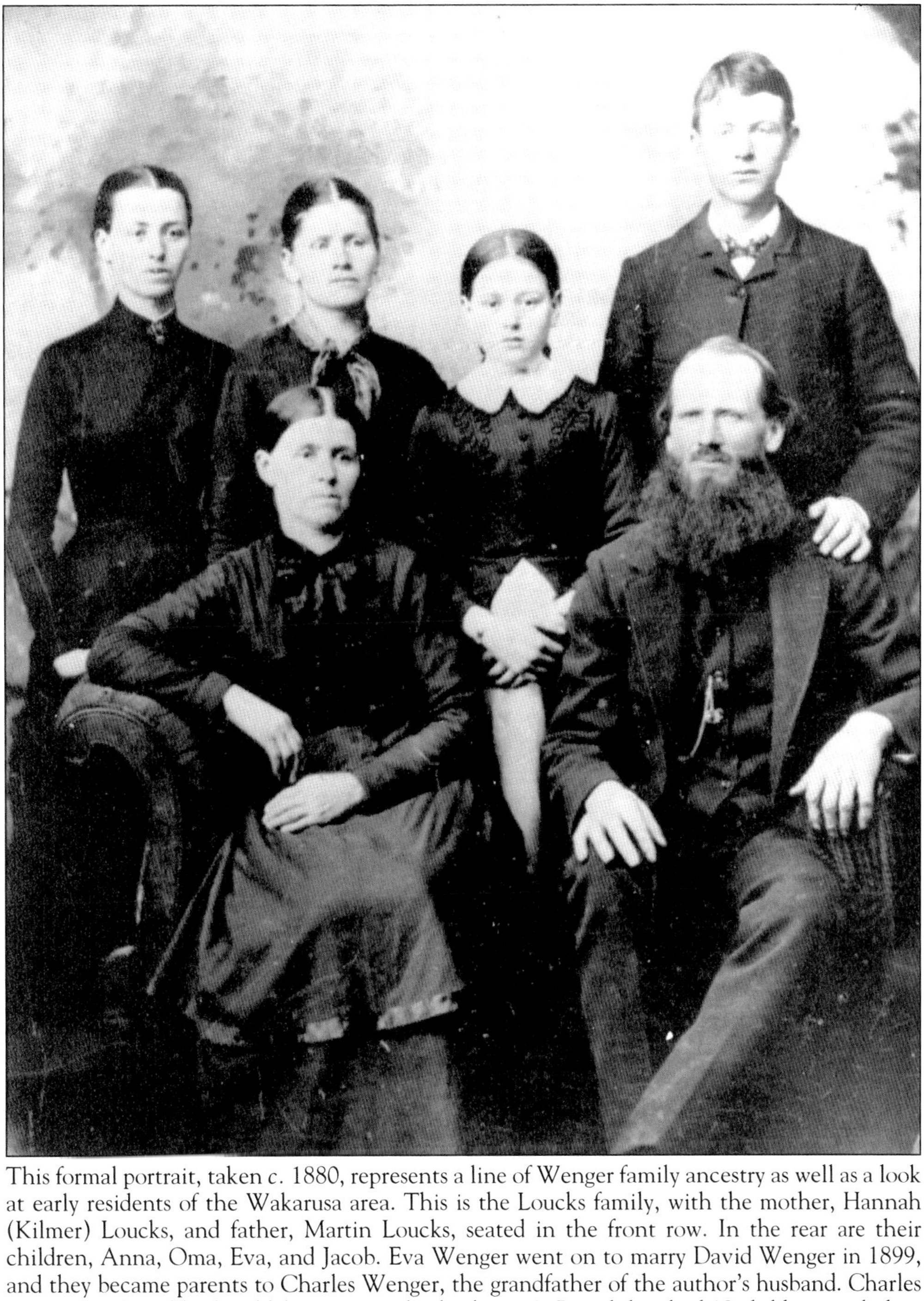

This formal portrait, taken *c.* 1880, represents a line of Wenger family ancestry as well as a look at early residents of the Wakarusa area. This is the Loucks family, with the mother, Hannah (Kilmer) Loucks, and father, Martin Loucks, seated in the front row. In the rear are their children, Anna, Oma, Eva, and Jacob. Eva Wenger went on to marry David Wenger in 1899, and they became parents to Charles Wenger, the grandfather of the author's husband. Charles Wenger took Goldie (Weldy) Wenger as his bride in 1917, and they had 12 children, including the author's father-in-law, Larry Dean Wenger. He is 11th in the line of Wenger siblings and the father of the author's husband, Larry Dean Wenger Jr. The author and her husband were married in 1993, and they have two daughters, Hannah Gabrielle and Rebekah Grace. (Photo courtesy of Mr. and Mrs. Kenneth Wenger.)

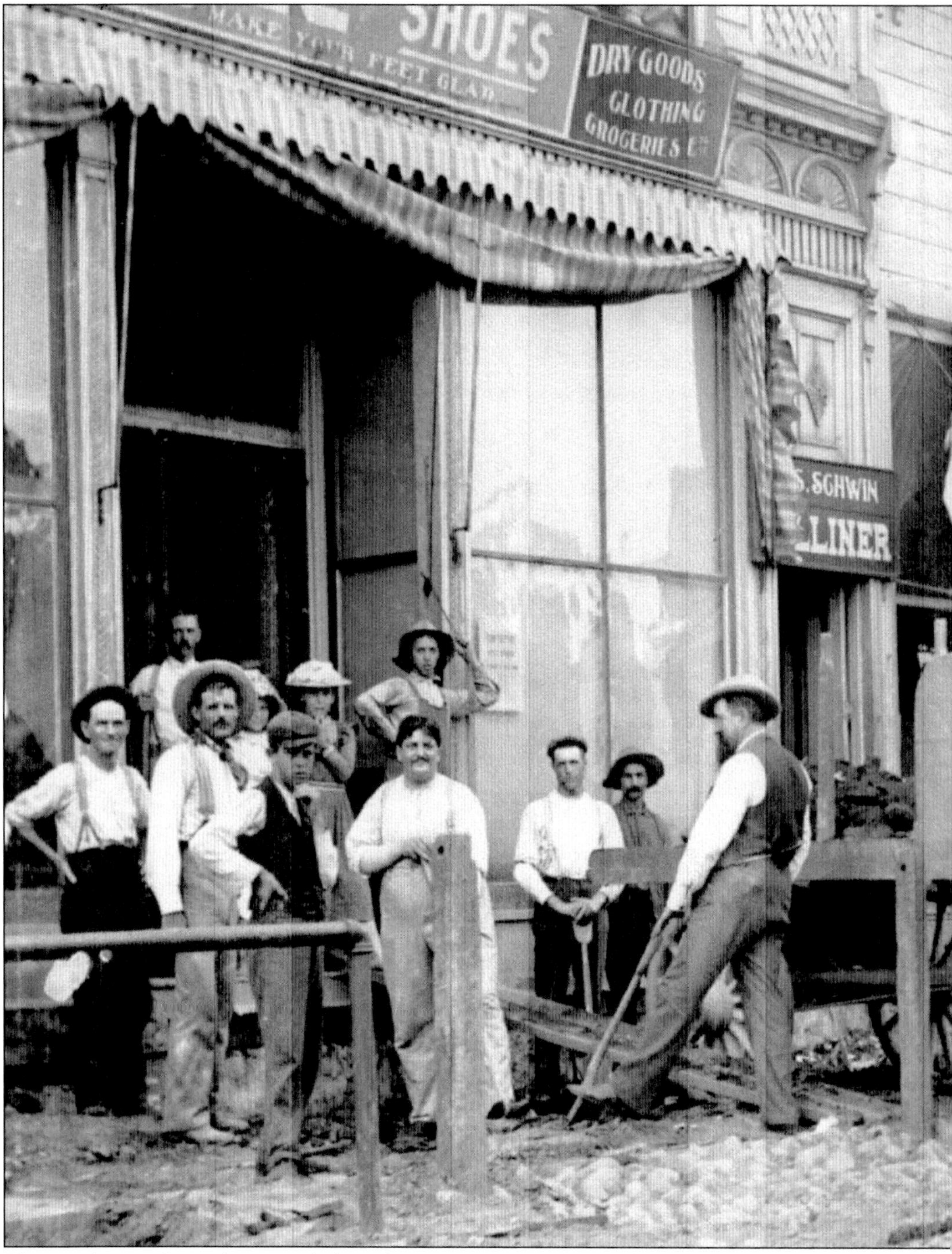

The gentlemen shown here are feeling the repercussions of one of Wakarusa's most legendary, and rather humorous, incidents. In the mid-1870s, the streets of downtown Wakarusa featured walkways fashioned of oak wood, and although the paths were not of particular concern to the men, they became a point of contention for the women, as the hems of their long garments and petticoats would often be snagged and torn by the shredding wood. When an elderly lady sprained her ankle after her foot broke through the treacherous trails, several of the local women

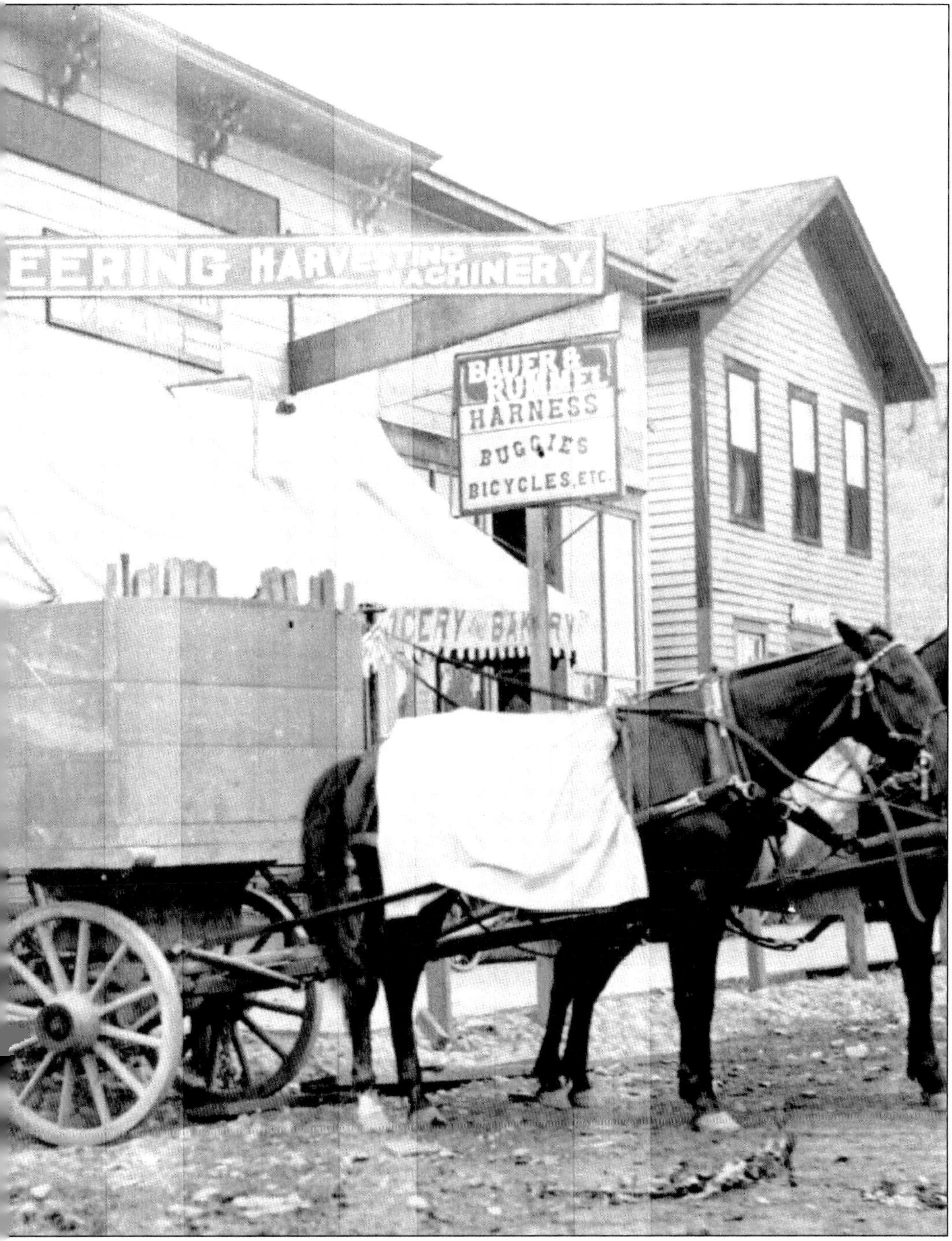

decided that it was time to take action. In the cover of darkness, they came wielding hammers and other tools and pounded the sidewalks into splinters. Shortly thereafter, a number of the townsmen banded together to remove the remains of the tattered boards, and new cement sidewalks were laid at last. Among those who assisted were Joe Mitchell, wearing a vest and standing by the dray wagon, Nicholas Cripe, behind the wooden post, and Joseph Eshelman, at the far left by the building. (Photo courtesy of Wakarusa Public Library.)

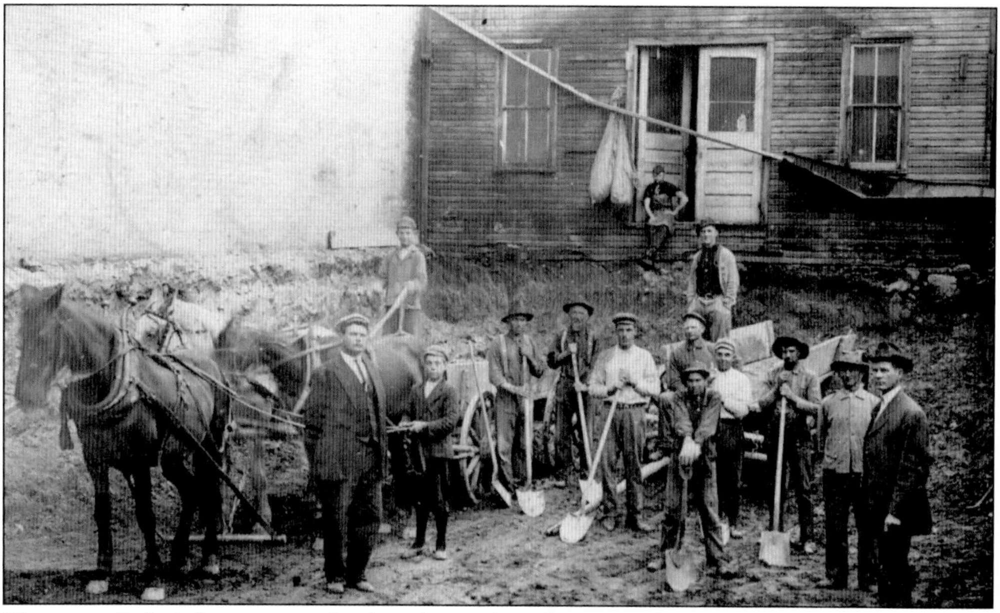

There was little information to be found regarding this scene, but it is interesting nonetheless. It is probably safe to assume that these men are working to raise a new building, perhaps shown in this image digging out some type of ground floor or basement. (Photo courtesy of Wakarusa Public Library.)

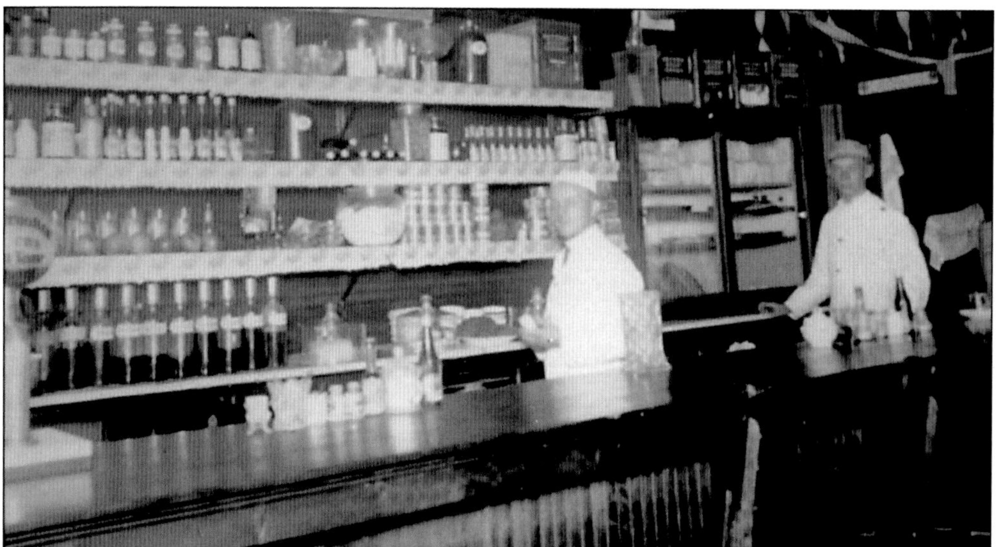

This is one of the only known photographs of a restaurant that once was located near the Wakarusa depot. S.Y. Weldy and a Mr. Fish are shown. Helen Klein, who with her husband Jay oversees the grounds of the Wakarusa Historical Museums, believes that the picture may have been taken in approximately 1893, just prior to the completion of the railroad. The restaurant was torn down sometime prior to 1940. However, a small piece of memorabilia remains at the east side of Wabash Avenue, where the establishment was situated. There is a tiny remnant of the original sidewalk burrowed into the ground—just across the street from the museums. (Photo courtesy of Mr. and Mrs. Jay Klein.)

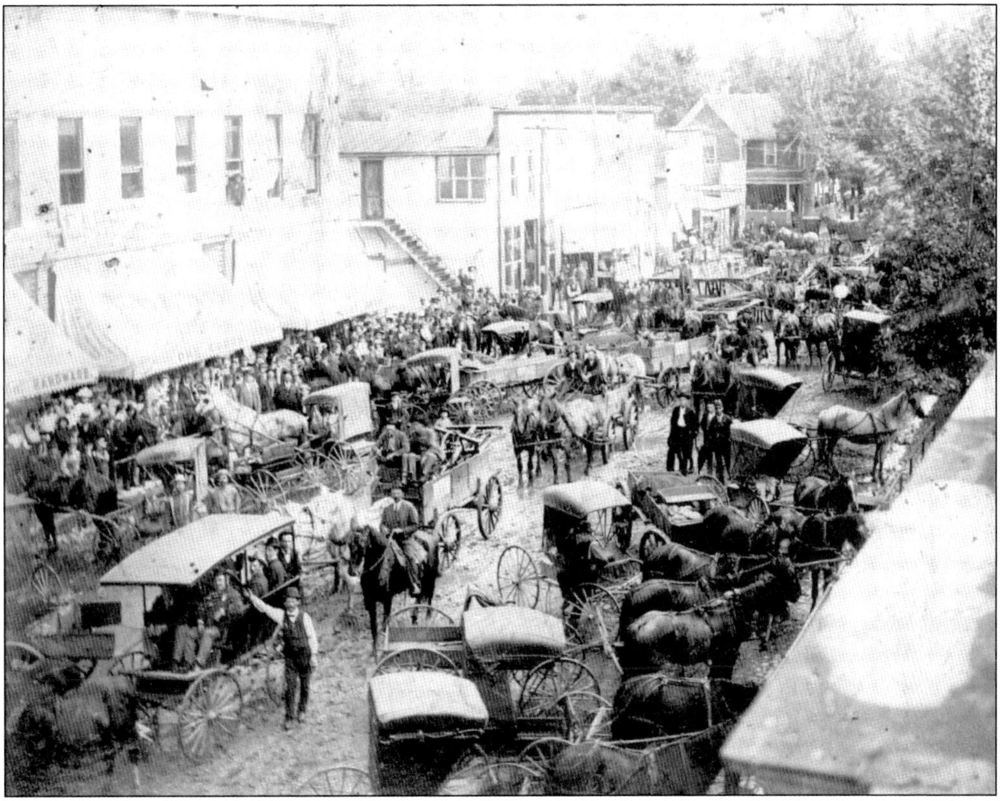

A hectic day for the downtown marketplace is illustrated in this undated overview. (Photo courtesy of Wakarusa Public Library.)

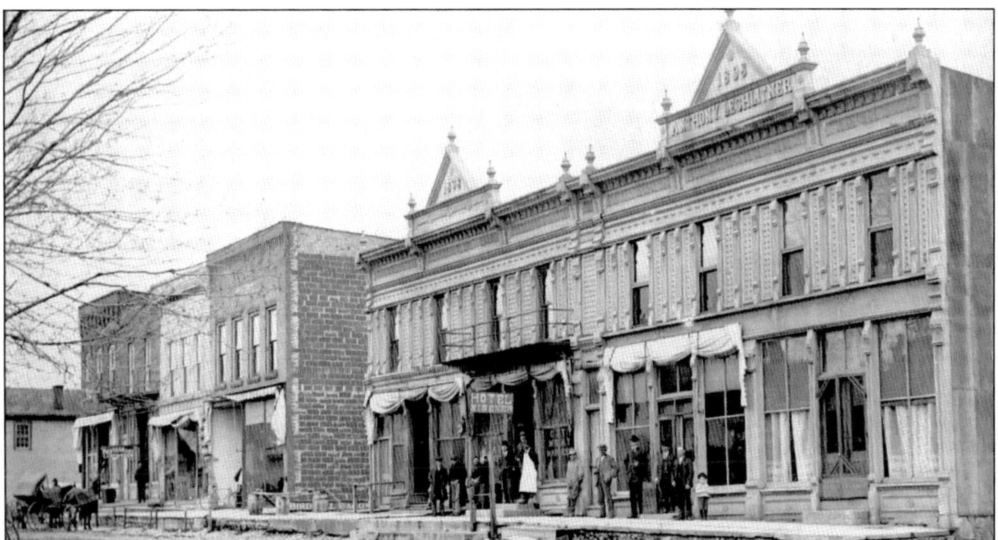

One of Wakarusa early hotels was the Elliott House, a downtown landmark of quite substantial nature, given the small size of the community in which it was located. (Photo courtesy of Wakarusa Public Library.)

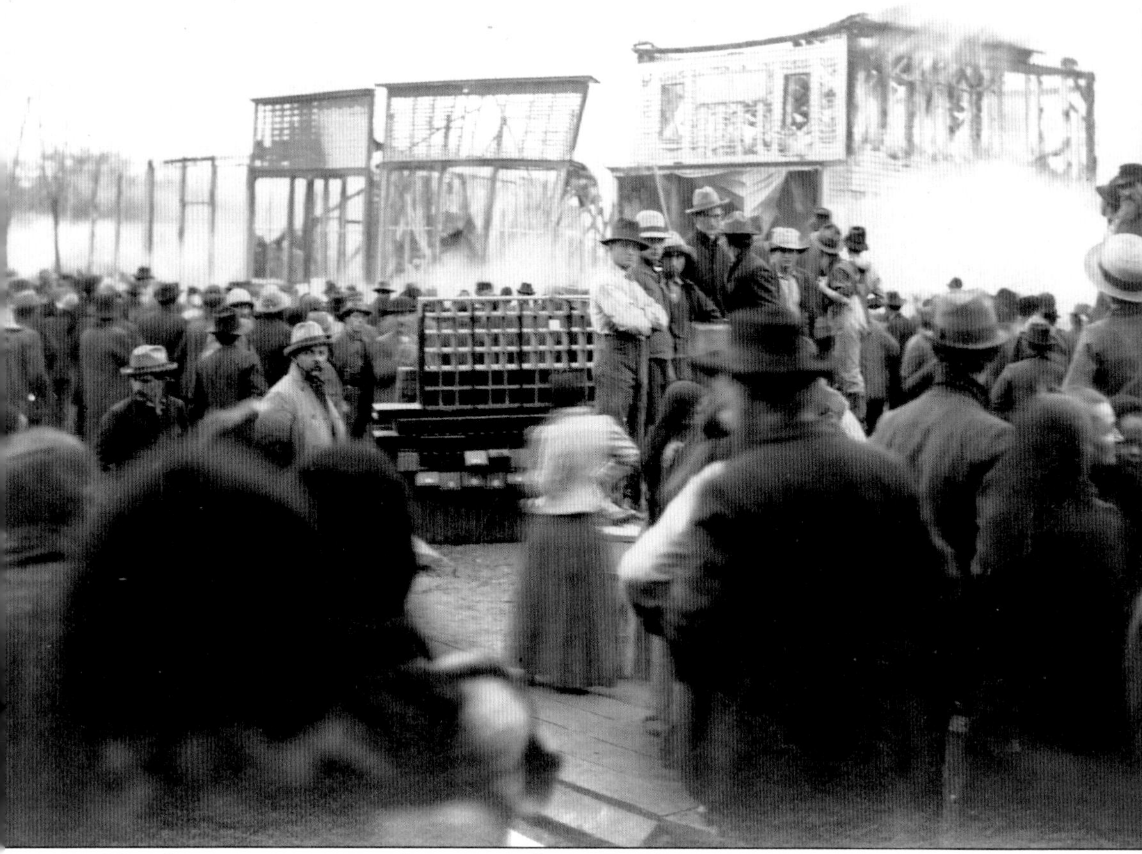

This chaotic scene captures the essence of one of Wakarusa's most sensational events, the great fire of October 29, 1899. The blaze was so massive and intense that there was serious threat of having the entire downtown Eshelman block decimated by the roaring flames. The fire was discovered at around 5 a.m. by one of the owners of Knisely and Burner's hardware store—Mr. Knisely was roused by his barking dog. When Mr. Knisely left his upstairs apartment to investigate, he came upon the fire in the rear of his store. After yelling "fire!" with a feverish sense of panic, many of the townsfolks arrived to begin the task of quashing the inferno. Because Wakarusa had no fire department at the time, men gathered to commence a "bucket brigade," where water was pumped into buckets and doused upon the fire. (Photo courtesy of Wakarusa Public Library.)

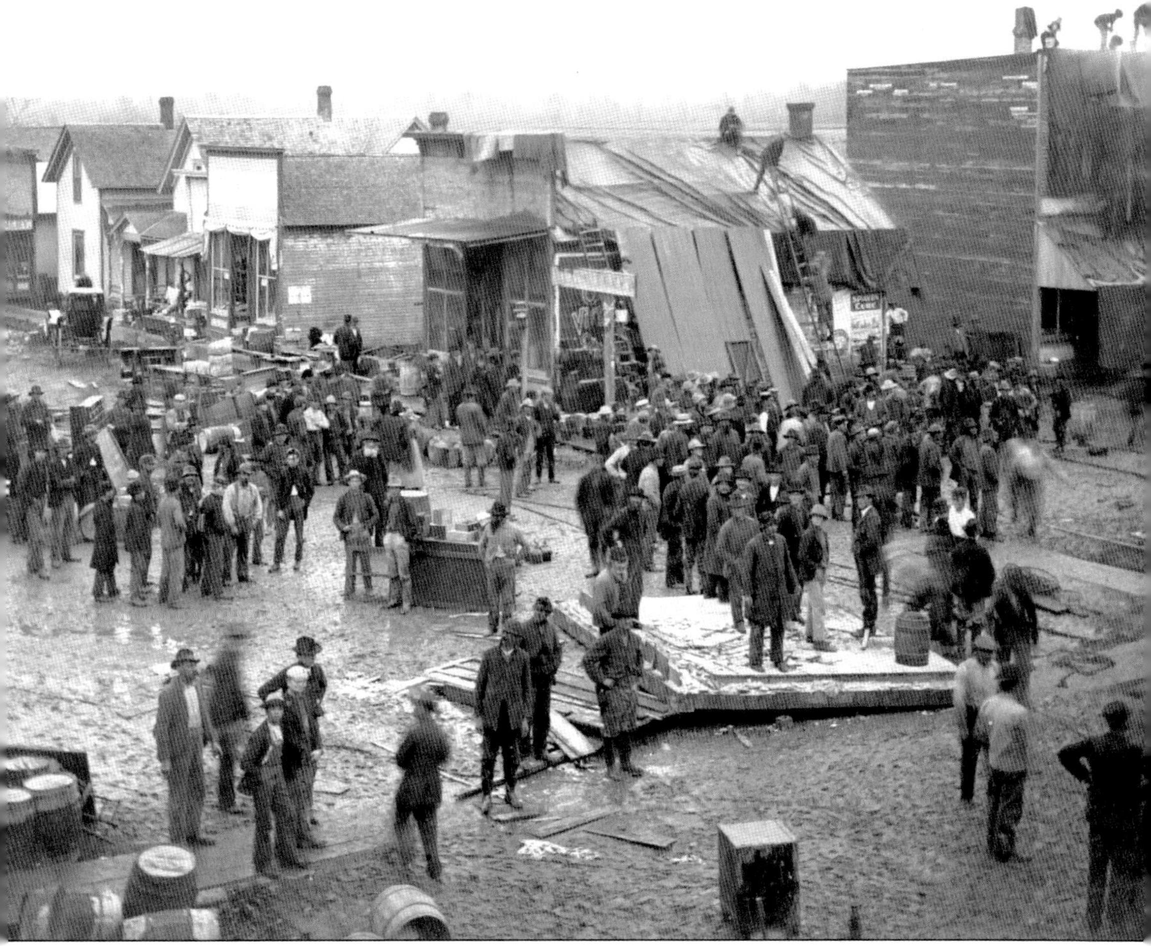

This is the smoldering view of the fire's aftermath. In all, 15 businesses, the post office, and the telephone exchange were casualties of the fire, and losses were tallied at more than $60,000. It was noted in the newspaper account of the tragedy that the winds and the quick actions of the "bucket brigade" were responsible for preventing the fire from spreading to the businesses across the street. Several of the storefronts, including that of Dr. Sensenich and the *Wakarusa Tribune*, were covered in wet carpet scraps and blankets to stave off the flames. There was some good that came from the disaster—by the beginning of 1900, a new volunteer fire brigade was established. (Photo courtesy of Wakarusa Public Library.)

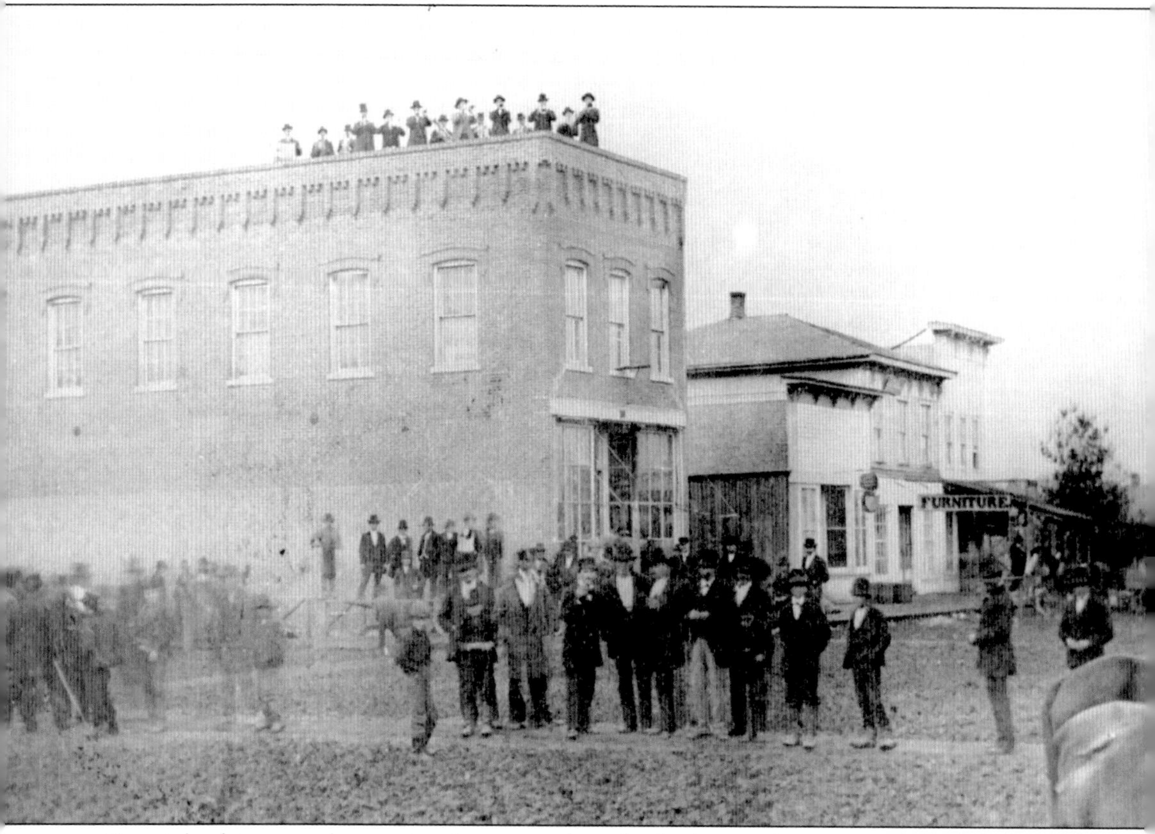

Certainly, this unusual attraction drew a number of onlookers to the town square where a rooftop band is clearly seen atop a building on the northwest corner of Elkhart and Waterford Streets. The date is unknown. (Photo courtesy of Wakarusa Public Library.)

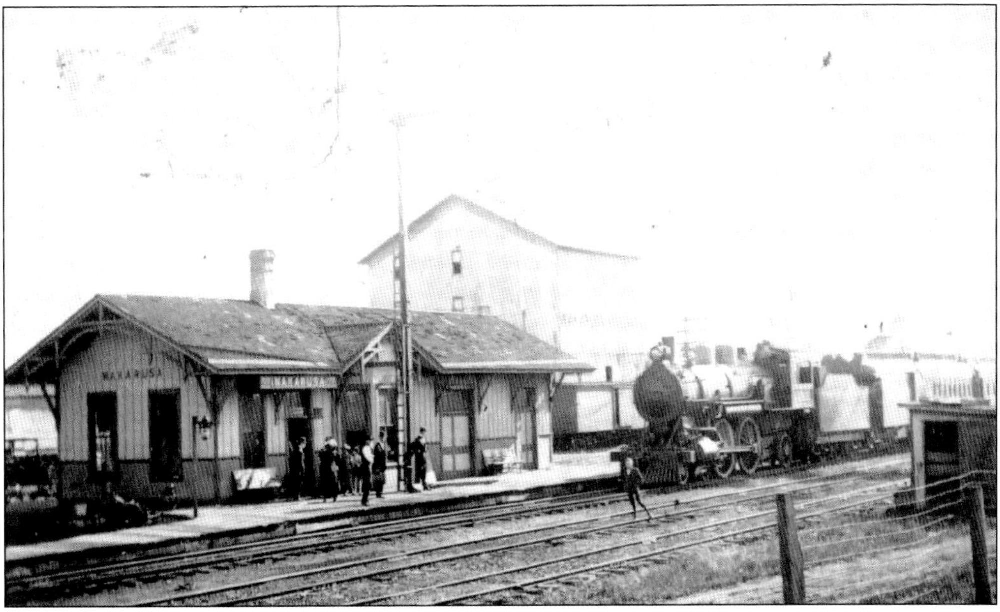

Wakarusa was a stop on the Wabash Railroad Company line when the tracks were laid in the early 1890s. The goal was to have a continuous railway connecting Detroit to Chicago, and Wakarusa, like several other rural communities in the region, was slated to become a stopping point. This depot was built in 1892, and the final run was conducted on January 30, 1990, with the tracks abandoned shortly thereafter. However, the depot is neither gone nor forgotten, as it is one of the centerpieces of the Wakarusa Historical Museum complex, where visitors can learn about the history of the depot and other local landmarks. (Photo courtesy of Wakarusa Public Library.)

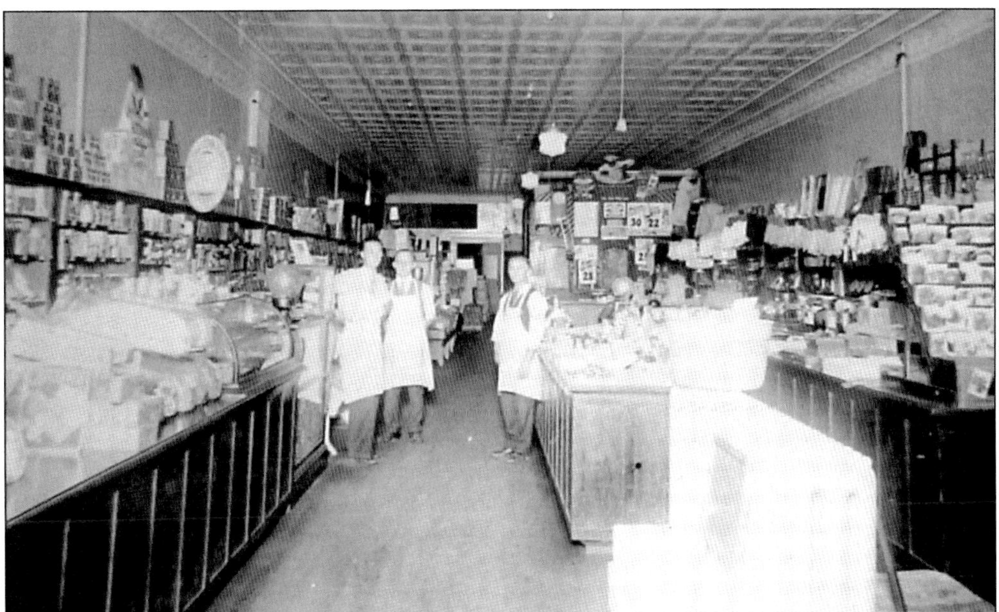

The S.Y. Weldy Grocery Store was a mainstay on the west side of Elkhart Street during the earlier part of the 1900s. S.Y. Weldy was the owner, and Elmer Metzler was employed as a clerk. (Photo courtesy of Mr. and Mrs. Jay Klein.)

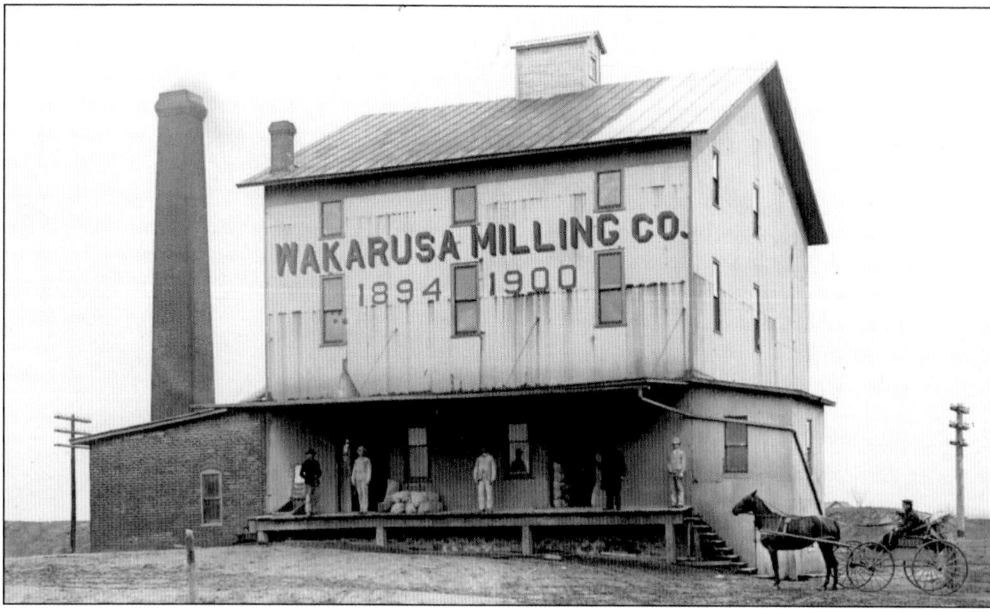

The Wakarusa Milling Company was also known as Jacob Weldy's mill. This facility had a small, but hardworking staff, where Joe Schryer was a miller, George Nettrour was an employee, and Leander Weldy, Jacob's son, served as a bookkeeper. One of the mill's specialty items was a pastry flour called "Fancy." Other items sold there included hard and soft coal for use in furnaces and heating stoves. The second floor of the mill had special machines, powered by steam engine, which could grind grain into flour. The grain was purchased locally and brought to the mill by way of rail cars. Once the flour was produced, it was funneled into a bin and then packaged. (Photo courtesy of Wakarusa Public Library.)

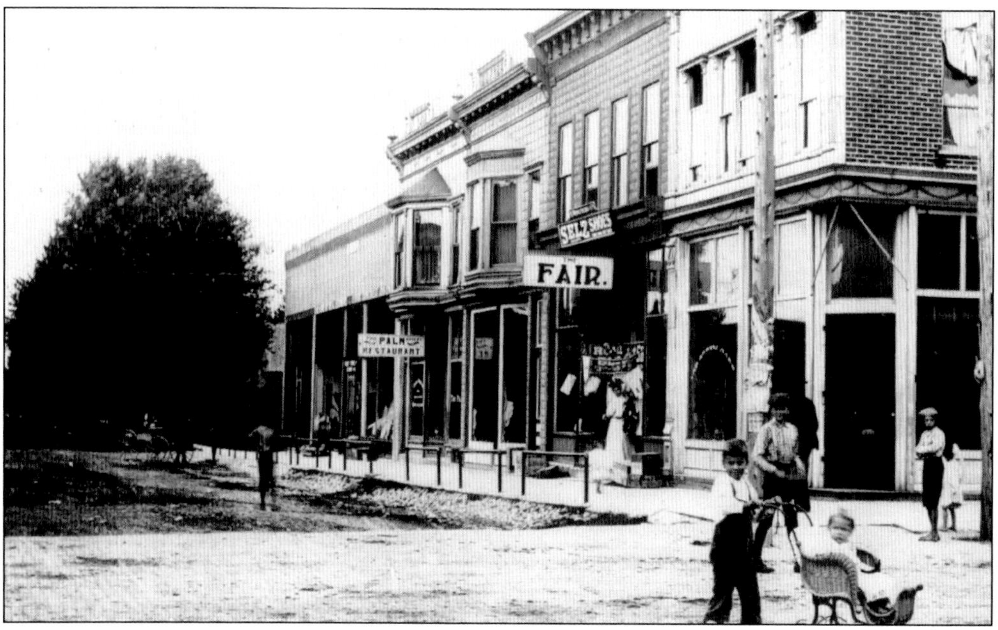

This photo shows the East Waterford Street corridor as it appeared in the early 1900s. (Photo courtesy of Wakarusa Public Library.)

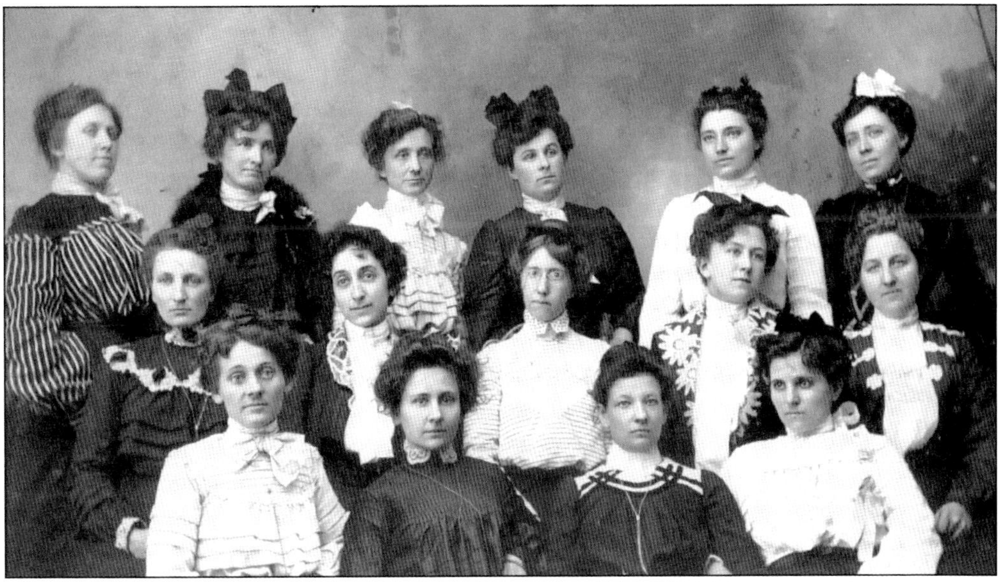

These genteel ladies were members of the Wakarusa Searchlight Club, a women's organization founded in 1900. The club's mission was to promote an atmosphere that was "literary, musical, and social." The women chose the rose as their club flower and their colors to be gold and crimson. The women would gather each Tuesday evening for a night of fellowship, a tradition which is still carried out today. This is the club as it was in 1903. Members shown, although not in order, are Mrs. Nicholas Cripe, Mrs. Frank Brown, Ida Rheubottom, Mrs. Henry Freed, Mrs. Etta Gore, Mrs. John Smeltzer, Mrs. Edna Freed, Mrs. Cleo Frash, Mrs. Dora Elliott, Mrs. Claud Smith, Mrs. Joe Mitchell, Mrs. Todd Knepple, Mrs. Frank Meisner, Mrs. John Fink, and Mrs. William Schwartz. (Photo courtesy of Wakarusa Public Library.)

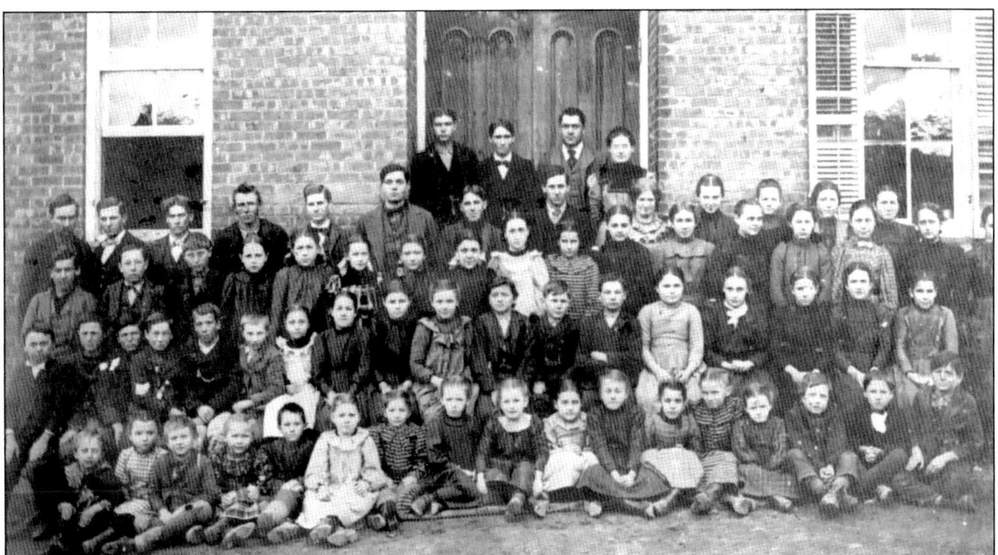

Students of the Harrison Center school pose for a photograph during the 1900 session. This one-room schoolhouse was located at the northeast corner of County Road 11 and County Road 36. It had the distinction of being one of the oldest and longest-serving schools of its kind in the region, opening in 1847 and having its final class in 1954. (Photo courtesy of Wakarusa Public Library.)

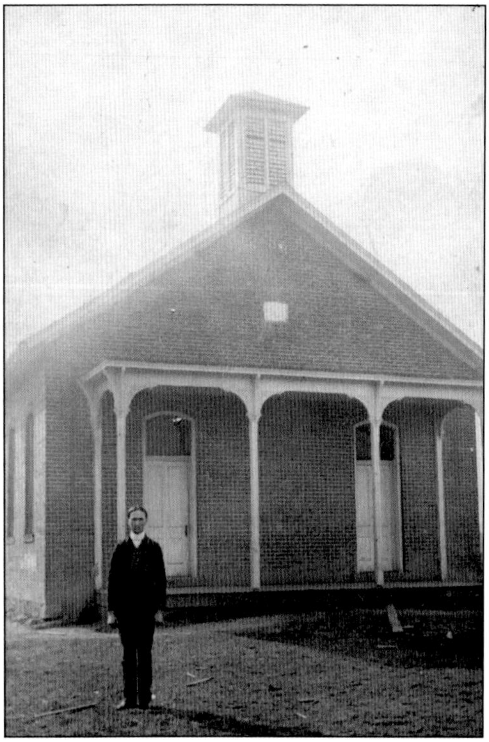

Another local one-room schoolhouse, the Lockwood School, sat at the southeast corner of County Road 1 and County Road 44. In the year that this picture was taken, 1903, Samuel Madlem was the director, George W. Ellis was the superintendent, and J.B. Pippenger was a trustee. It is not known which of the gentlemen is seen in the picture. The Lockwood School opened in 1850, and closed sometime in the mid-1920s. (Photo courtesy of Wakarusa Public Library.)

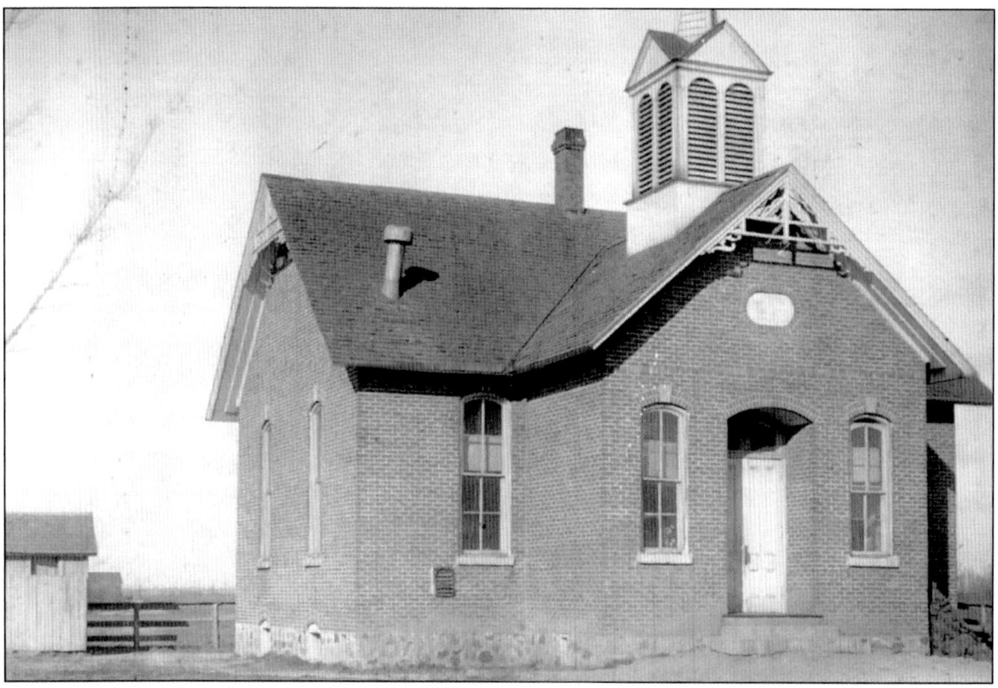

This is the Shriver School, which was two miles north and two miles east of Wakarusa. It served rural Wakarusa students at the dawn of the 20th century. One of the school's early pupils was Charles "Charlie" Wenger—grandfather of the author's husband. (Photo courtesy of Wakarusa Public Library.)

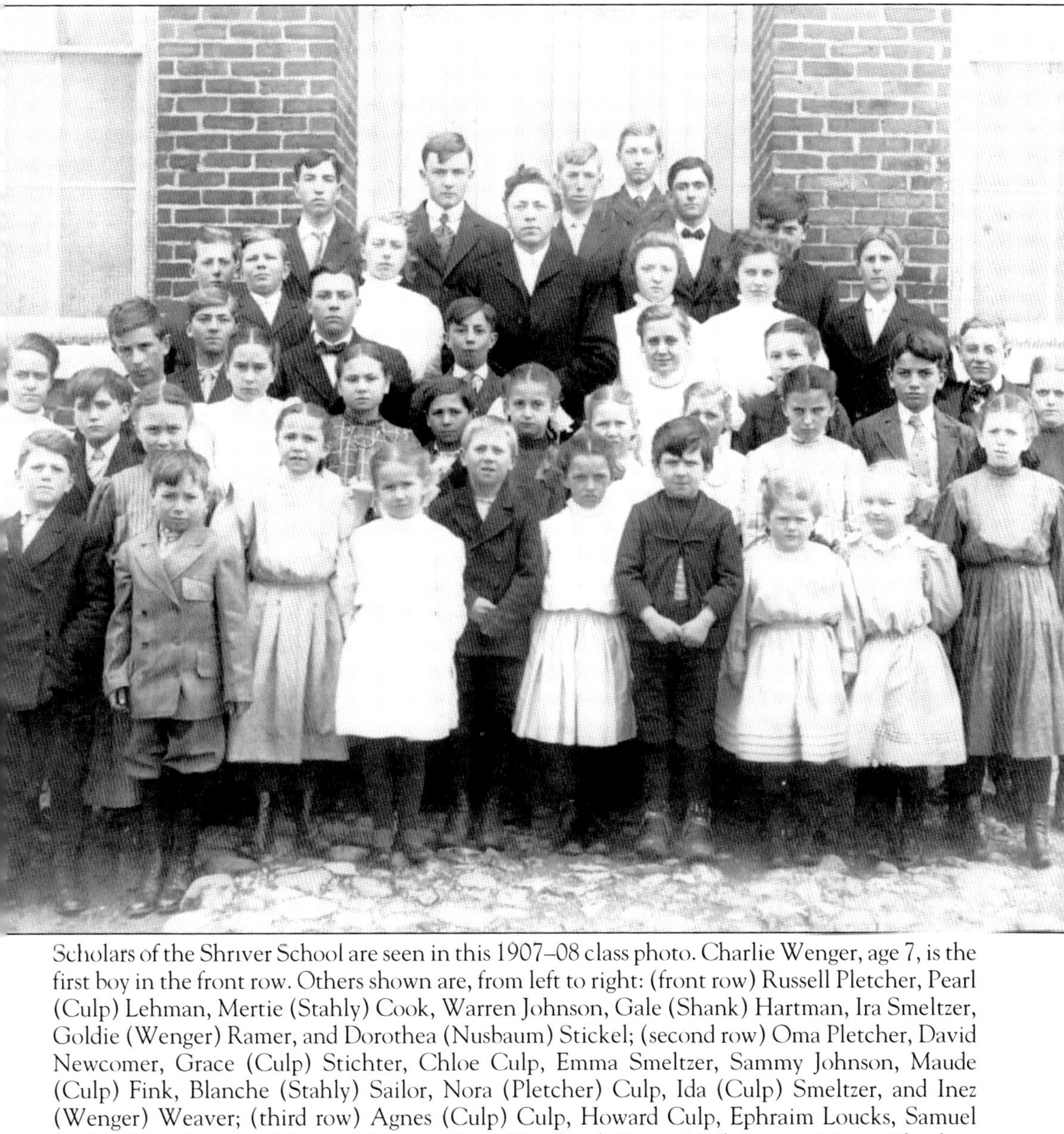

Scholars of the Shriver School are seen in this 1907–08 class photo. Charlie Wenger, age 7, is the first boy in the front row. Others shown are, from left to right: (front row) Russell Pletcher, Pearl (Culp) Lehman, Mertie (Stahly) Cook, Warren Johnson, Gale (Shank) Hartman, Ira Smeltzer, Goldie (Wenger) Ramer, and Dorothea (Nusbaum) Stickel; (second row) Oma Pletcher, David Newcomer, Grace (Culp) Stichter, Chloe Culp, Emma Smeltzer, Sammy Johnson, Maude (Culp) Fink, Blanche (Stahly) Sailor, Nora (Pletcher) Culp, Ida (Culp) Smeltzer, and Inez (Wenger) Weaver; (third row) Agnes (Culp) Culp, Howard Culp, Ephraim Loucks, Samuel Bixler, Stacy Morris, Salome Johnson, Nora (Smeltzer) Cripe, Voil Canen, Victor Pletcher, Martha (Wenger) Bixler, Orville Boyer, Nelson Fink, Goldie (Culp) Mast, David A. Yoder (the teacher), Clara Nusbaum, Beulah (Culp) Loucks, and Dan Johnson; (fourth row) Alpha Canen, Ralph Abel, Clayton Pletcher, Earl Nusbaum, Claude Culp, and George Newcomer. (Photo courtesy of Wakarusa Public Library.)

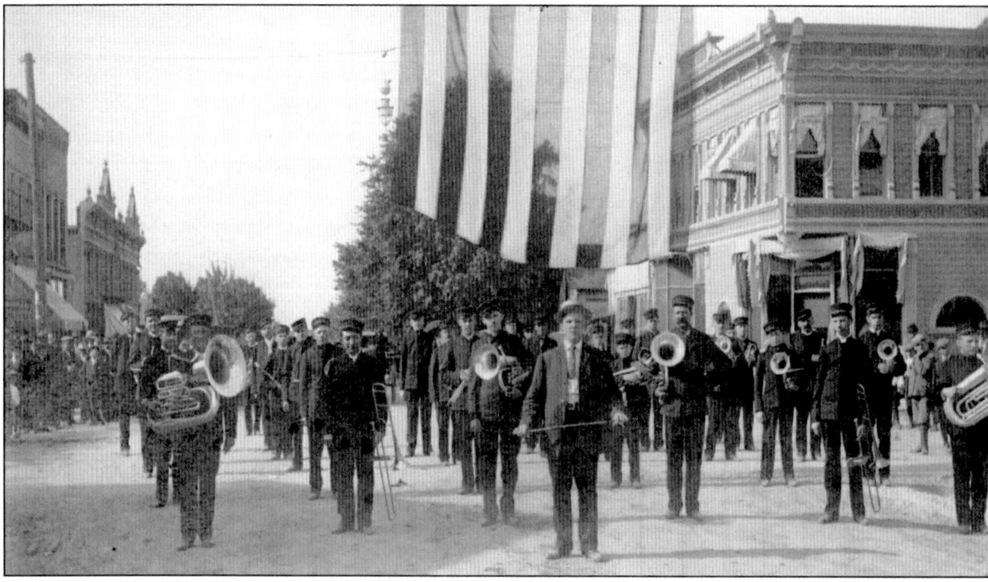

The Wakarusa Band stands at attention, poised for action in the downtown square. D.A. Rheubottom is shown with the baton, and the director, Mr. Lane, is the next to last gentleman in the second column from the left. (Photo courtesy of Wakarusa Public Library.)

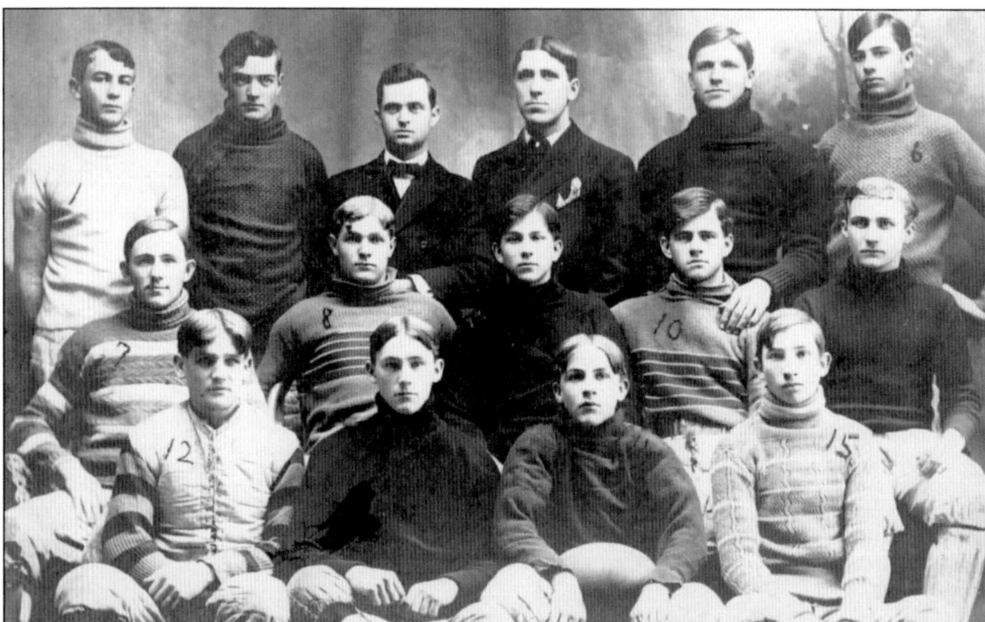

The Wakarusa High School football squad is pictured during the 1909 season. The team sport of football was a fairly new novelty for the time, with the school presenting its first year in 1907. Members shown here, though not in order, are Ed Strope, Warren Holdeman, Blaine Rheubottom, Daniel Nusbaum, Edgar Freed, Daniel Nye, Keith Knepple, Ralph Walter, Walter Lehman, Fred Craft, Thad Schalliol, Gladstone Rheubottom, Roscoe Miller, and Homer Roose. The principal, who served as the coach, is also in the photo. (Photo courtesy of Wakarusa Public Library.)

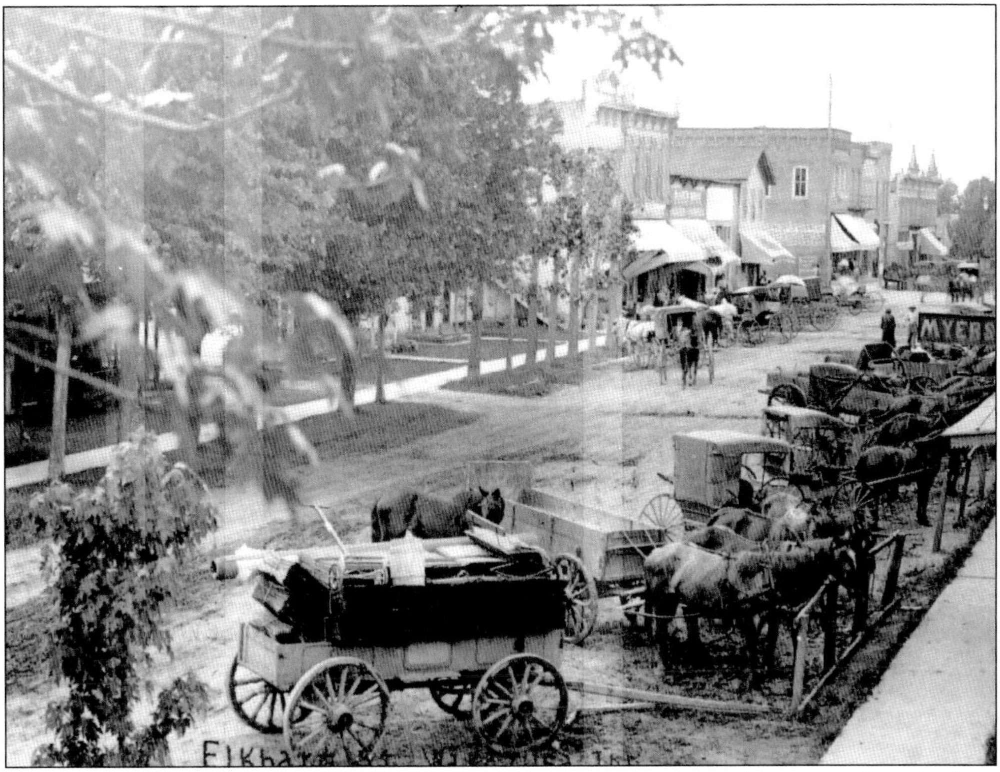

South Elkhart Street, which today is also referred to as County Road 3, is seen here looking northbound in an undated image. (Photo courtesy of Wakarusa Public Library.)

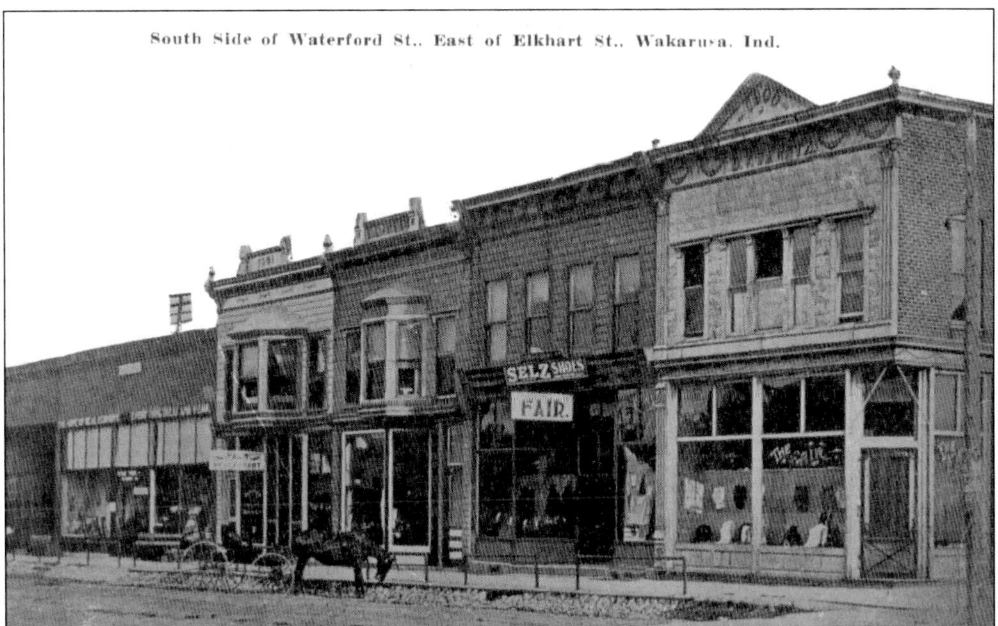

The south side of the East Waterford corridor is featured in this early town postcard. A message on the reverse side bears a 1911 postmark. (Photo courtesy of Mr. and Mrs. Dean Henry.)

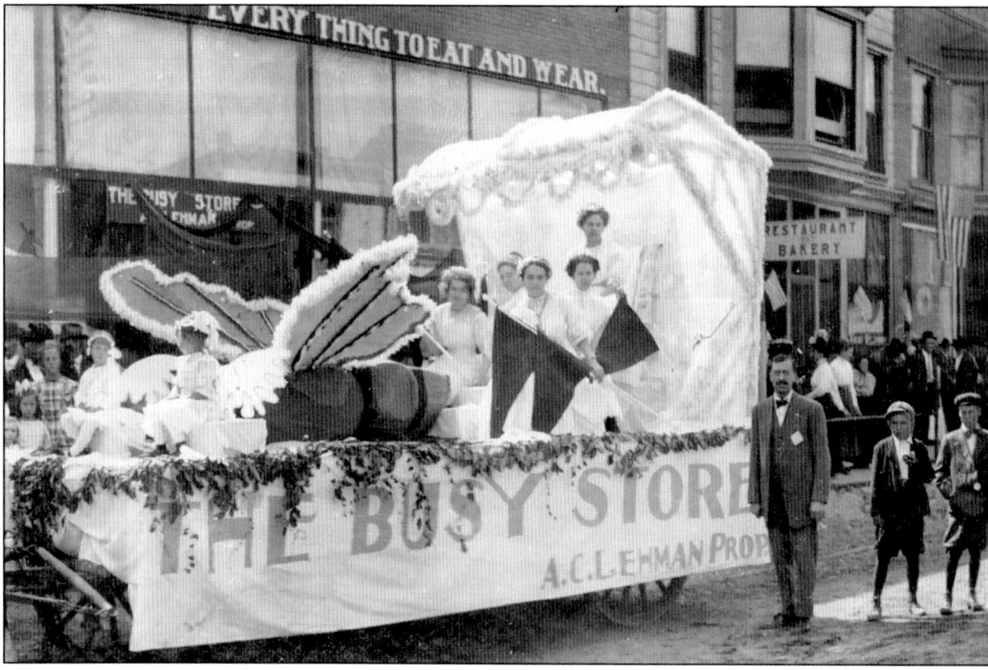

This parade float was designed in 1911 for the A.C. Lehman store, the "busy store." Lehman is seated at the rear of the wagon. Golda Clay, at the top of the float, is queen. The four queen candidates who rounded out the court are seen below Clay, from left to right, Omah Sensenich, unidentified, Emma Rheubottom, and Ruth Nusbaum. One of the little girls is Virginia Freed, believed to be on the right of the float. (Photo courtesy of Wakarusa Public Library.)

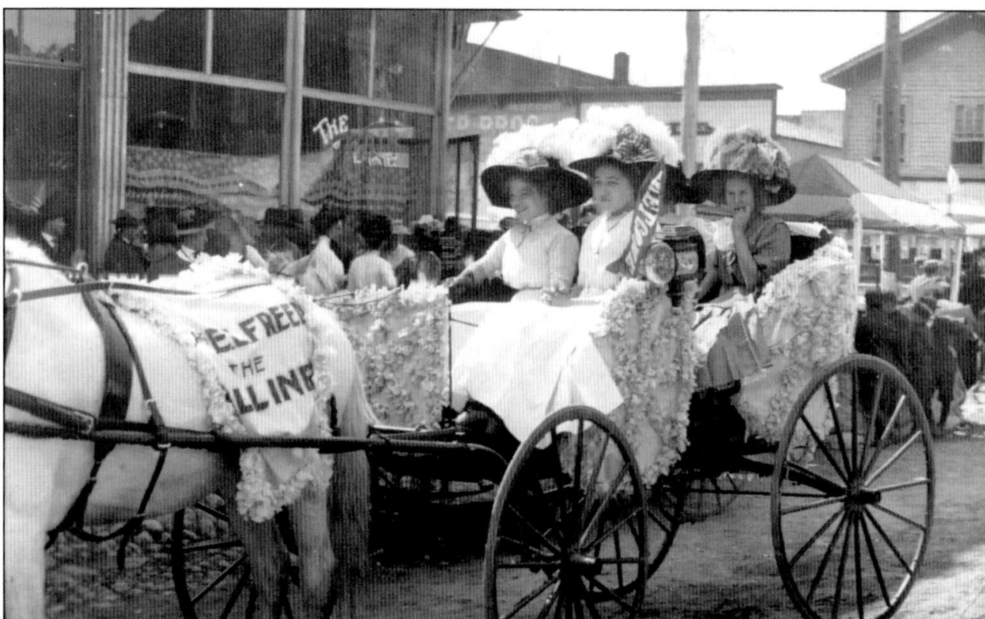

An elegantly adorned parade float glides down one of the town's thoroughfares during a 1911 parade. (Photo courtesy of Wakarusa Public Library.)

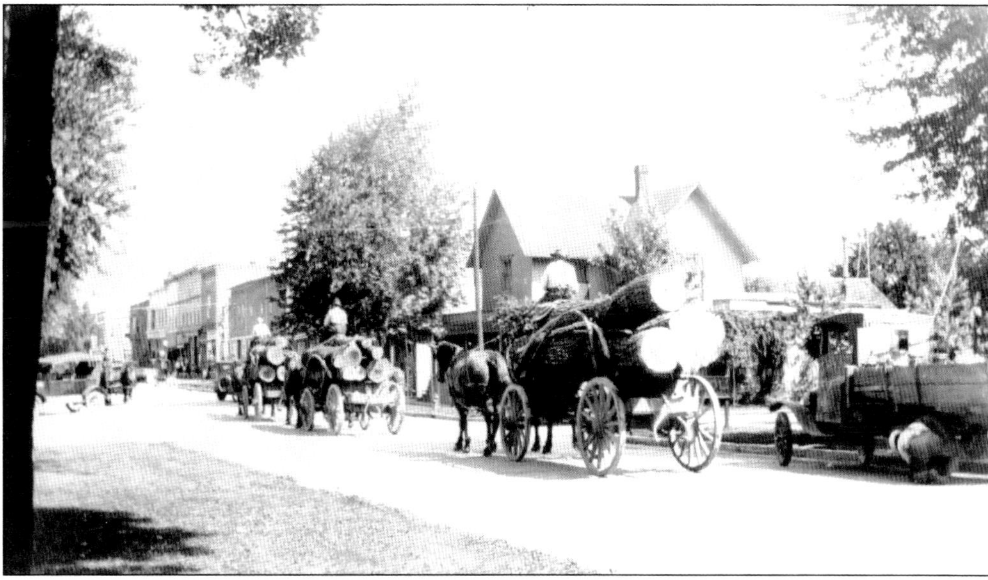

These floats are demonstrating the might and the competitive spirit of a local lumbering contest. Prizes were given to the sleds with the most board feet to haul the lumber. Among the top awards were sugar and flour. The "Keen Kutter" tools were provided through the sponsorship of Leonard Hardware. (Photo courtesy of Wakarusa Public Library.)

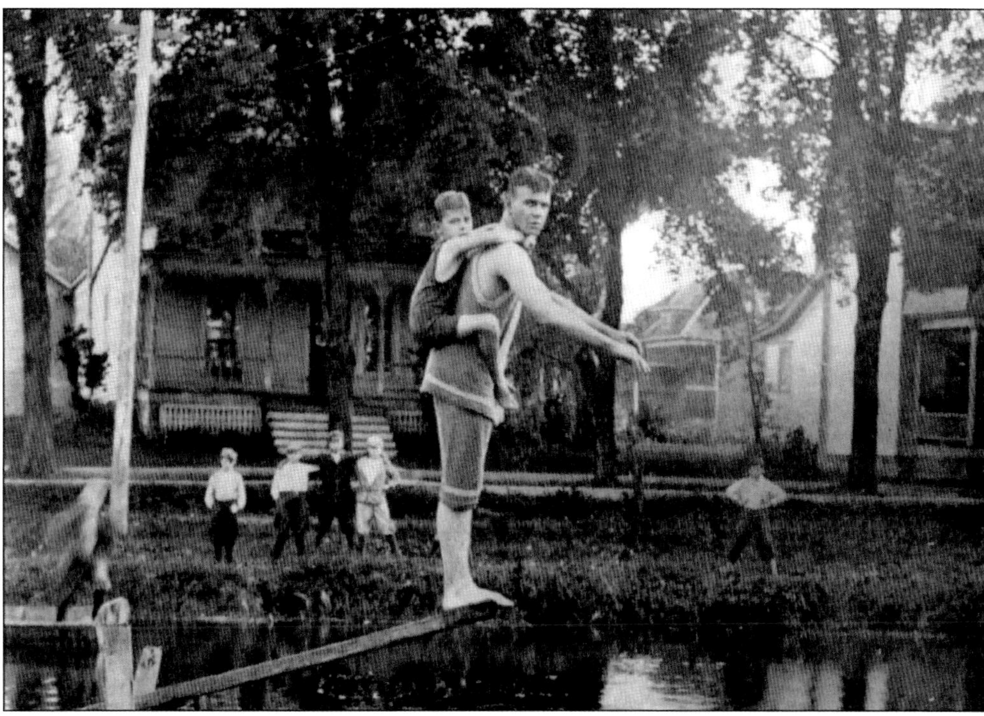

The man and the little tyke pictured are identified only as "Elliott and Lenard," seen just as they appear to be about to take a dive in the old town pond, built sometime between 1890 and 1900. Even though the pond is long gone, the area still serves a fine recreational purpose—it is the site of the current town park on Harrison Street. (Photo courtesy of Wakarusa Public Library.)

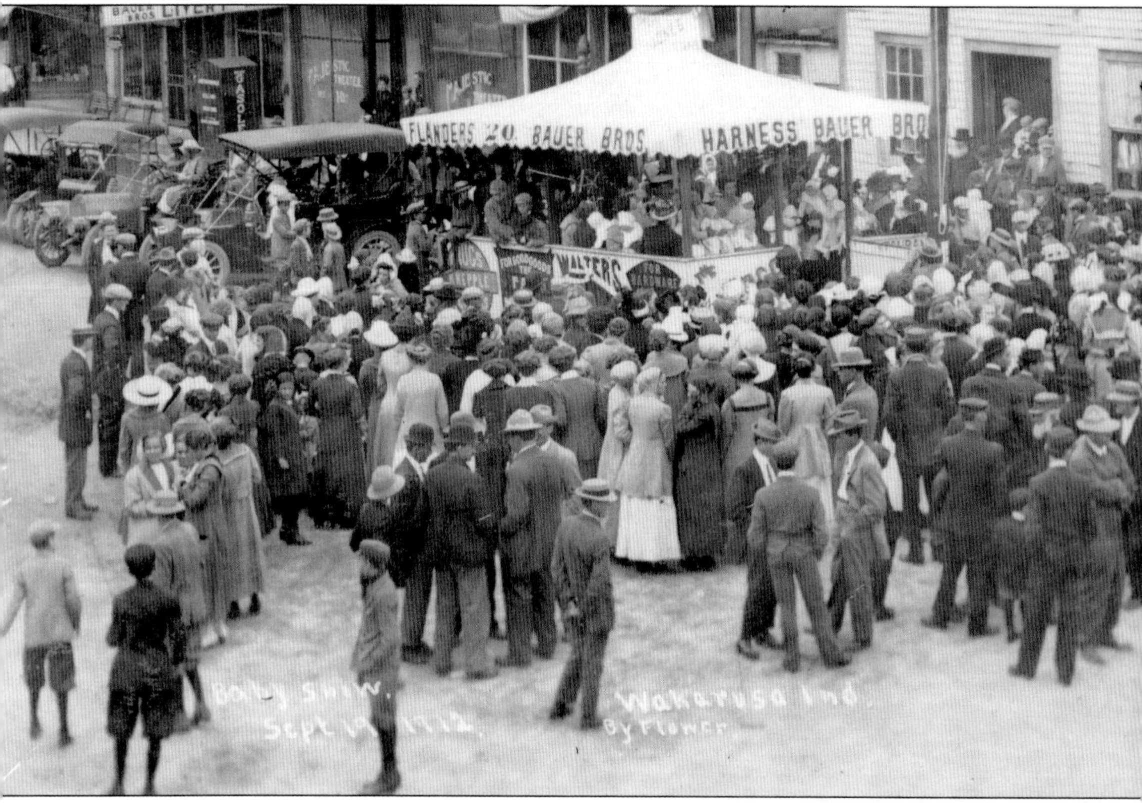

At first glance, the message on this canopy might imply that there is some type of advertising taking place. In fact, this was the scene of a beautiful baby contest, which was held on September 19, 1912. (Photo courtesy of Wakarusa Public Library.)

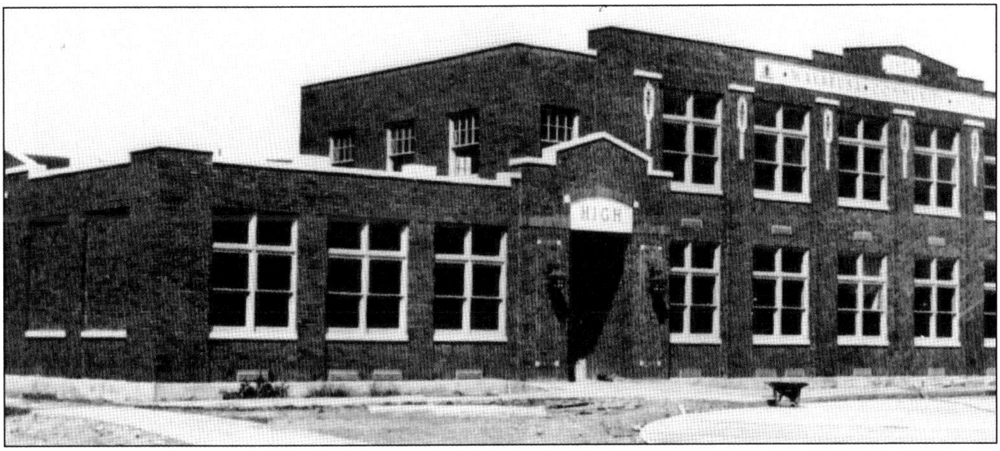

The completion of the Wakarusa High School building project in the spring of 1924 was an issue that polarized the community. While the new school had its share of supporters, there were many loyalists who felt that monies would have been better spent investing in adding on to the old school. When those who opposed the new building threatened an injunction to prevent the doors from ever opening at WHS, there was an uprising of sorts. Those who favored the new facility took action, choosing the blackest part of night to make their move. They transferred materials and furniture into the new building, knowing that if they could have the new classrooms operational by dawn, the injunction could never be signed. The mission proved successful, and Wakarusa High School was part of the community for several more decades. The school served its purpose for nearly 80 years, until, in a sad event for historians, alumni, and townsfolk alike, the Wakarusa High School building was demolished in March of 2003. (Photo courtesy of Wakarusa Public Library.)

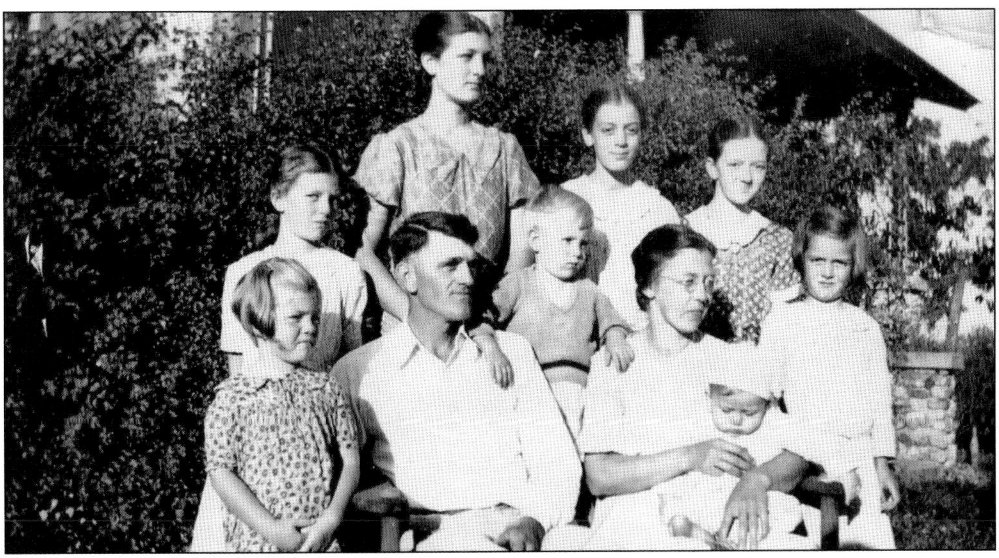

This is the family of Charles and Goldie Wenger. They are shown here with eight of their children, posing at the family's farmstead at the northeast corner of Indiana 19 and County Road 38. Pictured from left to right are: (front row) Doris, Charles (Charlie), Charles Jr. (Chuck), Goldie holding baby David, and Vada; (back row) Helen, Fay, Leota, and Myrtle. In all, there would be 12 children to bless the Wenger household—the ones who were not yet born at the time of this photo are Kenneth, Phyllis, Larry, and Lester. (Photo courtesy of Mr. and Mrs. Merrill Yoder.)

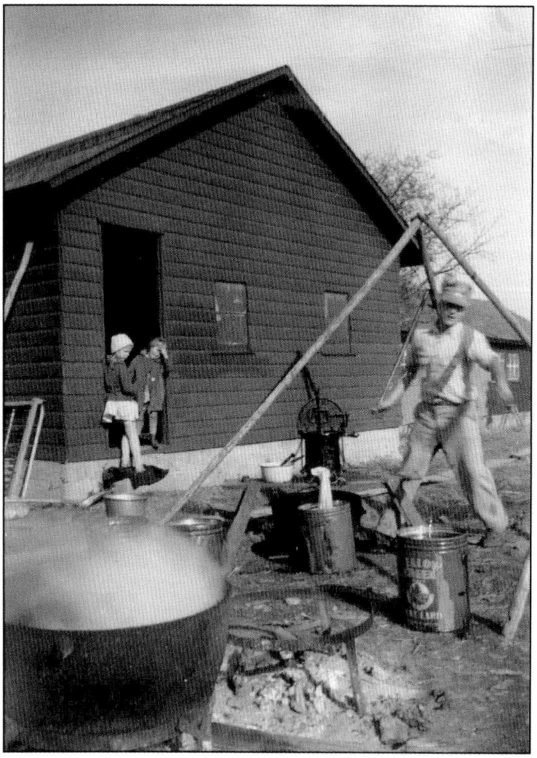

It was butchering time, which made for many busy days, as illustrated during this scene from approximately 1933. The young man is Merrill Yoder, who is the husband of Fay (Wenger) Yoder. He was working at the Dave Wenger farm, one mile north of Wakarusa, when this picture was taken. (Photo courtesy of Mr. and Mrs. Merrill Yoder.)

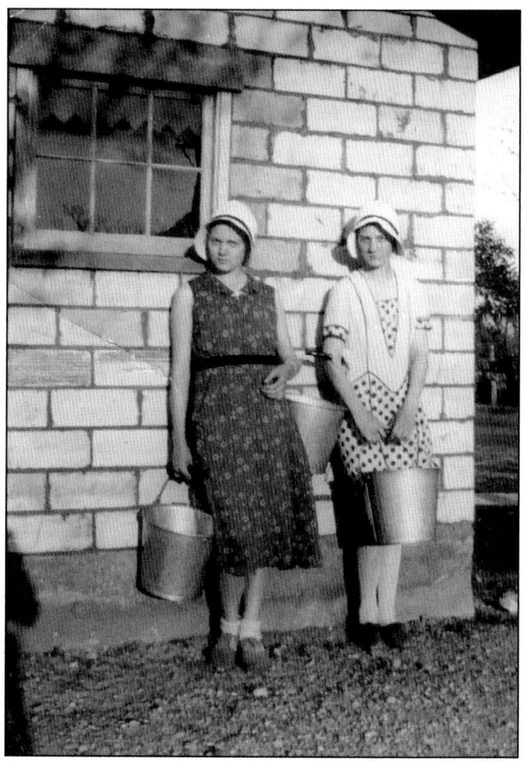

Mary (Wenger) Miller and Fay (Wenger) Yoder on the Wenger farm, c. 1933. (Photo courtesy of Mr. and Mrs. Merrill Yoder.)

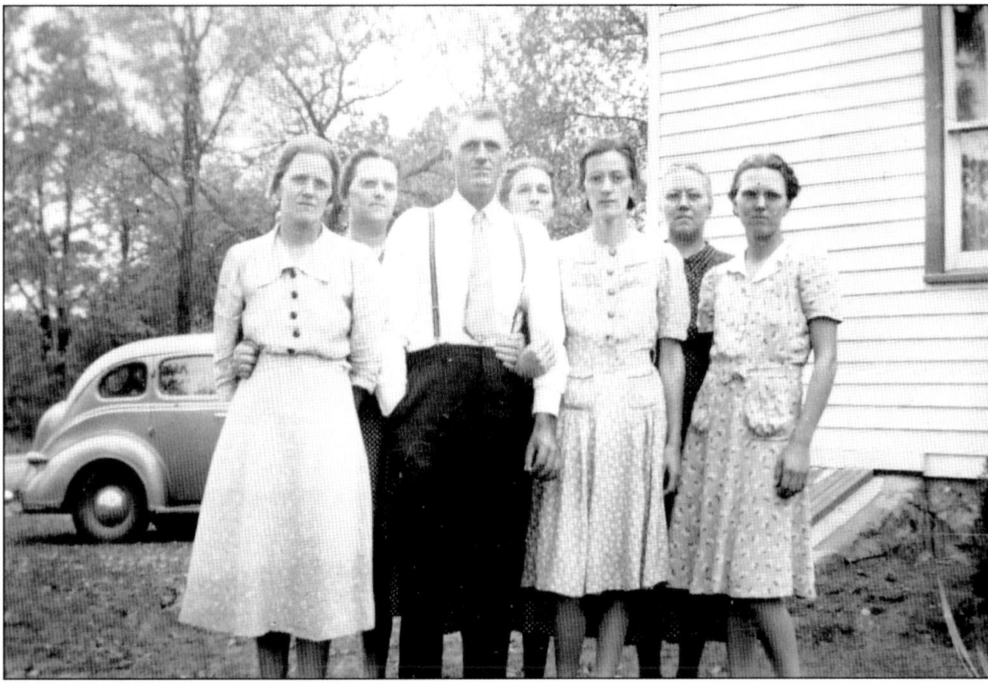

Charlie Wenger is surrounded by his sisters in this moment captured from the late 1930s. Pictured from left to right are: (front row) Golda (Wenger) Ramer, Charlie Wenger, Florence Schrock, and Mary Miller; (second row) Martha Bixler, Inez Weaver, and Oma Martin. (Photo courtesy of Mr. and Mrs. Merrill Yoder.)

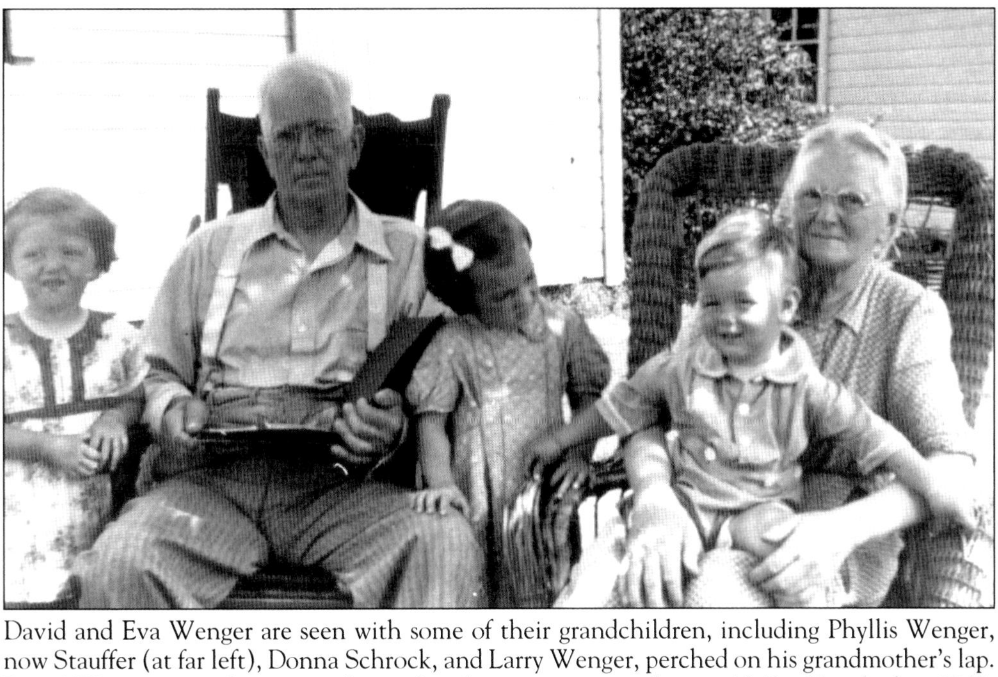

David and Eva Wenger are seen with some of their grandchildren, including Phyllis Wenger, now Stauffer (at far left), Donna Schrock, and Larry Wenger, perched on his grandmother's lap. David Wenger passed away not long after this picture was taken in 1942—Eva died in 1963. (Photo courtesy of Mr. and Mrs. Kenneth Wenger.)

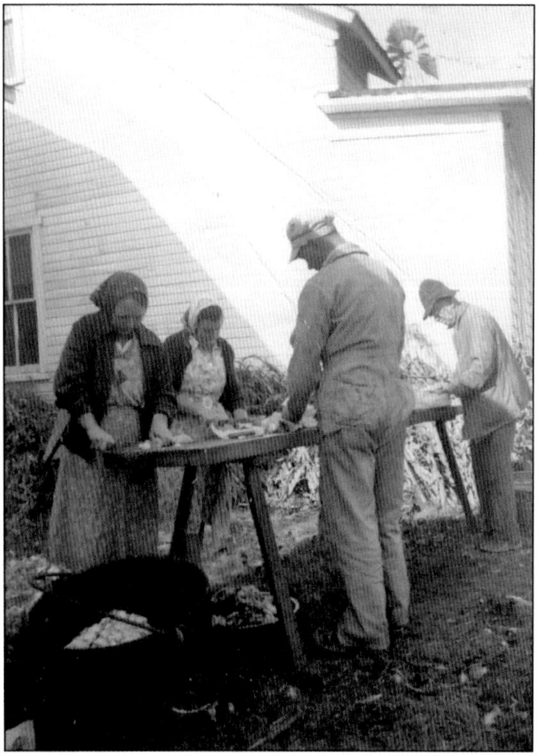

Several members of the Wenger clan gather for a day of work on the Wenger family farm in approximately 1942. Shown are Nina Weaver, Marian Martin, Dave Wenger, and David Martin. (Photo courtesy of Mr. and Mrs. Merrill Yoder.)

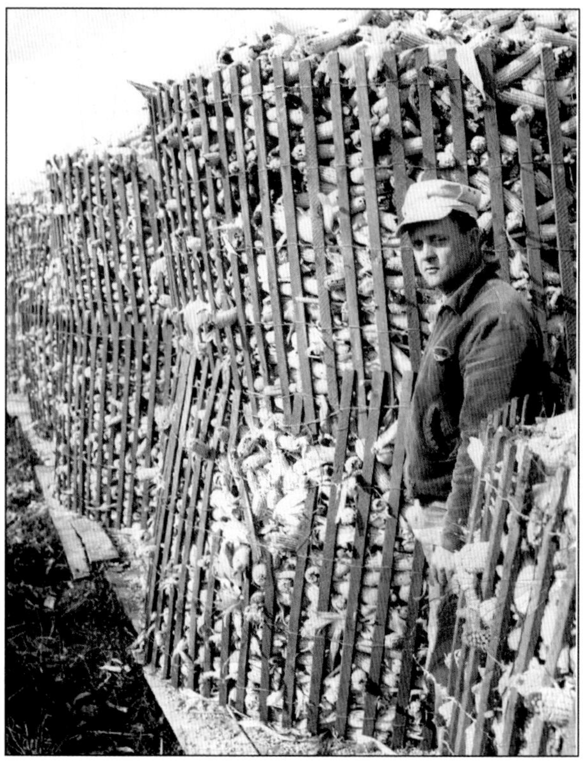

Merrill Yoder is seen in this 1952 image, flanked by an abundance of the corn harvest. At the time, he was working on a farm located along County Road 28, just east of County Road 7. (Photo courtesy of Mr. and Mrs. Merrill Yoder.)

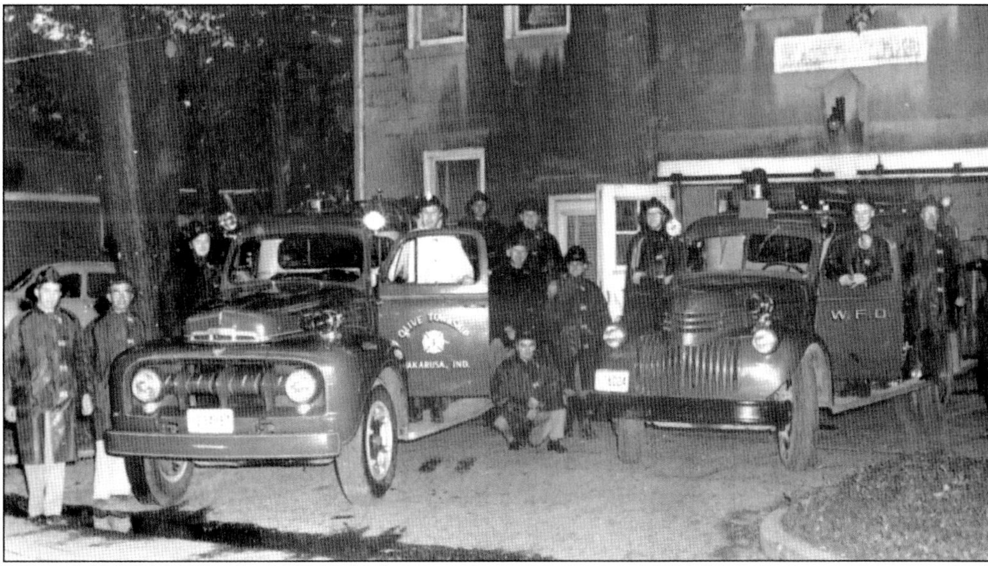

The Wakarusa Fire Department, as the company looked in 1952—pictured from left to right are LaMarr Strycker, Meloin Myers, David Anglemeyer, George Doering (chief), Milton Brown, Cleson Weldy, Walter Klein, Dale Metzler, Willfred Hunsberger, Ray Brubaker, Carl Hunsberger, Jr., Walter Myers, and W.K. Brown. Not show are Tully Obenhoff, Nelson Lehman, Mel Flory, and James Freed. (Photo courtesy of Wakarusa Public Library.)

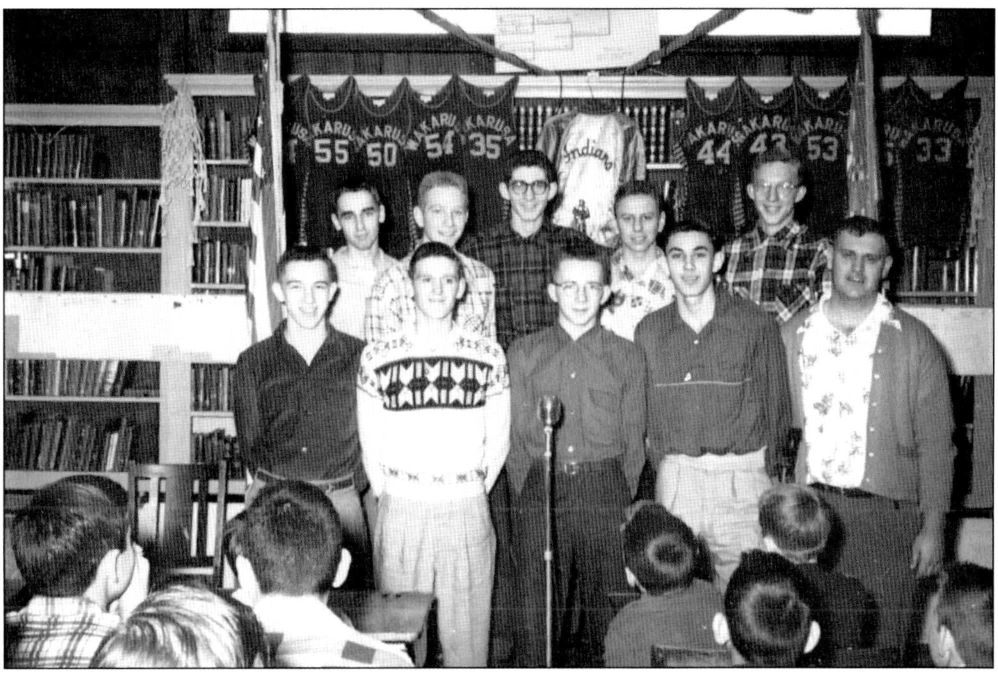

During an assembly in 1952, the students of Wakarusa High School presented a special salute to honor their basketball team, winners of the Elkhart County Holiday Tourney. Team members were, from left to right: (front row) Bill Eslinger, Kenneth Wenger, Larry Sawyer, Lee Weldy, and Harold Bollman; (back row) Lee Hartman, Stanley Holdeman, Tom Evans, Stan Smeltzer, and Jim Horein. (Photo courtesy of Mr. and Mrs. Kenneth Wenger.)

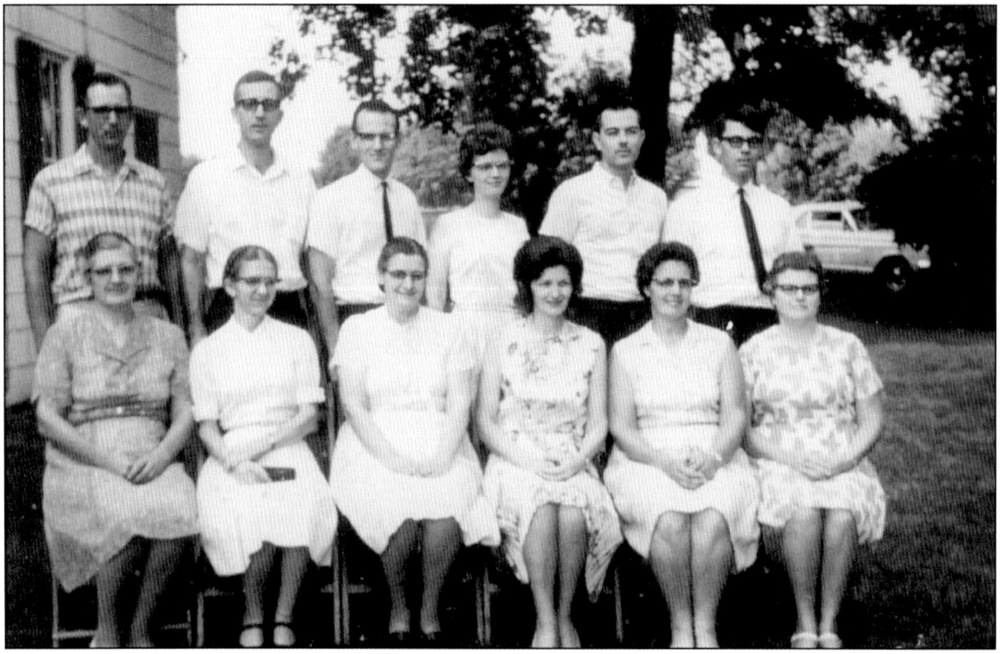

The Wenger siblings, all 12 of them, convene for this familial scene from the 1960s. Pictured from left to right are: (front row) Fay Yoder, Myrtle Kehr, Leota Yoder, Helen Alexander, Vada Blosser, and Doris Nunemaker; (back row) Charles Jr. (Chuck), David, Kenneth, Phyllis Stauffer, Larry, and Lester. (Photo courtesy of Mr. and Mrs. Kenneth Wenger.)

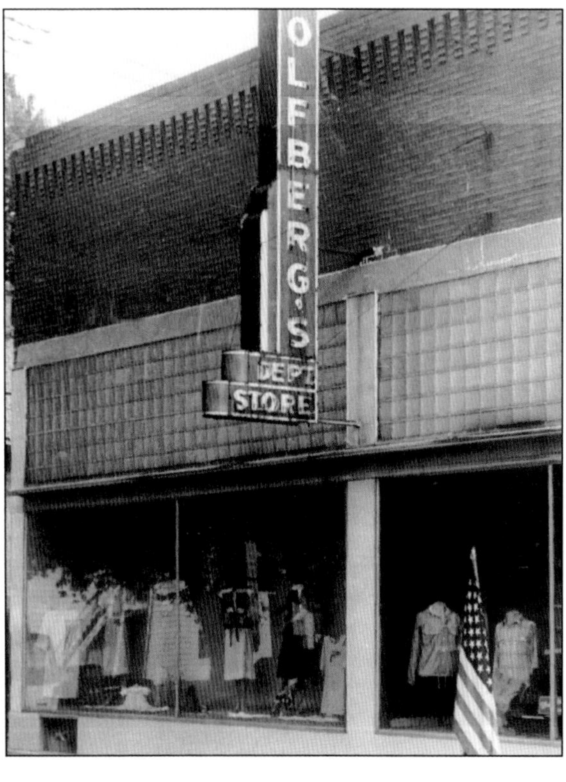

This is the former Wolfberg's store, once located at 109 East Waterford Street. The business was founded by Moses Wolfberg, who in the earliest part of the 20th century was something of a peddler and would sell his wares on the streets of Wakarusa using a horse and a wagon. He chose to provide his sales career with a permanent home in 1907. The store was later owned by Wolfberg's son Louis, then his daughter and son-in-law, Mr. and Mrs. Loren Smith. The latter kept the enterprise in the family until 1979, when it was purchased by Michael Dallek. Wolfberg's closed its doors in May of 1983, after more than 75 years of service. (Photo courtesy of Wakarusa Public Library.)

Three

NEW PARIS
Risen From a War, Triumphed by Prosperity

It was known as the War of 1812. Who could have imagined that such a cataclysmic event on the timeline of our nation's history would allow for the founding of the small farming community known as New Paris?

Colonel John Jackson, leading a detachment of General Anthony Wayne's troops, was sent on a special mission to stake out what was then called the Elkhart Prairie. The goal was to have an Indian camp begin relocation efforts away from the area. As the brigade made their approach, the startled Indians fled, leaving behind kettles of hominy still cooking over open fires.

Jackson was taken with intrigue, and promised to himself that when the war was over, he would make the territory his home. But it wasn't until after embarking on a period of prospecting that Jackson was able to return to the land, in January of 1829. He was surprised to discover that two men had already become established homesteaders on the fledgling farmland. Elias Riggs and William Simpson sold their property right to Jackson for a price of $50 apiece. Finally, Jackson settled into the northeast corner of the newly formed township, which would be christened Jackson Township in his honor.

In 1834, another man came along who would soon become a pivotal influence. Isaac Abshire moved his family from their Preble County, Ohio, home to join the flourishing population. "One cold night in January, these two men sat in a log cabin owned by Abshire, and by the light of a fat lamp, considered the advisability of laying out a town," documented an article in the Milford Mail newspaper. On March 1, 1836, the pair, armed with poles and other tools worthy of surveying, set about platting the new town. They called the town New Paris, for the Ohio city which Abshire had once called home.

One fellow who is talked of at length in the earliest annals of New Paris history is Frederick Harriman. He was the son-in-law of founder Enoch Wright. Harriman is credited for establishing the first homestead in the New Paris town limits. He operated his wheelwright business, noted as the first New Paris industry, out of his log cabin home, where he lived with his wife, Mary, and their seven children. The house was unique, in that it captured some of the pioneer spirit that Harriman still harbored—it was a log cabin with a small fireplace and greased paper over the spartan windows. While still turning out spinning wheels in his home shop, Harriman also served a 10-year stint as the town's first constable, beginning in 1831.

It was during one of Harriman's excursions that Mary Harriman had an unusual encounter with a young Indian squaw, the outcome of which saved untold numbers of lives. The young woman, who was said to be from a neighboring Pottawatomie/Miami mixed tribe, had become a treasured acquaintance of the Harriman family. One day, she arrived at the cabin, frantic with the news that some of the renegade braves were planning a rebellion against some of the white settlers. She then opened her apron to display a wealth of weaponry, with ample knives, arrowheads, and tomahawks, said to be readied for battle. The squaw implored Mrs.

Harriman to hide the weapons in an attempt to avoid conflict. Mary Harriman willingly obliged, opening a trap door leading to a tiny cellar underneath the cabin, and the contraband weapons were concealed.

The threat of an uprising was never mentioned again. Thanks in part to that friendly alliance with the Indian woman, the Harrimans and other New Paris citizens were soon able to forge a solid and trustworthy relationship with their Native American neighbors.

As the 1800s progressed, the New Paris area continued to grow and thrive. Colonel John Jackson is said to be the one responsible for creating the first township school, sometime between 1830 and 1838. An etched stone marker at the site commemorates the occasion. The school was constructed of round logs, with an ample fireplace and a chimney fashioned of sticks.

By 1881 a brick four-room schoolhouse had been built, and the membership of the student body had risen to approximately 100 students. In those days, students had only one textbook—a spelling primer.

A new high school was to open in 1927, but delays meant teachers would sometimes conduct classes wherever they could—the basements of churches, in the hallways of the school, and sometimes even outdoors under the shade of trees. By Christmas of 1927, the new school was officially opened.

In the late 1960s, the New Paris schools were consolidated with nearby smaller communities. The school system became Fairfield High School for the 1968–69 academic year. The former high school building now serves as the New Paris Grade School. There are also students in the region who attend Bethany Christian High School, which has been an institution of faith-based education since 1954.

Another harbinger of change that was a boon to the growth of New Paris was the arrival of railroads. As far back as the 1860s, a north-south rail line was built that was designed to connect the Michigan city of White Pigeon to the north, Warsaw, Indiana to the south, and points in between. This railway passed right through the center of New Paris. By the early 1890s, New Paris was again earmarked as a site for the Wabash Railroad, extending west to east, from Chicago to Detroit. The easternmost segment of the former Wabash line, which encompassed 47 miles between Steuben County and Wakarusa, was officially abandoned in 1985.

New Paris was also an arrival and departure point for the Winona Interurban line, a network of tracks that connected a number of cities in northern and southern Indiana, and included such major cities as Elkhart, South Bend, and Mishawaka. New Paris was the scene of the Winona's historical final run in 1952, as gondola cars transported local dignitaries from Warsaw to New Paris and back again.

There are those who will always think of New Paris and its legendary Burger Dairy facility in a synonymous fashion. Originally known as the New Paris Creamery when it was formed in 1919, the dairy itself was built in 1920 and named for Robert Burger, the patriarch of the family who ran the business. Burger Dairy was the source of this area's premium dairy products, such as milk, butter, and ice cream, for more than 80 years. It was purchased by National Dairy Holdings in 2001, but due to changes in the industry, the New Paris site met with a bittersweet farewell on February 1 of 2003.

An Elkhart County plat book from 1874 notes of New Paris, "This is a fine farming section, well watered and timbered, and the farmers have fine barns and good houses, and the most of them are in a comfortable situation." The statement seems as relevant today as it did a century ago.

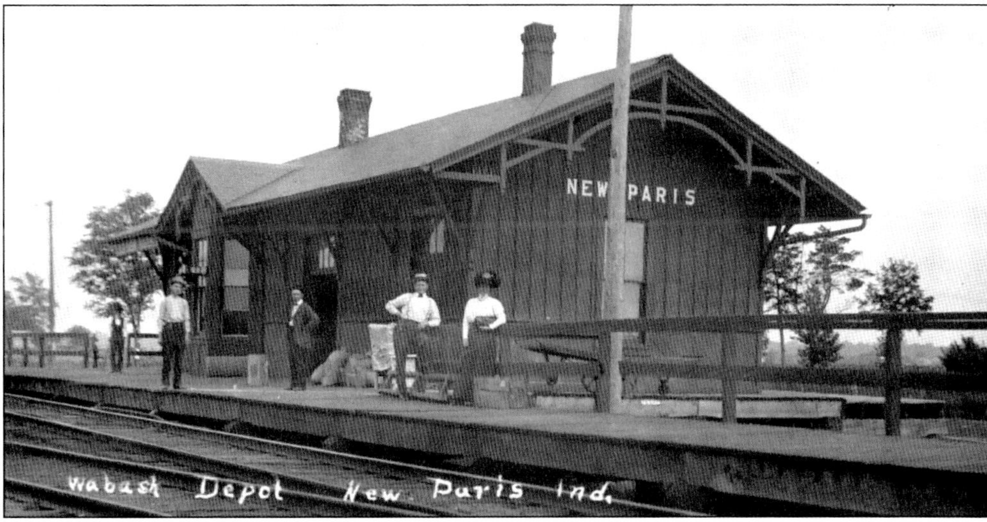

The Wabash Depot was built not long after the Wabash Railroad Company instituted a new railway through New Paris in the 1890s. The line was a major connection of three states, beginning in Detroit and ending in Chicago. A stockyard and shipping area were added to the New Paris area to facilitate the comings and goings of freight, and once the area was instituted as a key shipping point, the growth of the town accelerated. The Wabash line fell by the wayside of changing times, and the tracks were removed in 1985. (Photo courtesy of Mr. and Mrs. Dean Henry.)

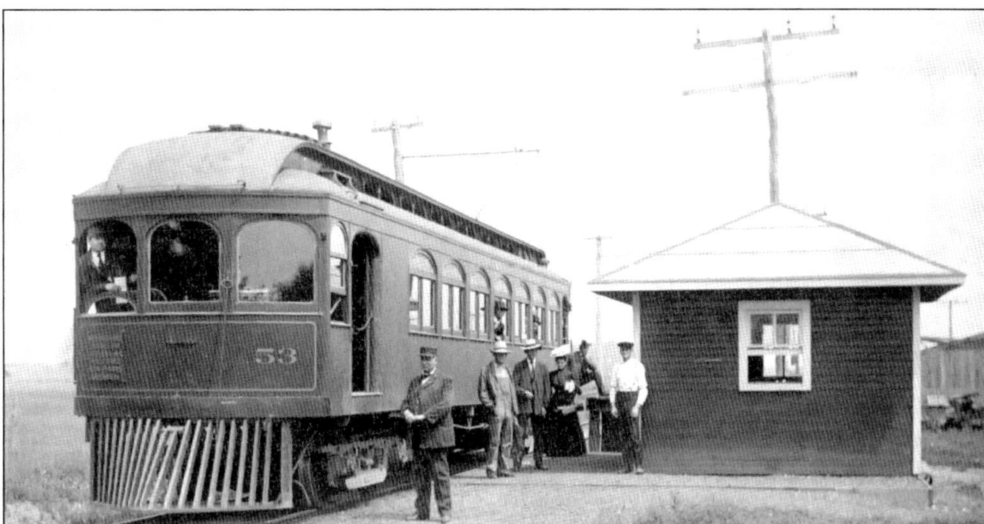

Quickly embraced by folks as "a godsend," the Winona Interurban Railroad made it possible for people to venture to nearby cities, and even as far south as central Indiana, without the means of horse and buggy, or by foot, as they would have done before. Work on the electric line began in July of 1905, for the price of $500,000. The railroad started as a three-mile segment of track to transport people from Warsaw to the Winona Assembly, a religious settlement at nearby Winona Lake. It was financed in part by automotive magnate J.M. Studebaker of South Bend. The line proved so successful that additional stops were created, and at the height of its worthiness, the Winona Interurban line carried thousands of passengers daily. The Winona Interurban line made its last journey on May 31, 1952. (Photo courtesy of Mr. and Mrs. Dean Henry.)

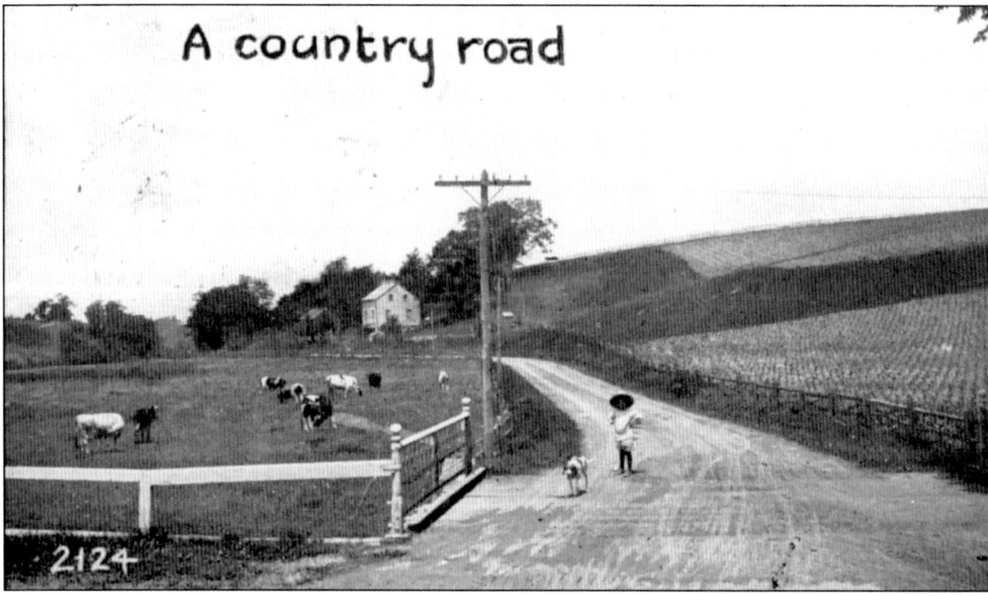

One of Elkhart County's many country roads, this one made a path near the New Paris area in the early part of the 1900s. Such a fetching image made for a lovely postcard, and it was used by one youngster to write to a friend in the Mishawaka area—it is postmarked October, 1912. (Photo courtesy of Mr. and Mrs. Dean Henry.)

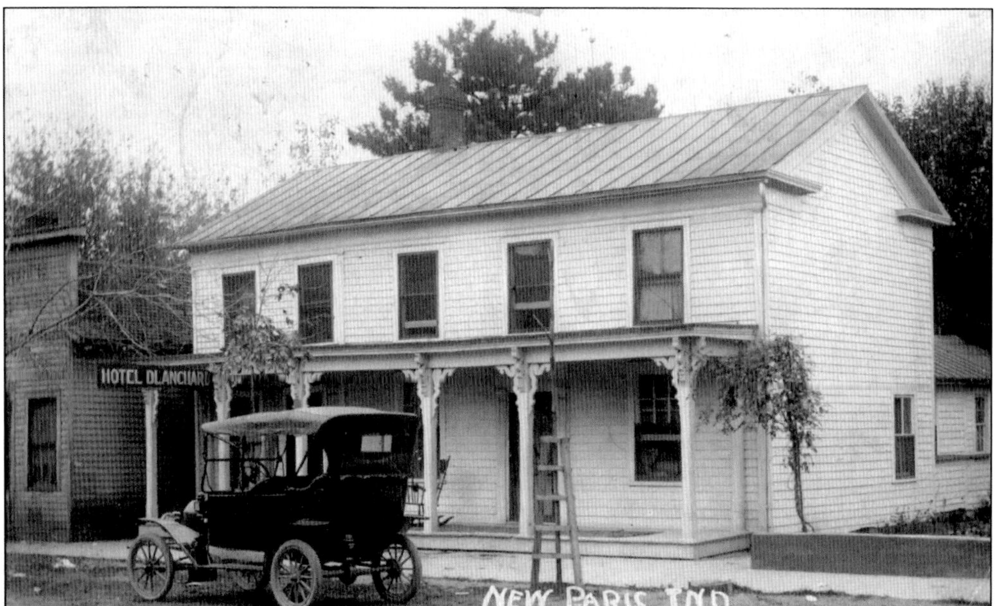

Edson G. Blanchard and his wife, Menerva, were the landlords of the Hotel Blanchard, which was located on North Main Street in New Paris. Blanchard was one of the town's first residents, settling in 1836, and was also a veteran of the Civil War. Blanchard's father, Abram, built the vicinity's first brick house in the same year his son made New Paris his home. When E.G. Blanchard passed away on April 6, 1914, he was the town's oldest resident, having lived to 80 years of age. (Photo courtesy of Mr. and Mrs. Dean Henry.)

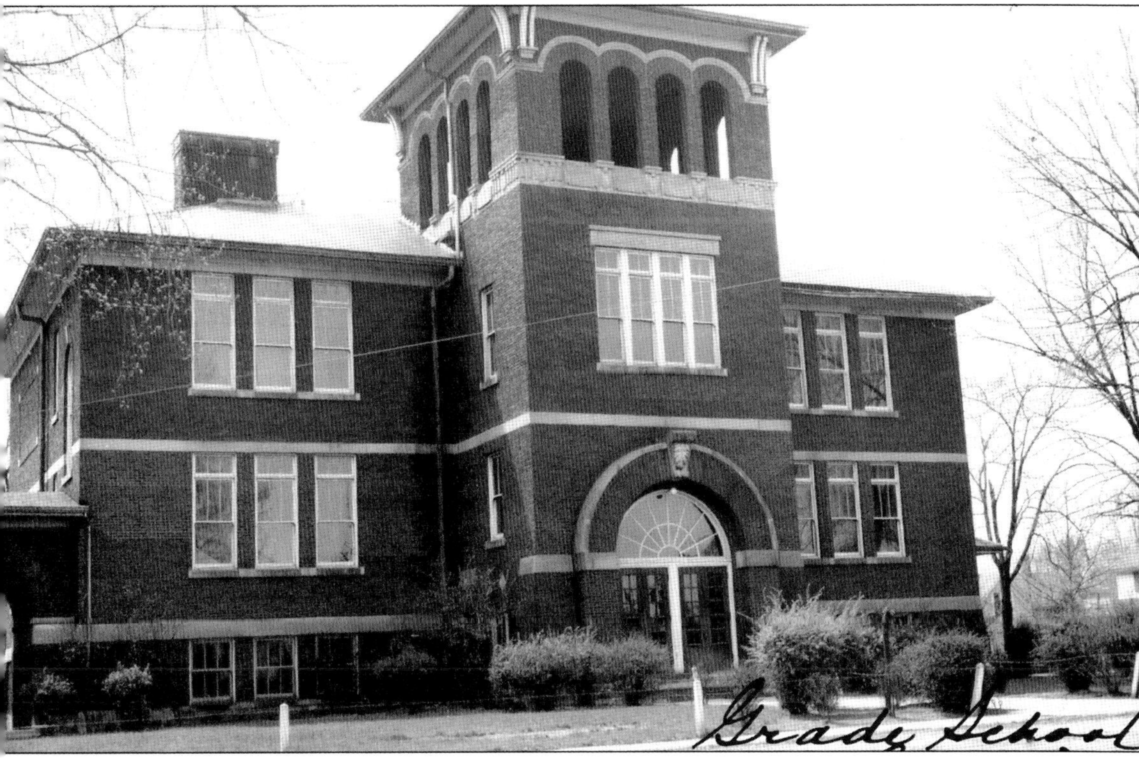

This is the New Paris Grade School, once situated along the southwest corner of Division and Fourth streets. It was a predecessor to the New Paris High School, but this building housed area students in all grade levels. It was built in 1912, and abandoned in 1927, when the new high school facility debuted. Mr. Raymond Dausman, a New Paris resident who helped compile a history of Union and Jackson Township schools, notes that directly behind this structure, there was once another, older brick school building that had been torn down in 1912. Although no one is quite sure when that particular building was erected, students of that period sometimes referred to the original schoolhouse as the "red building." (Photo courtesy of Mr. and Mrs. Dean Henry.)

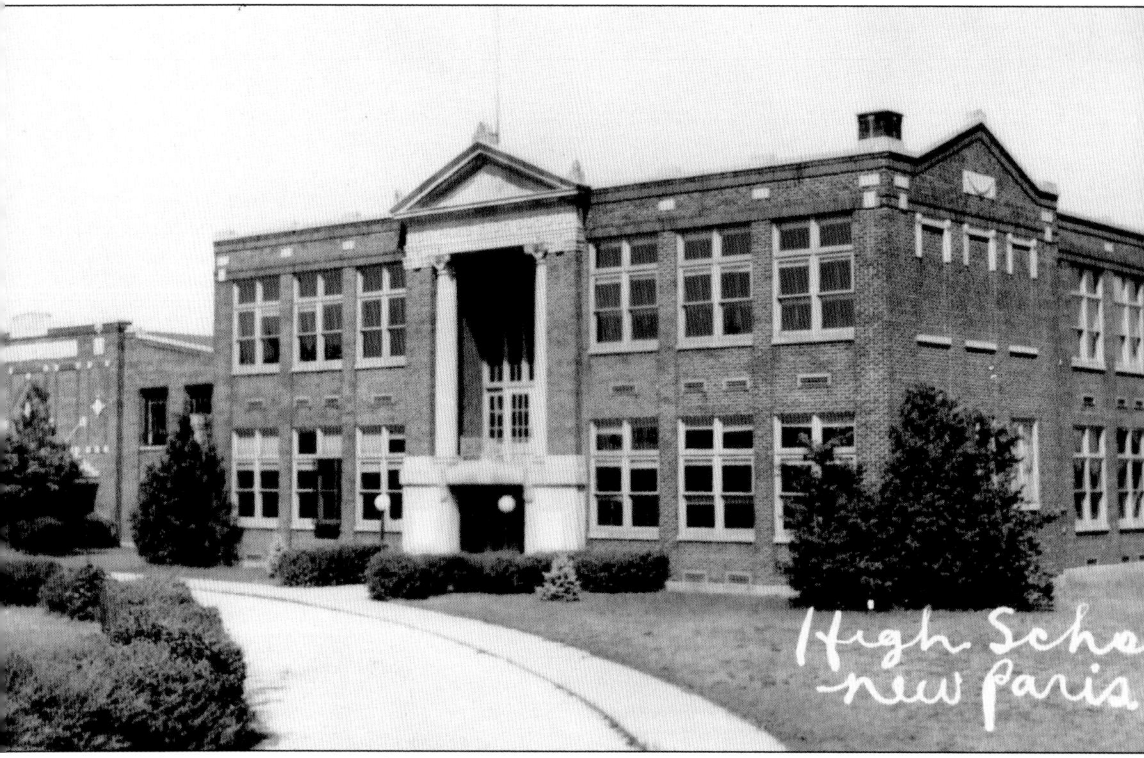

The former New Paris High School, as it looked shortly after it was built in 1927. Junior high and high school students of the New Paris community now attend the Fairfield Junior–Senior High School, but this building is still in use as the New Paris Grade School, located on Division Street. (Photo courtesy of Mr. and Mrs. Dean Henry.)

Four

FORAKER
A Tale of a Crossroad That Followed a Railroad

In 1891, when the Wabash Railroad made plans to install a new rail corridor between Toledo, Ohio, and Chicago, it was rumored that the tracks would pass through Elkhart County. This news caused only a ripple of interest for residents of that area. It was a project that had been spoken of for some 20 years, and no one took it very seriously, even when the surveyors came and staked out the proposed land. To the people, the railroad would have to be seen to be believed.

So it must have generated quite a commotion when construction began on the Wabash line 1892 and it was completed in 1893. With this new mode of transportation, there surely would be unlimited potential, convenience, and opportunities for business and for travel.

Meanwhile, along the crossroads of County Road 44 and County Road 15, a tiny group of businesses had just been established, and land freshly platted, for a community called Foraker. But the town never achieved its permanence—at least not at that location. Realizing that it would best serve their interests to be closer to the railroad, the townspeople simply packed up and moved on—to a new destination at County Road 142 and County Road 13, which is where Foraker remains today.

The original Foraker was born of a plan belonging to Samuel Yoder. There was a general store operated by Noah Kauffman, as well as a post office, a saw mill, a blacksmith, and an additional store. These were the businesses that made the pilgrimage to the second Foraker when it was founded in 1893, also on land owned by Yoder. The buildings were moved by teams of horses pulling the structures on log rollers. A Mr. Blosser from Waterford and a Mr. Bechtel from Wakarusa were the two men responsible for mapping the boundaries of the new town. The name of Foraker was chosen in honor of Ohio senator Joseph B. Foraker, a popular politician at the time.

Within a short while of Foraker's latter establishment, there were around 25 families in residence, and business was moving along in a respectable fashion. The town welcomed the arrival of the first westbound freight train on April 27, 1893, and the next month, on May 30, an eastbound passenger train made an appearance. That same year, Foraker became a stop along the route which carried travelers to and from the World's Fair in Chicago.

By the early part of the 1900s, events transpired which led to the advent of some of Foraker's longest running businesses. Samuel Yoder had sold his general store to B.P. Bollinger, who by 1912 elected to sell the store to a newlywed couple—Mr. and Mrs. Henry S. Weaver. The Weavers would become among the community's most beloved and enterprising families. The H.S. Weaver General Store was a mainstay in the heart of the town for many decades, and Weaver allowed his store to house the post office, beginning in the summer of 1921. He served as the town's postmaster until his retirement in 1955, after which time his wife succeeded him. She held that position until her death in 1965. The local post office branch closed in 1966, then the city of Goshen began operating a substation based in Foraker. The community retained its own zip code, until the sad day in 1983 when the last batch of rural mail would bear the Foraker postmark.

Other significant businesses that were part of Foraker included a pickle factory, where 23 vats kept pickles in storage and were processed for later shipment to Chicago. A cream station, which was an ancillary of the George Freese Creamery in Nappanee, was also situated in Foraker for a time. In 1908, a fellow named George Werntz purchased the local cider mill and worked solely from his residence for a number of years. There was the Foraker Grain Elevator, which was destroyed in a fire in 1932. Abe Shelly and Henry Weaver also shared responsibilities of running a local stock yard, where they assisted in the buying and shipping of cattle.

In 1921, a group of farmers banded together to form the Farmers and Merchants Bank, but its tenure was fairly short-lived. When the Depression struck in 1929, the federal government closed all of the banks. Some of the banks were able to reorganize and reopen, but others, like the one in Foraker, were casualties never to achieve posterity. Other businesses have weathered well over time and crises, and are still an active part of the Foraker community. One such example is the lumber yard that began at the dawn of the 1900s as Culp and Weaver Lumber Yard. It was later bought by Amos and Henry Hoover, thus becoming Hoover Lumber and Coal, the name the firm still bears today. Then there is Hess Brothers, which originated in 1931 as a garage and filling station. In its earliest days, the establishment sold Studebaker and Willys automobiles, then later added Case farm implements and machinery to its inventory.

It would be remiss not to make mention of one of Foraker's most notorious figures—the individual who ran the workings of the Wabash railroad depot from 1918 all the way through the 1940s. Her name was Jennie Wiley, and she was a staff of one. She took on the dealings of the ticket office, freight department, express agency, and Western Union telegraph operations. It is thought that she may well have been the only woman station agent on the Wabash line during her later years of service.

The passage of time did not hasten a boon in population nor in the growth of new business; still, the Foraker of yore gave its people a sense of belonging and a resounding communal spirit that could never be silenced. Those sentiments have been passed on to younger generations, and they still dwell in the hearts of those who take great pride in having once called Foraker home.

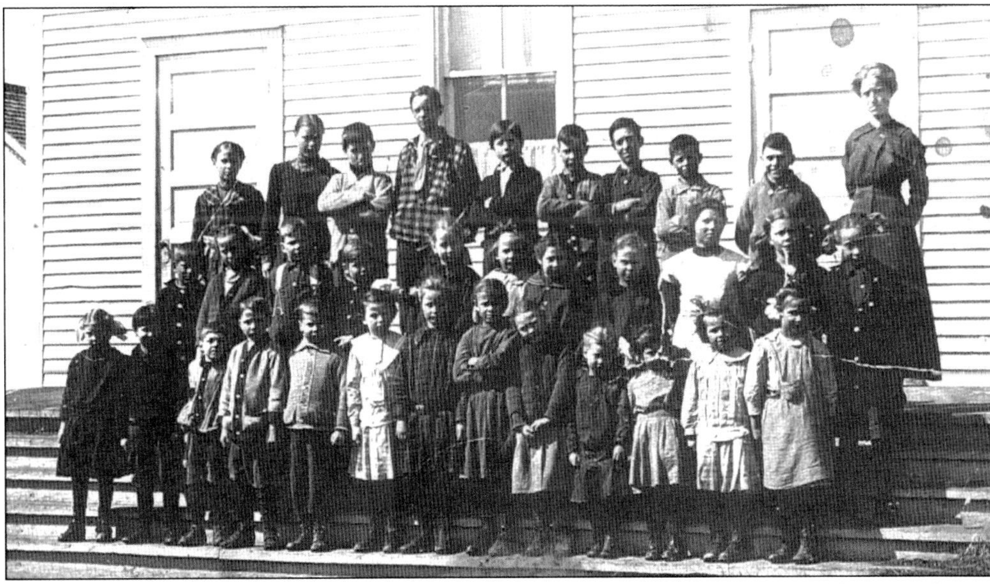

Although the town of Foraker did not have a school within the boundaries of the town limits, there were two rural schoolhouses in the immediate area. There was the Miller School, where the children of the west side attended classes, and the Swoveland School, which housed the pupils of the east side. This is the Swoveland School as it looked between 1912 and 1916. It was located on County Road 44, between County Roads 13 and 15. The building still stands, but has since been remodeled into a house. The Miller School was lost to a fire. (Photo courtesy of Mr. and Mrs. Howard Hochstetler.)

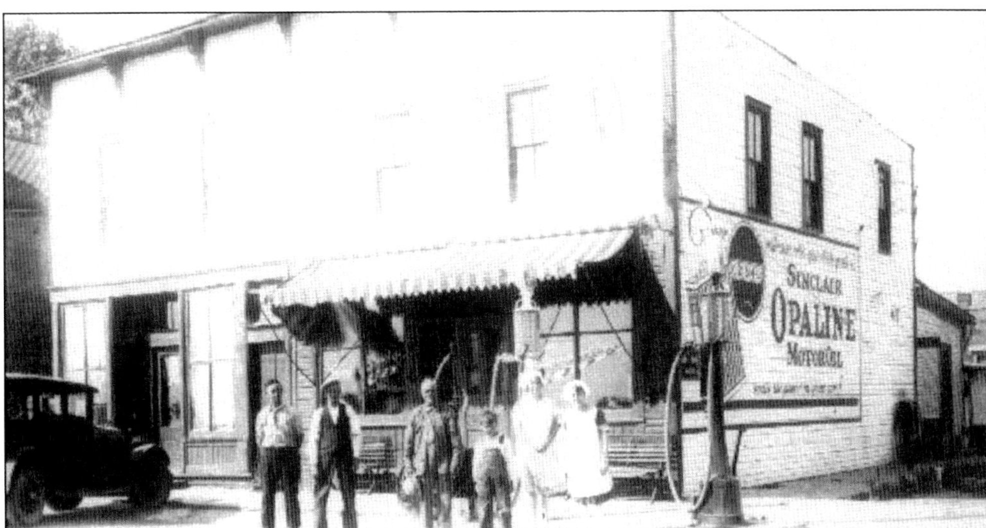

Located in the heart of Foraker, this is the general store of Henry S. Weaver, in a picture from the 1920s. Customers could find sundries of all sorts, such as clothing and shoes, hardware and tools, and various types of food. The store had no set hours—employees simply kept the business open until all of the farmers completed their chores for the day. Weaver was also the town's first postmaster, establishing the Foraker post office within the store. He maintained his position as postmaster for 34 years before stepping down in 1955. His wife was his successor, and she carried out the postmaster duties until her death in 1965. (Photo courtesy of Mr. and Mrs. Robert Culp.)

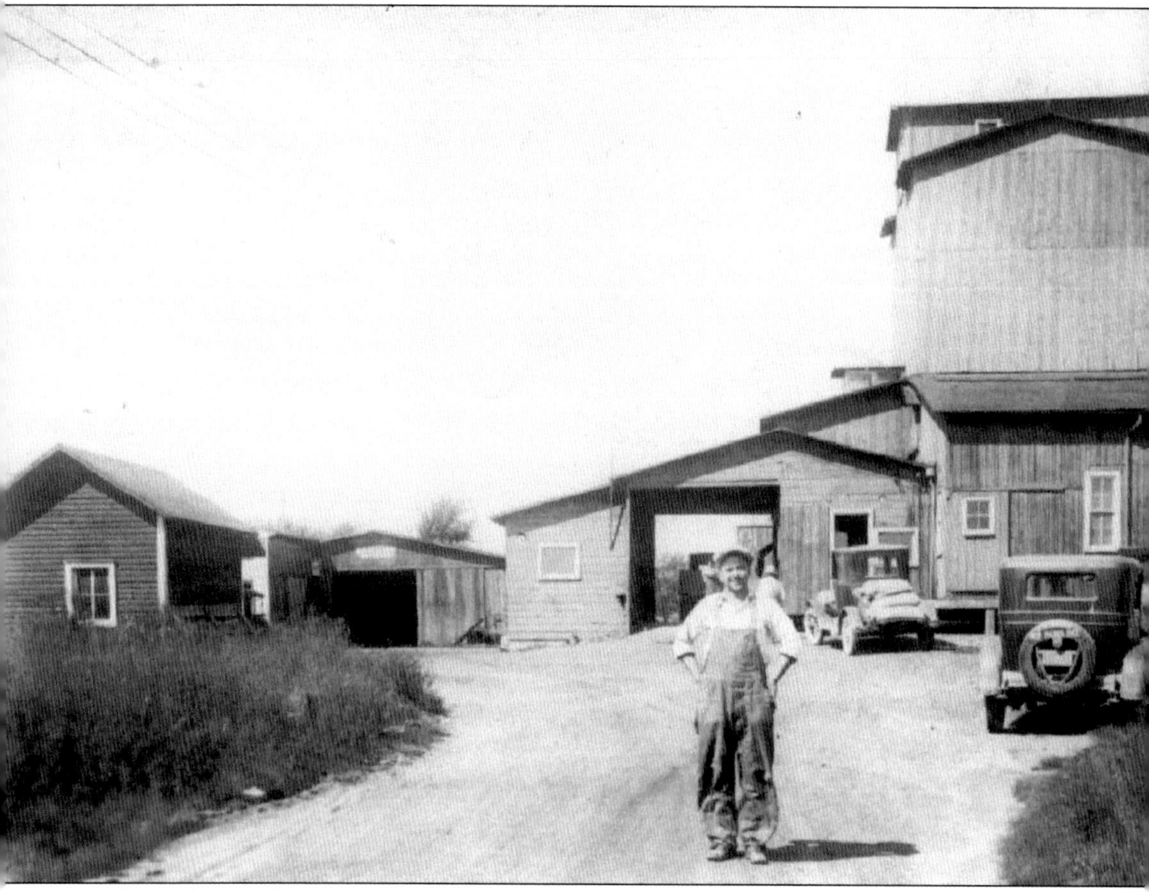

This is the Foraker Grain Elevator, in a photo from the late 1920s. The fellow standing in the foreground is Aura B. Culp, father of the gentleman who shared this picture. The Culp ancestry includes the first family to raise a farm in the Foraker area. The building was destroyed in a massive 1932 fire that exceeded $12,000 in damages to the facility and equipment. The fire started when H.S. Weaver, the owner, and Isaiah Shaum dropped a lantern while working in a wheat bin. Because the storage unit was filled with grain, chaff, and dust, it did not take long for the entire 60-foot structure to become engulfed in flames. Firefighters from the neighboring towns of Goshen, New Paris, and Wakarusa teamed up with the forces from Foraker to help extinguish the blaze. Thankfully, the loss was almost entirely offset by insurance. (Photo courtesy of Mr. and Mrs. Robert Culp.)

Five

LOCKE
The City That Was—
Noble Souls and Able Hands

The tiny hamlet of Locke, though no longer recognized as a certifiable town, is as much a community in name and in spirit presently as it was in its formative days. A picturesque patchwork of homes and rural businesses can be found dotting the countryside where the crossroads, the "downtown" intersection, is defined by County Road 50 and County Road 3. Locke, despite its diminutive stature, is definitely a worthy contributor to Elkhart County history, and can certainly be credited with helping in the foundation of its neighbor to the southeast, the city of Nappanee.

Locke's history actually begins with the formulation of Locke Township, officially organized in June of 1841. It was named for the area's first settler, Samuel Lockwood, who arrived with his wife and children in 1836. Sadly, Lockwood died in December of that same year. Other pioneers would come upon the land and establish homesteads—by 1839, Abner Hibray, John Pitts, James Berry, Morlan Albin, Daniel McCoy, Philip Reed, and David Salisbury were residents of Locke Township. The following year, those families were joined by Samuel Wilson, John Burns, Jacob Burns, Joel Farlay, and Franklin Stevenson.

Over the course of the next several years, the fledgling township would observe and celebrate many firsts. The wedding of Lucius Lockwood and Hannah Hibray in 1840 was quite an event, as the young bride and groom were children of the area's premier families. The township held its first election in 1842, with nine voters casting ballots. By the mid-1860s, Locke Township was the site of a regional post office, a sawmill was up and running (courtesy of the Lockwood family), and John Wolfe debuted a new general store.

By 1867, the decision was made to plat a specific section of Locke Township, the 24th section precisely, and create a new village, which for a very short duration was known as Whistlertown. George W. Eby, M.H. Morlan, and L.B. Winder were the three men credited with the town's founding. Within a fairly short period of time, there was a significant amount of growth and change, and it seemed that prosperous times were a certainty. In just a few years, Locke had approximately 40 residences and a wide spectrum of businesses, including a drug store, a grocery store, three dry-goods stores, a hardware store, a tinsmith, two boot and shoe shops, a furniture maker, two sawmills, a wagon shop, a steam grist and flouring mill, a hotel, three blacksmiths, three physicians, a church, a shingle mill, and a public schoolhouse.

A written history of Elkhart County, published in 1880, details how the business interests of Locke were thriving and establishing quite a rapport with nearby cities. The Miller and Rickert sawmill produced barrel-heads and staves and had clientele based as "far away" as Elkhart, Goshen, Warsaw, and Ligonier. A fellow by the name of W.L. Tucker took a former dwelling and turned it into an active sawmill industry, where the facility turned out shingles, staves, bedstead slats, table fixtures, and other items.

Meanwhile, just a short distance to the south, there was a stir of activity taking place in a section of the county that didn't seem to outwardly bear much promise. It was a swampy terrain, thick with woods and brush, but to the powers that be of the Baltimore and Ohio railroad, it was their ideal for a new passenger train line. Work was beginning as far back as 1872, when surveyors were meeting with property owners, negotiating purchases of land, and clearing a swath of clean land.

By the summer of 1874, the B & O railroad was completed, a new city was about to rise, and the fellowship of Locke carried their fair share of responsibility to assist in the goings on. Although the citizens of Locke felt somewhat defeated, knowing that the railway project had literally passed them by, they realized that in order to secure a solid stream of business, their assistance on the railroad would be a must. It was suggested that perhaps Locke should spearhead the efforts to create a station, by which passengers and freight could come and go, establishing this new area as a reliable point of access.

Interestingly enough, Locke had initially made a pledge to the B & O that the town would donate five acres of land adjacent to the tracks, and in exchange, the B & O would see to it that a depot would be built. However, that may well have been a commitment spoken out of turn, because part of those five acres were owned by Daniel Metzler and John Culp—two of the founders of what would very soon become a little town christened Nappanee. Needless to say, those men were not about to relinquish the rights to their newly acquired land, since their sights were set on creating a city apart from Locke.

Yet somehow, several businessmen of Locke rallied enough support that a passenger depot was indeed erected under Locke leadership. For a time, the depot was known as the Locke-Eby passenger station, and train schedules from this particular point in time show that the route included "Locke," which was in fact Nappanee in its infancy.

It would not be long until the savvy businessmen of Locke discovered that there would be far greater potential to be had by relocating closer to the railway. Many of those early entrepreneurs literally packed up their merchandise, buildings, and moved their entire lot to Nappanee. And so in essence, what proved to be a blessing for Nappanee would result in the slow decline of Locke as a town. The township as an entirety did continue to offer its share of opportunity for at least a few more years—records of an 1880 history of the area show that there were still more than 75 residences and farms, along with a church, a school, two physicians and surgeons, and approximately a dozen other businesses. But any possibilities for future growth in Locke were diminished once Nappanee etched its way into the Elkhart County landscape.

Perhaps it could be said that the good people of Locke, while such an instrumental part of the evolution of Nappanee, sacrificed a bit of their own homeland along the way.

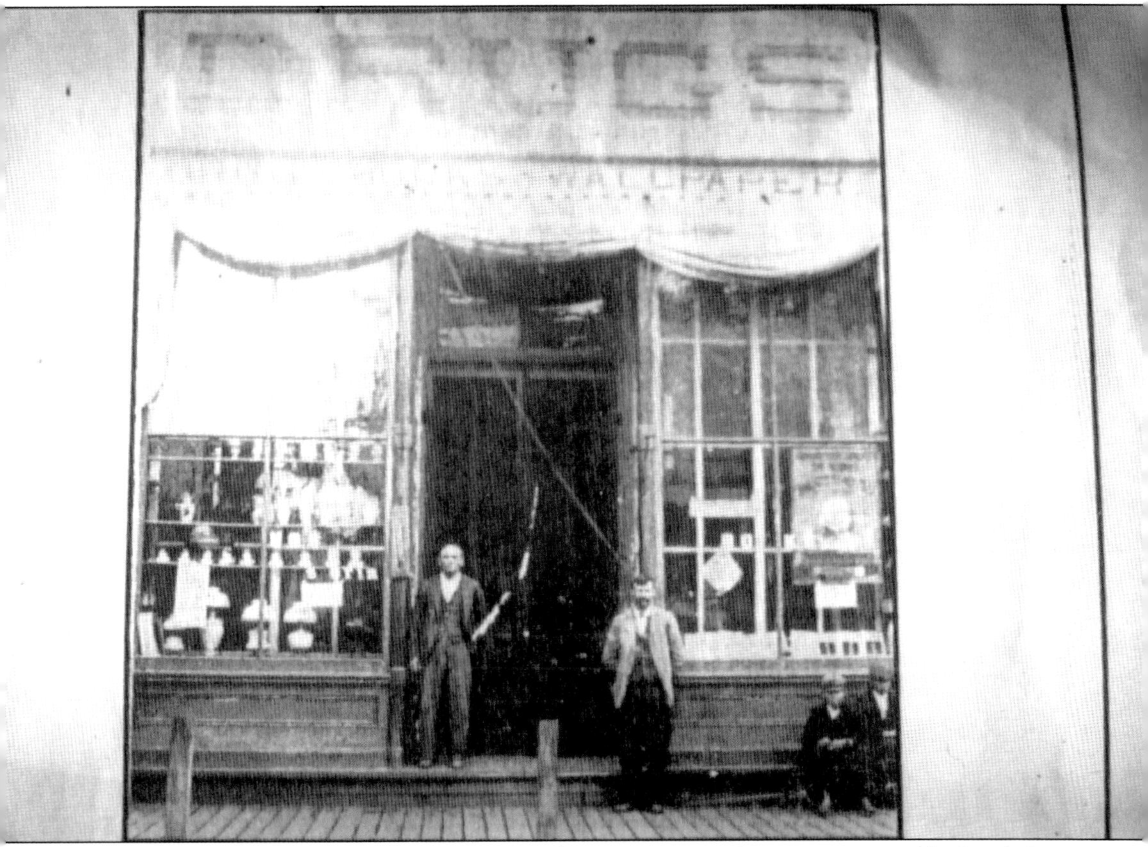

In its day, this was known as the "one first-class drug store" in Locke—it was owned by Jacob S. Walters. Walters began his business in 1876 and kept ample stock of groceries and medicines. Sales were brisk in the first few years, with annual sales running in the vicinity of $4,000. When the city of Nappanee was laid out in 1874, Walters opted to relocate his enterprise, building and all, to the new place. His became a name often mentioned in the workings of early Nappanee business and social organizations. By 1914, he opted to sell in his interest in the drug store to his son, Arthur and his nephew, Thomas, and the drug store was known as Walters and Walters until 1936. Walters also helped to establish the First Nappanee Bank, which was originally situated in a corner of his drug store, and he was the bank's first president. He was known in the community of Nappanee for having on his farm what would be the city's only animal park. It was located one mile north of the town square and offered visitors a chance to see deer, elk, buffalo, and ponies. Jacob S. Walters died in 1929. (Photo courtesy of Mr. and Mrs. William Johnson.)

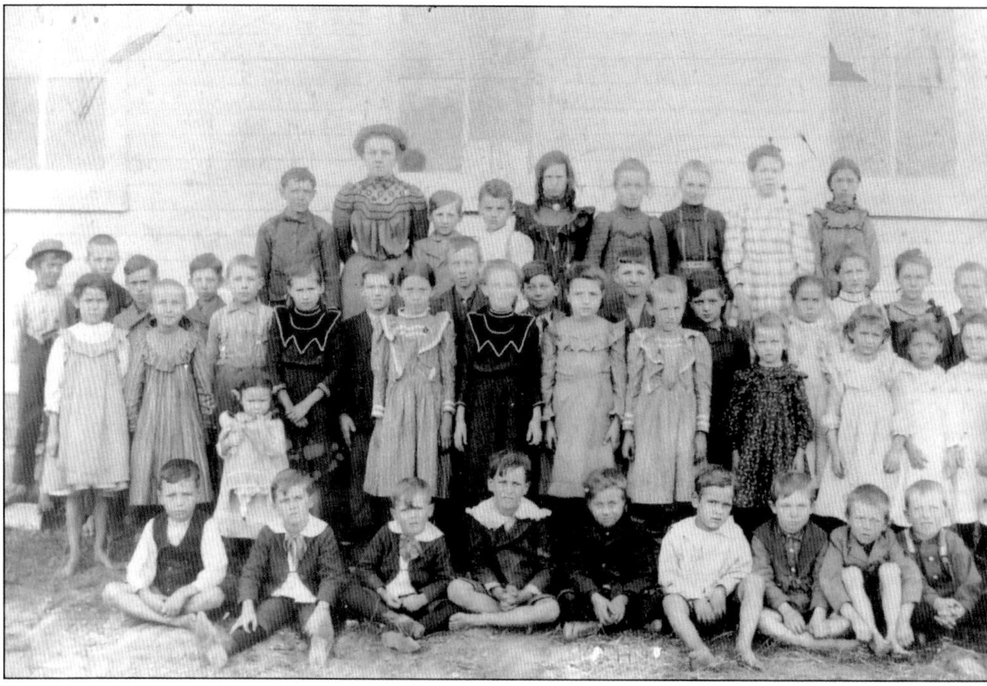

Youngsters of the Locke Township School pose for a class photograph in 1904. The school was fairly new at the time, having been built in 1890. It was situated at the corner of County Road 50 and County Road 3, and today the structure has been renovated and remodeled to serve as a private residence. (Photo courtesy of Nappanee Public Library.)

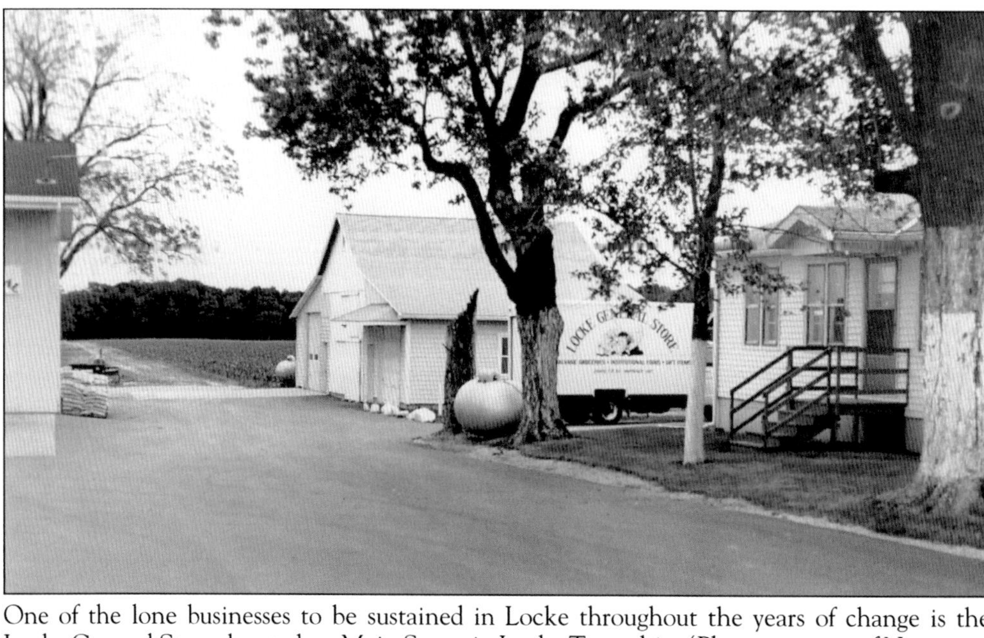

One of the lone businesses to be sustained in Locke throughout the years of change is the Locke General Store, located on Main Street in Locke Township. (Photo courtesy of Nappanee Public Library.)

Six

SOUTHWEST
A Scenic Sight on a Legendary Trail

One of the region's most well-known roadways, and perhaps one with the greatest deal of folklore, is the Plymouth-Goshen Trail. For more than two centuries, it's been known as the path that begins in the city of Plymouth, in central Marshall County, and travels northeasterly through Elkhart. It ends in the Goshen area, located in the heart of Elkhart County. According to most local accounts, the Pottawatomie and Miami Indians who once resided here used the trail as a means of travel, having discovered some merit behind the old adage, "the shortest distance between two points is a straight line."

It is along the Plymouth-Goshen Trail that one can find the tiny community of Southwest. It is situated five miles southwest of Goshen—hence its name. One of the more time-honored riddles of the area tells of a lost traveler who asked a farmer for directions. The farmer replied that the befuddled wanderer was "a mile north of Southwest," which of course, was cause to thoroughly confuse.

The earliest known permanent resident of the region known as Harrison Township dates back to 1831, with the arrival of a spirited pioneer named Daniel H. Stutsman. He became the first man who was not of Native American descent to erect a homestead in the township—a house fashioned of logs. As he worked tirelessly to clear the abundant forestry that was so prevalent at the time, it is said that the sound of his ringing axe was the first gesture from a white man to make an attempt for a settlement.

Stutsman was not alone for long. He would soon be followed by David Y. Miller, Conrad Brumbaugh, James and William Stewart, Samuel Buchanan, James McDowell, and Christian S. Farber. Miller, in particular, was noted as a virtuous ally to his Indian neighbors, and the sentiment was reciprocated in noble fashion. When Miller would venture to Ohio on business excursions, the gates to his stockade would be opened, and the Indians would come to stand guard over the property until Miller's return.

The first mention of a schoolhouse in the district reaches back to the 1840s, and was apparently located where the Yellow Creek Church of the Brethren now stands. Another school housed pupils sometime prior to 1873, with a building along the southwest edge of the town. The structure was later moved to the northeast portion of the square. The final schoolhouse was the Southwest School, nestled at the junction of what is now State Road 119, the former Plymouth-Goshen Trail, and County Road 40. Records vary somewhat on when exactly this schoolhouse was in use, but most documentation supports the notion that the building was serviceable from 1889 until 1932.

An article in the Goshen Democrat from December of 1847 spoke of a new post office being raised in a western section of Harrison Township regarded as Cabin Hill, with one Solomon Yeoman as the postmaster. When that office ceased to exist after a brief period, a new postal facility was erected and operated by Aaron Craig, who was also a justice of the peace. The mail was transported from the larger cities by way of horse and cart—quite often, the load of mail was so immense that the rider of the cart would have to resort to walking and simply lead the horse along. Farmers would stop by the Southwest post office on a weekly basis to retrieve their mail.

There was some type of general store owned by Henry Garbrick during the latter part of the 1800s, and another store sprung up under the ownership of Wess and Moses Hartman, the latter lost to a fire after only one year in operation. Another early resident by the name of John Smith was granted the nickname of "Double Smith" by virtue of being a "smith" by trade—he was a blacksmith. A fellow named Jacob Goble was such an expert in the building and repairing of firearms that his customers traveled from miles around to have their firearms professionally attended to.

Because the land which cradled Southwest was, and still is to some extent, quite rolling, any low places in the road were filled in logs and soil in the hopes of evening out the path. This makeshift construction gave the main thoroughfare a unique look so as to be labeled a "corduroy road." The bumpy byway sometimes carried teams of oxen, whose drivers would pass through Southwest to let their animals drink from a large watering trough, cobbled together with an old wooden tub and water siphoned in from a vast open well.

Despite these early harbingers of palpable growth, it seemed that Southwest was not destined to be a large, bustling city. It seems that the town reached a bit of a peak around the mid-1940s, when there were a handful of timely businesses to be found. There were two churches, one school, a veterinarian, a service garage, a carpet weaver, and one store. The population? Just 32 residents, happily ensconced in 12 homes.

But there were enough folks on hand to form a softball team, which won a Goshen city league tournament. And the youth of the town came together to establish a 4-H club, with a grand total of seven members.

So although Southwest never achieved the status of a bona fide city, or even officially a town, there is still that aura of community around those who live there, and a touch of serenity as well. Never mighty in size, but impressive in faith, it would seem fair to say that the people of Southwest are content with life just the way it is.

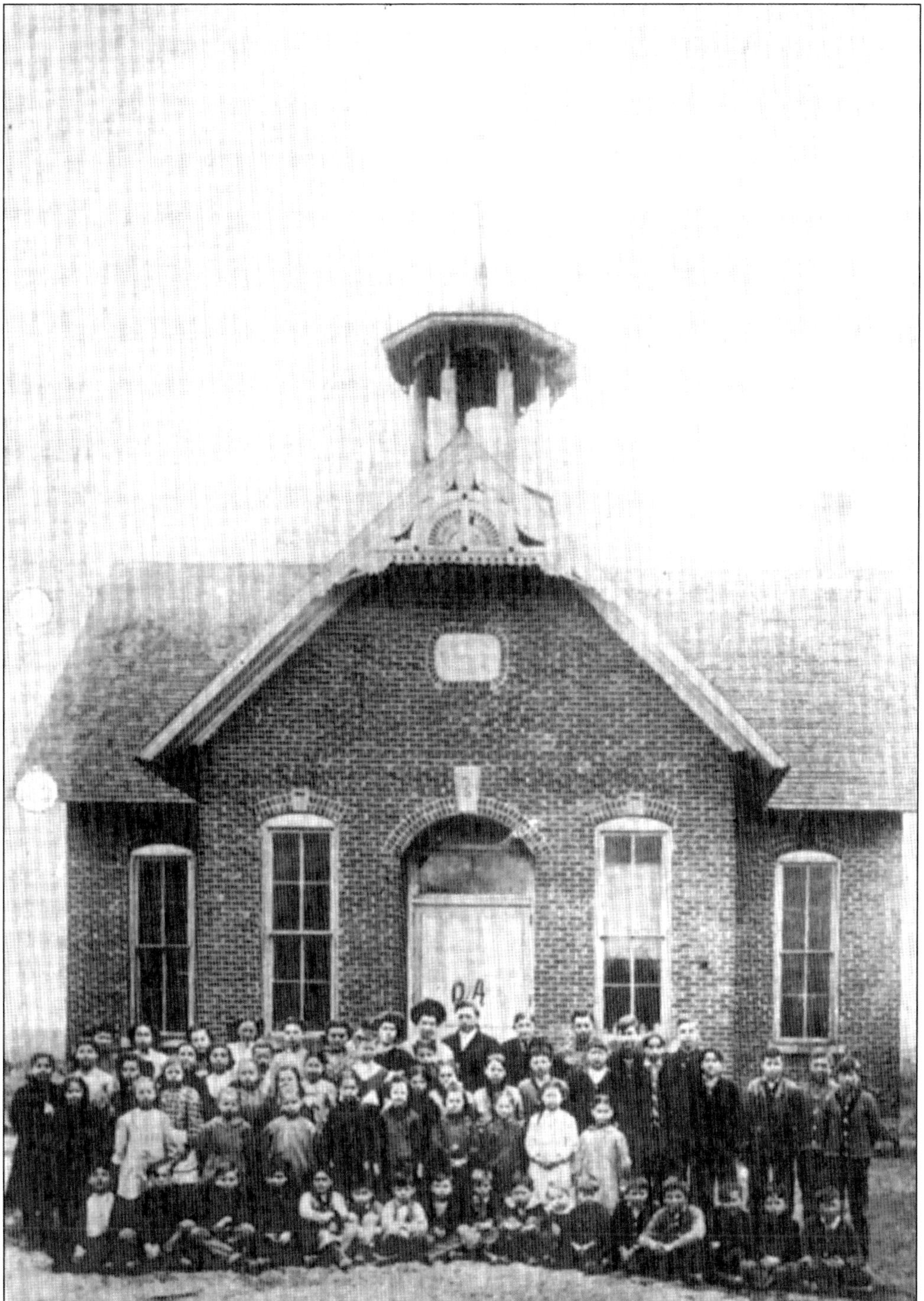

At the junction of State Road 119 and County Road 40, there is a little sewing notions shop called Calico Point. A century ago, it was the site of the Southwest School, a one-room schoolhouse built in 1889. It served the children of Harrison Township until 1932. (Photo courtesy of Mr. and Mrs. Melvin Crilow.)

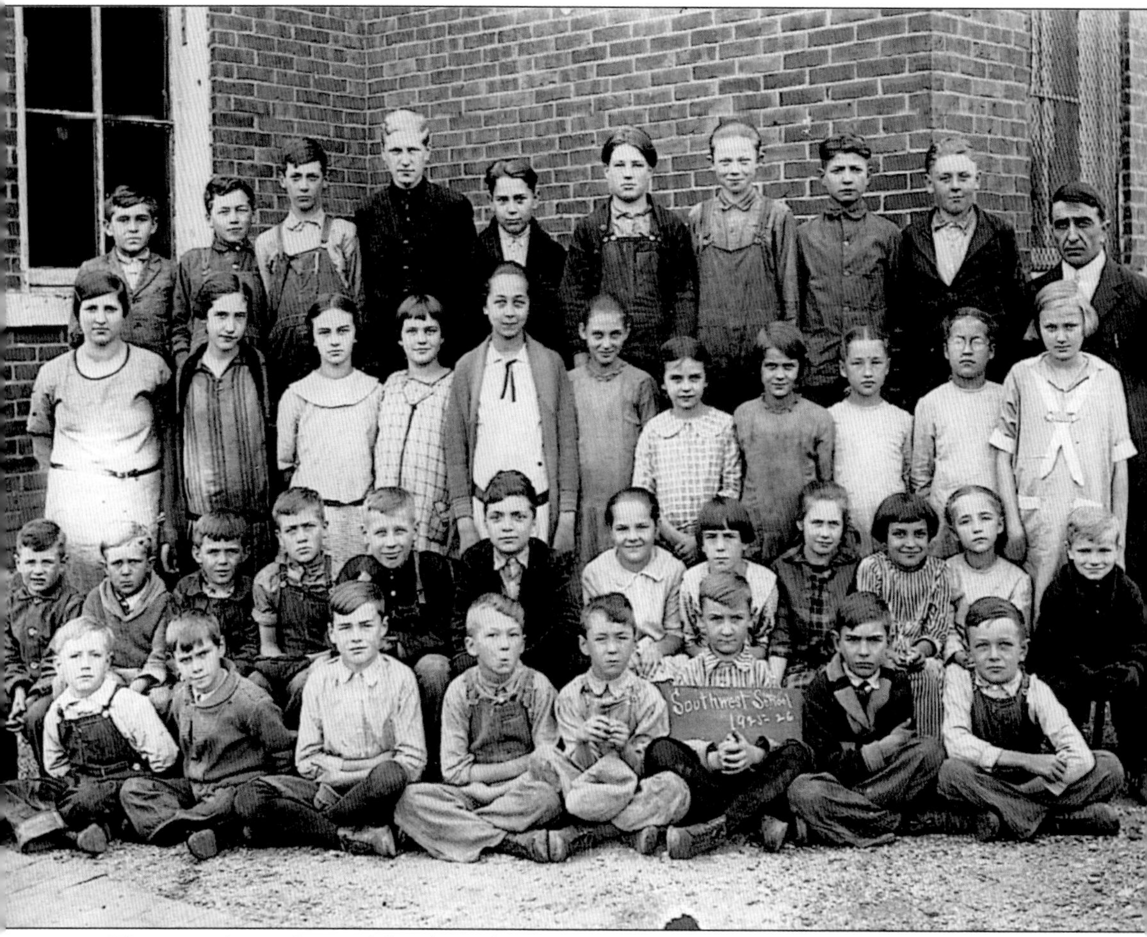

These are the students of the class of 1925–26, at the former Southwest School. Pictured from left to right are: (front row) Raymond Hoover, John Bean, Emmert Herr, Marvin Cripe, Alph Cripe, Clarence Stahly, Ned Farber, and Warren Christophel; (second row) Kenneth Blosser, Earl Leinbach, Theron Christophel, Carlyle Hoover, Charles Huffman, Ralph Neterer, Edith Leinbach Stauffer, Bessie Hoover Eash, Erma Blosser Crilow, Evelyn Wise, Martha Weaver Burkholder, and Chester Detwiler; (third row) Dessie Wise, Christena Weaver, Anna Weaver Winters, Florence Hoover Wingard, Frances Christophel Stauffer, Lois Christophel Reuter, Nora Weaver Hoffman, Annabelle Christophel Su, Anna Weaver Martin, Mary Weaver Imhoff, and Laura Culp; (fourth row) Oscar Leinbach, Elam Weaver, Everett Christophel, Elmer Detwiler, Russell Neterer, Seth Hoover, Arthur Hartman, Clifford Wise, and Darlo Miller. The teacher was Allen B. Christophel. (Photo courtesy of Mr. and Mrs. Melvin Crilow.)

Seven

JIMTOWN
In the Harmony of Men Begat a Steadfast Spirit

Of the seven small cities, towns, and villages that are being lauded in this book, the tiny burg which is about to be introduced holds the distinction of being one of the oldest of its kind in Elkhart County. Baugo Township, with a meticulously detailed and fascinating connection to Indian heritage, is the site of Jamestown, generally better known today as Jimtown.

Some 200 years ago, the area which would become Jimtown was one of the most breathtakingly beautiful sites in the county. With its vast forests, flowing waters, and plentiful wildlife, it was an attractive place for a community. The Pottawatomie Indians who populated the region knew this, and had already established themselves there long before the presence of the white men who would come to raise a settlement. The "thick woods," as they were called, boasted an impressive variety of native trees, such as poplar, maple, elm, and black walnut, while deer and wild turkeys roamed the nearby plains.

And then there was the unbridled, wildly winding stream which was christened Baubaugo, the "Devil River." It was so aptly named because of the unruly banks and swift currents. When the seasons ushered in the river's highest levels, the noise of the rushing waters could be heard for miles. Aside from being a challenge to navigate, it was a great source of food for the people—legend has it that sturgeons as long as eight feet could be found there.

It would stand to reason that a land of such promise would not remain undiscovered by pioneers. It was in the year 1830 that eight families came to the vicinity to make their homes. They were John Barnes, a minister; James Davis and William Richardson, both carpenters; Daniel Richardson, a tailor; and John McNay, William Mote, Joseph Noffsinger, and Isaiah Rush, all farmers.

The men wasted little time in raising a number of businesses. Davis and William Richardson erected the first sawmill in 1932, and Davis also built the first grist mill on the shores of the Baubaugo the following year. Other buildings which sprung up around that time were a distillery, a tannery, and cider mill, and several houses and farms. Samuel Cotterel is the man credited with opening the first general store in 1835. That same year, Davis became the one who would officially establish Jamestown as a village. It was also during this era that the name of the Baubaugo River was shortened to become simply Baugo.

Just a short distance to the east of the newly formed town, a group of Pottawatomies had a small community of their own, and they easily struck up friendships with their neighbors to the west. The Indians often traveled to the general store, willing to exchange their wares of baskets, maple sugar, venison, and honey for groceries, salt, and sundries. Because the Pottawatomies were people of a pacifistic nature, most of the transactions were carried out quite smoothly. However, there were occasions when some members of the tribe spent too much time partaking of the spirits to be found at the distillery. They called the liquor "hot fire."

There are records from those founding days that indicated a possibility for a new railroad to forge through the town. The Buffalo and Mississippi railroad company had purchased several right-of-way privileges on a handful of properties, with the intention of laying tracks in 1835. At the time, a community called Elkhart was coming together to the north, and because Jamestown was a larger, more populated area, it seemed a certainty that the rail project would literally come to pass. But the Buffalo and Mississippi charter was transferred to the Lake Shore and Michigan Southern Railroad, and the company chose to place the line just north of Jamestown, still in Baugo Township, where the town of Osceola is today. It was quite a bittersweet venture for some of Jamestown's early settlers as they journeyed to the new railroad to see a wood burning engine begin its maiden voyage in October of 1851.

Once the town was certifiably founded, and the business progressing well, the next priorities were to create places of worship and education. The first schoolhouse was a log cabin, built in 1839, followed a few years later by a frame structure. A Methodist church, also a building crafted of logs, was raised in 1854 by Zenas Belden. It did not serve a lengthy period as a church, because it was deemed too small and too low, so it later functioned as a livery stable.

Mail service of the early to mid-1800s was more than a small nuisance—it was an all-out major excursion. Back then, the closest post office was located in Fort Wayne. The trip sometimes took anywhere from four to seven days, so there were very few residents who volunteered to go that distance. When it became necessary to trek to Fort Wayne, travelers often returned with groceries and other supplies, and usually took advantage of the opportunity to mill. It did not help matters in that during this time, the postage was paid by those to whom letters were addressed—a fee of 25¢. If the intended receiver did not have the necessary funds, the mail had to be shuttled back to Fort Wayne. After a fairly short period of this aggravation, the settlers helped with the initiative to create a post office in nearby Elkhart Plain.

The people of early Jamestown were said to have had a true affinity for one another, and the kindred souls were always counted upon to gather in the spirit of generosity. Whenever a new home or barn needed to be raised, men would come from all across the township, tools in hand. The feeling of benevolence was not lost on the women, as they convened frequently for quilting bees, or to sew carpet rags. All members of the community often enjoyed the camaraderie of husking bees, singing schools, spelling contests, and debates.

Life in modern day Jimtown bears some resemblance to those yesteryears. There is still a small network of business in the rural setting, and the Jimtown school system is reputed as one of the finest in the area, both academically and in the realm of sports. And whenever one of its own is in need, the call is answered without fail by the townsfolk, always willing to share in the blessings of good fortune and guide each other in faltering times.

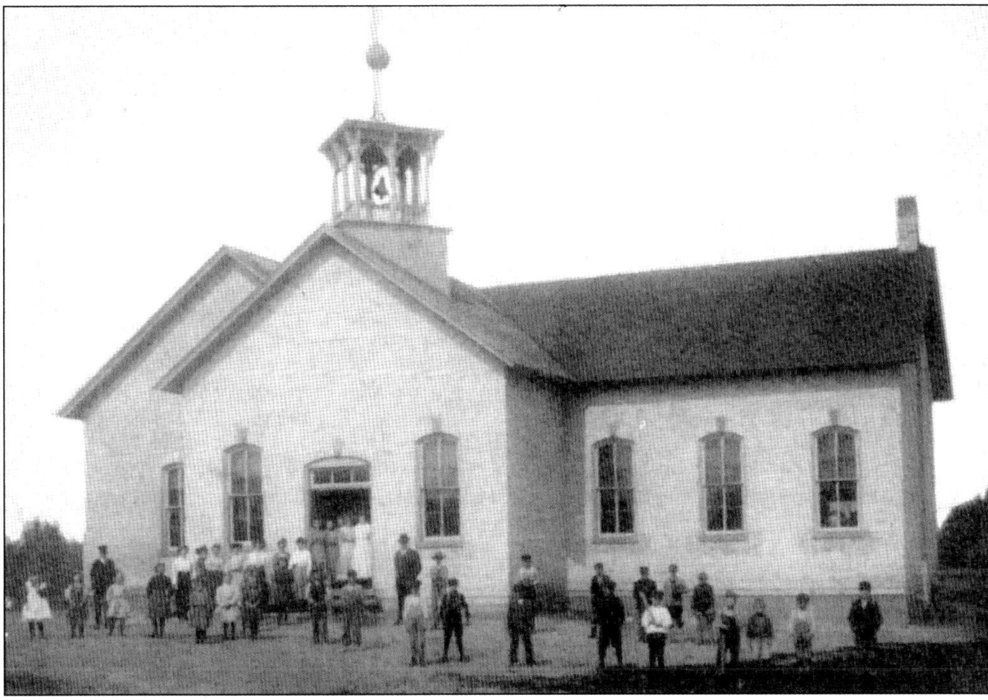

This is the original Jamestown Schoolhouse, built in 1877. It was used as a grade school until 1909, and it housed both elementary and high school students until 1913. (Photo courtesy of Mr. and Mrs. Richard Shigley.)

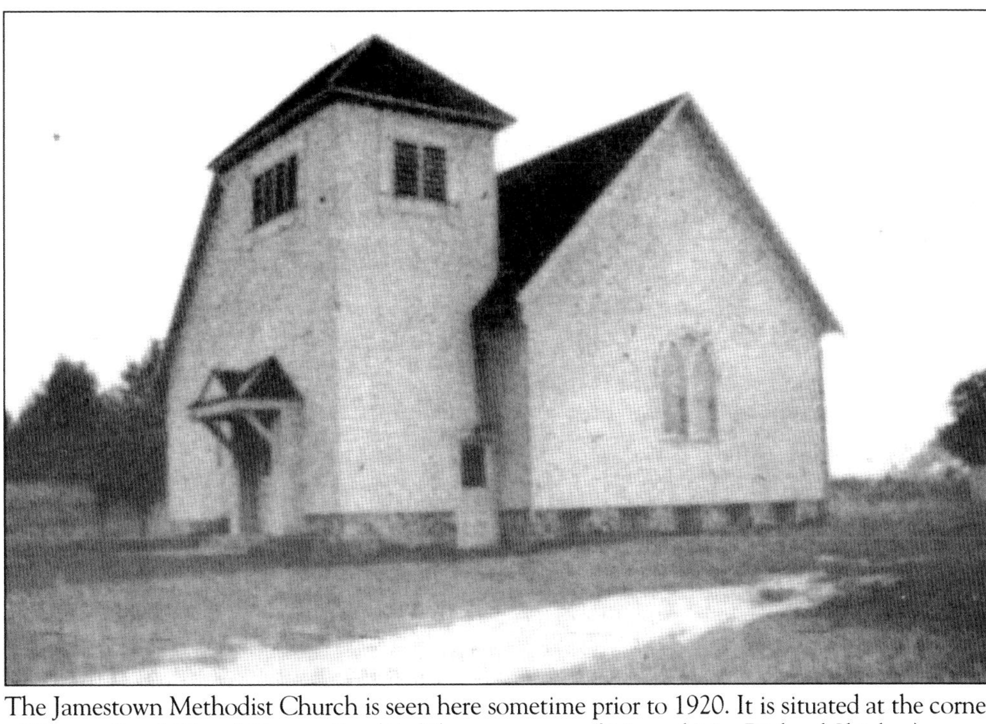

The Jamestown Methodist Church is seen here sometime prior to 1920. It is situated at the corner of County Road 22 and County Road 3. (Photo courtesy of Mr. and Mrs. Richard Shigley.)

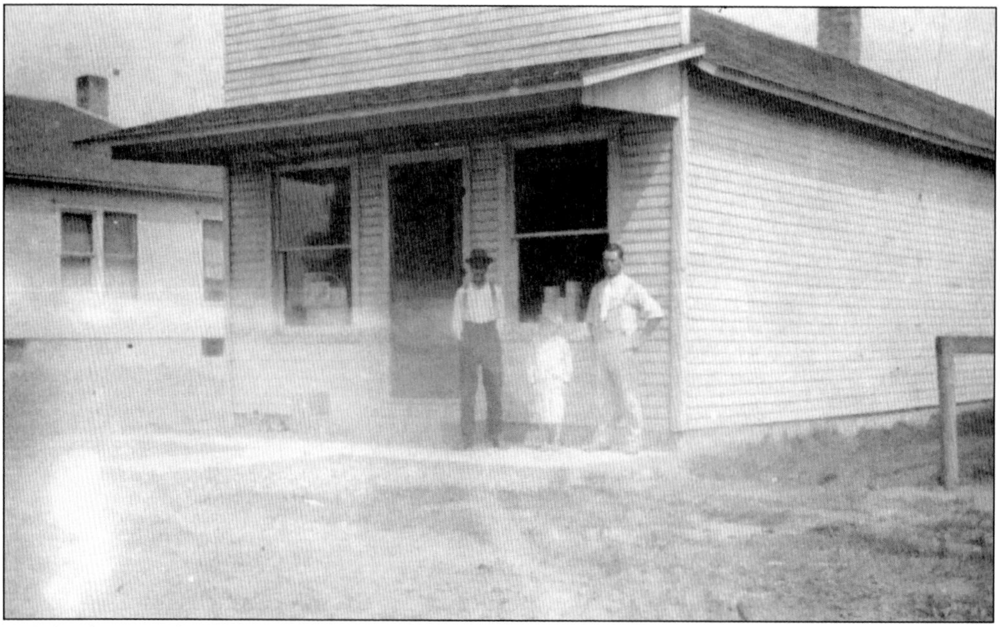

Ralph Sheets is the man who built this simple grocery store during the course of 1914 and 1915. Known then as the Jamestown Store, it was originally run by Dayton and Mary Miller. The building remains at the intersection of County Road 22 and County Road 3. (Photo courtesy of Mr. and Mrs. Richard Shigley.)

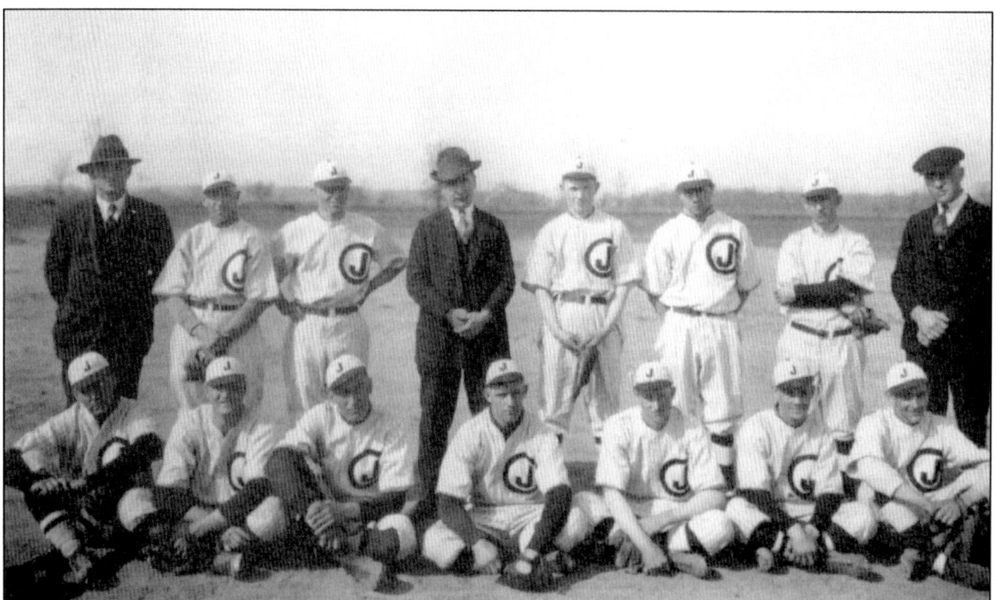

Members of the Jamestown Tigers independent baseball team pose for a photograph during their 1920–21 season. (Photo courtesy of Mr. and Mrs. Richard Shigley.)

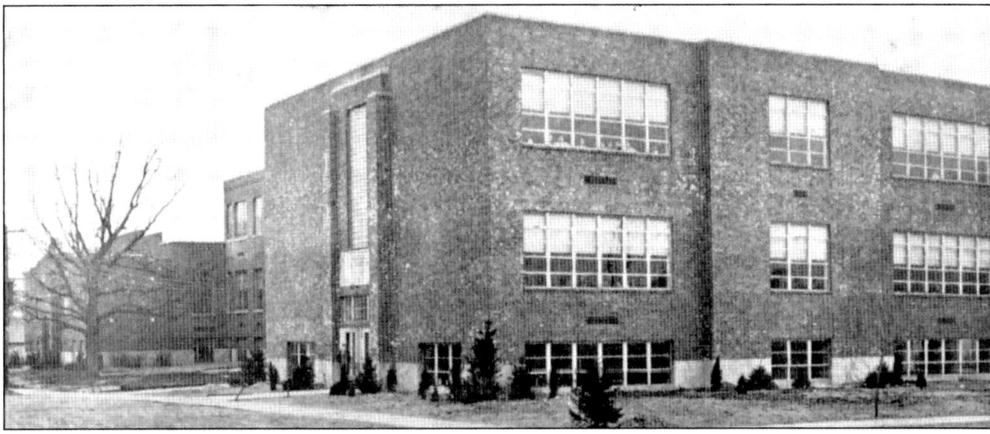

The brand new Baugo Township High School premiered just in time for the senior class of 1940 to enjoy the new facilities. (Photo courtesy of Mr. and Mrs. Richard Shigley.)

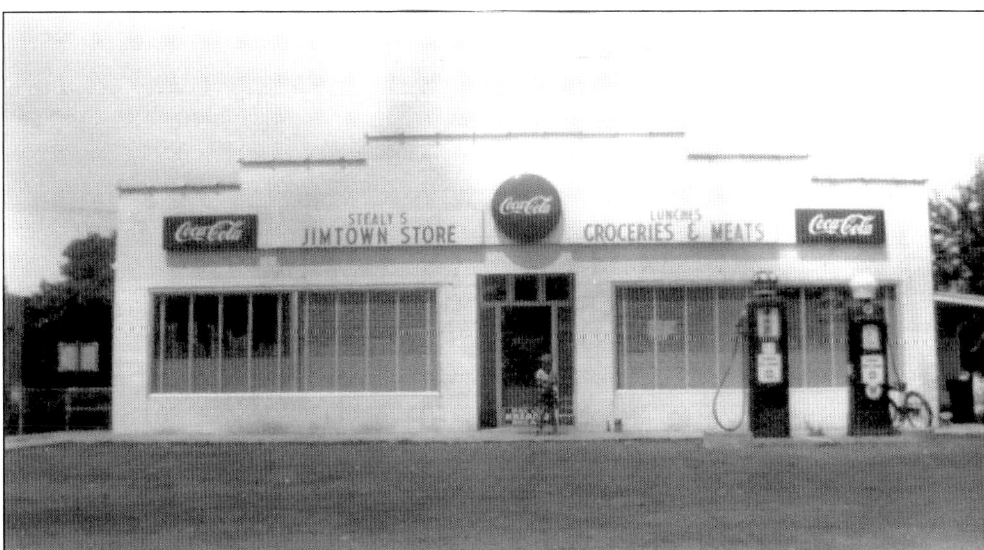

In the year 1950, this new business opened to cater to residents of Jamestown—a grocery store, eatery, meat shop, and filling station. (Photo courtesy of Mr. and Mrs. Richard Shigley.)

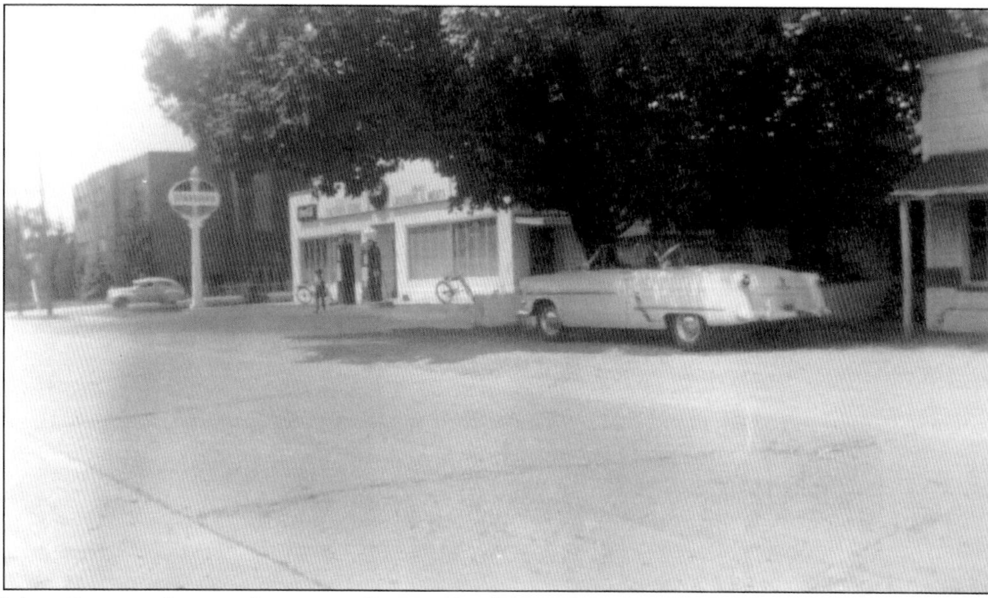

Main Street, otherwise known as County Road 3, in downtown Jamestown, is featured in this 1950 scene. (Photo courtesy of Mr. and Mrs. Richard Shigley.)

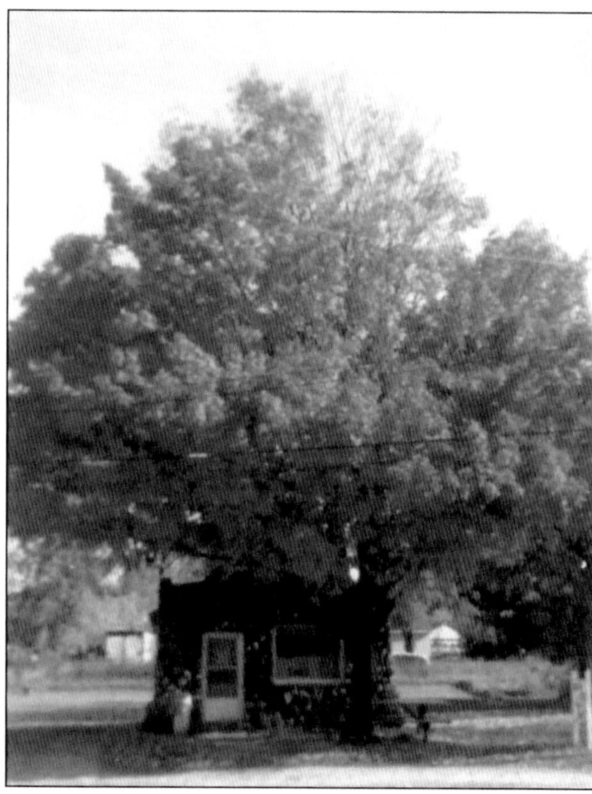

This tiny building just happens to offer some of the best pizza in the county—carry-out only, of course. This is Jimtown Pizza, located at 59176 County Road 3. When it was first built, it was home to Hoover's Barber Shop. (Photo courtesy of Mr. and Mrs. Richard Shigley.)